SOCIAL STUDIES
Detecting and Correcting
Special Needs

Joyce S. Choate/Series Consulting Editor
Northeast Louisiana University

LANA J. SMITH

DENNIE L. SMITH
Memphis State University

ALLYN AND BACON
Boston / London / Sydney / Toronto

THE ALLYN AND BACON
DETECTING AND CORRECTING SERIES
Joyce S. Choate, *Series Consulting Editor*

Editorial Production Service: Karen G. Mason
Copyeditor: Susan Freese
Cover Administrator: Linda K. Dickinson
Cover Designer: Susan Slovinsky

Library of Congress Cataloging-in-Publication Data

Smith, Lana J.
      Social studies
      (The Allyn and Bacon detecting and correcting series)
      1. Handicapped children—Education—Social sciences
      2. Social sciences—Study and Teaching (Elementary).
I. Smith, Dennie L.,   II. Title.   III. Series
LC 4029.5.S64 1989   371.9'04483   89 18273

ISBN 0-205-12151-9

Printed in the United States of America

10 9 8 7 6 5 4 3 2 1   94 93 92 91 90 89

Contents

FOREWORD
ABOUT THE DETECTING AND CORRECTING SERIES

Social Studies: Detecting and Correcting Special Needs is one of several books in an affordable series that focuses on the classroom needs of special students, both exceptional and nonexceptional, who often require adjusted methods and curricula. The purpose of this book, as well as the others in the series, is to supplement more comprehensive and theoretical treatments of major instructional issues—in this case, teaching social studies—with practical classroom practices.

The underlying theme of each book in the *Detecting and Correcting* series is targeted instruction to maximize students' achievement. Designed for informed teachers and teachers-in-training who are responsible for instructing special students in a variety of settings, these books emphasize the application of theory to everyday classroom concerns. While this approach may not be unique, the format in which both theme and purpose are presented is in that it enables the reader to quickly translate theory into practical classroom strategies for reaching hard-to-teach students.

Each book begins with an overview of instruction in the given subject, addressing in particular the needs of special students. The groundwork is laid here for both Detection and Correction: observing students' difficulties and then designing individualized prescriptive programs. Remaining chapters are organized into sequentially numbered units, addressing specific skill and topical needs of special students. Each unit follows a consistent two-part format. Detection is addressed first, beginning with a citation of a few significant behaviors and continuing with a discussion of factors such as descriptions and implications. The second part of each unit is Correction, which offers a number of strategies for modification according to individual students' learning needs.

This simple, consistent format makes the *Detecting and Correcting* books accessible and easy to read. Other useful features include: a) the Contents organization, designed for quick location of appropriate topics and problem skills and behaviors; b) a concise explanation of skills, special needs, and guiding principles for implementing instruction; c) a "Reflections" section ending each part, providing discussion and application activities; and d) an index of general topics and cross-references to related subjects.

Social studies, much like science (the topic of the most closely related book in the series), represents an area in which special students often can be accommodated with minor but important instructional adjustments. Together, these and the related books on basic mathematics, classroom behavior, instructional management, language arts, reading, and speech and language, comprise an expanding series that simplifies teachers' tasks by offering sound and practical classroom procedures for detecting and correcting special needs.

Joyce S. Choate
Series Consulting Editor

PREFACE

Social Studies: Detecting and Correcting Special Needs is designed to address the social studies needs of special students who are functioning on an elementary skill level. It is intended for use as a supplementary text and field resource guide by teachers and prospective teachers who are concerned with teaching and improving knowledge of social studies content and skills of special learners in both regular and special education classrooms. A practical complement to theoretical texts and teaching wisdom, this book is deliberately brief and concise. The intent is to enable the reader to quickly translate the theory, knowledge, content, and skills of social studies and special education into practical classroom strategies to improve the social studies skills of special students.

ASSUMPTIONS

This text is designed specifically to address the needs of special students in learning the skills and content of social studies. It is intended for use as a modestly priced supplementary text in several settings: as the special education module in social studies methods courses; as the social studies module for special education courses; as a resource text for field-based experiences in both regular and special education settings; and as a resource for inservice teachers. The basic assumptions underlying the structure and content are these:

- By definition, special students have special needs that may necessitate adjusted instruction in social studies.
- Varying the instructional emphasis renders much of the content of the regular social studies curriculum appropriate for many special students.
- Mastery of social studies skills evolves through the acquisition of language-related skills and opportunities to apply these skills in meaningful social contexts.
- Certain instructional principles facilitate the selection of topics and adjustment of instruction to meet the individual learning needs of special students.
- The social studies classroom should be a microcosm of the real world, in which students learn and practice important social coping behaviors.

These assumptions are incorporated into the Detection and Correction model for identifying the special skill needs of individual students and then correcting those needs with targeted instruction in the social studies.

ORGANIZATION

The Contents is designed to provide an at-a-glance guide for locating specific social studies topics and the needs of special students. The book is divided into four major parts. Each begins with an overview and concludes with suggestions for reflecting on its content. "Reflections" are intended for reader clarification, discussion, interpretation, application, and extension. The final item in each "Reflections" section lists additional resources for further information.

The three chapters in Part I describe the social studies needs of special learners and provide the framework for the corrective strategies in the remaining chapters. Chapter 1 explains the goals of social studies instruction and the specific skill strands that characterize instruction in this content. Chapter 2 outlines categories of special students, both exceptional and nonexceptional. Chapter 3 presents ways of detecting special needs, as well as 12 basic principles of instruction that guide the selection and implementation of corrective activities. The order of this presentation is by no means intended to diminish the focus of this book on the special student. Rather, it is intended to reflect the integration of a specific content area into a context for teaching special-needs children that will enhance both the achievement of social concepts and skills and the individual abilities and social adjustment of the students.

Parts II, III, and IV present corrective activities within an expanding communities framework commonly presented in many social studies curricular designs. Topic content was derived from a wide sampling of textbook series and curriculum guides to ensure that topics would closely match the concepts most often taught and emphasized across social studies curricula.

FEATURES

These detecting and correcting strategies are grounded in theory and research and, most importantly, shaped by practice. Their uniqueness resides in their versatility. Most can be implemented in both regular and special education classrooms with individuals or both small and large groups of students. Because the strategies must be adapted to fit individual students and teachers, only the most salient features are described. To keep the text clear, succinct, and practical, social studies and special education theories are built into the strategies.

As a study and reference aid, a consistent format is used throughout. Each of the strategy chapters (4–10) includes a diagnostic section entitled Detection which contains a Description of the content and concepts related to the chapter topic, a Causation unit that identifies etiological factors contributing to learning deficiencies, and an Implications unit that presents a rationale for inclusion of the topic in the intellectual and social development of special students. The second section, Correction, identifies an activity title, the skill strand, and the most directly related skill within that strand that the activity addresses.

ACKNOWLEDGMENTS

These strategies have been selected and developed over many years of experience and with many modifications from teachers and students who have field tested, critiqued, and improved them. We appreciate the contributions and expertise of these practitioners.

A special thank you is extended to Joyce Choate; without her guidance and inspiration, this text would never have been accomplished. We are also grateful to our field reviewers: Richard L. Dickson (Rhode Island College), Judith Hakes (Angelo State University), and Ed Lerner (Newton, Massachusetts Public Schools).

To our editorial team at Allyn and Bacon, Mylan Jaixen, Ray Short, and Karen Mason, we extend our thanks for their professionalism and dedication to quality in education. And to our families who have supported, tolerated, and encouraged, we are indebted.

PART I

SOCIAL STUDIES
AND THE
SPECIAL LEARNER

Social studies is a combination of studies drawn from the social sciences and related disciplines and as such is considered a content subject. Mastery of this content requires the utilization of not only basic skills, such as reading, writing, and arithmetic, but also skills endemic to the discipline itself.

All students have individual instructional needs, and, on occasion, all students need specific instruction to meet these needs. Some students, however, require more specialized instruction. This section briefly outlines the content and skills of the social studies and describes some of the special problems that certain categories of students experience in learning these skills. Common types of problems are shared by many of the students in each classification, as they often exhibit similar needs in social studies instruction.

Chapter 1 discusses the multifaceted nature of the content field commonly grouped and taught in schools as social studies. The primary goals of the field are delineated and placed in context for teachers who are responsible for teaching social studies to students with a broad range of ability levels, including those who are special-needs learners. The skills framework for social studies instruction is outlined and adaptations for the special learner are generally discussed.

Social studies content, as noted in Chapter 1, is distilled from a wide range of social science areas, presenting somewhat of a challenge in selection of topics appropriate for building basic skills. The discussion of content is followed by a description of the three major social studies strands, or skill groupings: acquiring information; organizing and using information; and participating socially. Chapters 2 and 3 apply this skill model to the needs of special learners and integrates these needs with the most widely accepted principles of effective social studies instruction.

In Chapter 2, two sets of special learners are described: regular and remedial learners, who typically experience some difficulty achieving, and students who are eligible for special education services by virtue of their learning differences. The first set includes those students who teachers informally categorize according to the assumed cause of their learning difficulties; the second set includes those students classified according to their diagnosed handicap. Gifted students are treated as a separate group because of their unique exceptionality and because the classification of these students varies so widely across regions. The implications of social studies instruction are outlined for each category of special learners based upon the logical inferences from the most frequently cited learning characteristics. Although never applicable to every student in any group, each cursory description presents the most likely instructional needs of the different types of special learners.

Some argue that social studies instruction for the special student detracts from the time and effort needed by these students for basic subjects, such as reading and math. Proponents of a strong social studies curricula recommend its inclusion because of the need to reflect the nature and composition of the world students live in now and will enter as adults. It is through this microcosm that students can explore and learn the coping behaviors needed to survive as adults.

Chapter 3 presents ways to detect special social studies needs, including the use of available data, formal and informal assessments, interviews, and observations of students inside and outside of the social studies classroom. Classroom observations utilizing a structured checklist are recommended because they offer the most realistic reflection of a student's performance. The interpretation of all available diagnostic data should provide direction for both specific skill instruction and topic selection.

Twelve basic principles of instruction are recommended for adjusting social studies instruction to meet the needs of special learners. Noted as particularly important are 1) selecting topics that are related to students' real-life needs and experiences, 2) establishing cooperative learning environments where students can practice their social skills, and 3) teaching and adjusting for special skill needs. These principles are intended as guidelines for implementing the special strategies that are suggested in Part II, Chapters 4 through 10.

CHAPTER 1 /
SOCIAL STUDIES SKILLS DEVELOPMENT
FOR THE SPECIAL LEARNER

Special instruction in the social studies is designed not only to develop a foundational knowledge base but also to accommodate the diversity of developmental, academic, and social levels of students who have special learning needs. These students are likely to have more difficulty meeting the demands of a larger social world if they are unable to use social science knowledge in a technological and changing economic world community. And at the very least, these students must be able to cope and function effectively in all social milieus, including home, school, work, and the larger society.

The scope and complexity of social science knowledge and content are enormous and somewhat nebulous to identify. The vast amount of information makes it difficult to determine what is most important, interesting, and provocative for students to learn. Also, many groups—including academicians, practitioners, parents, special interest groups, and students—constantly influence and change social studies curricula. Developers make scrutinized decisions in selecting content from the various social science disciplines for a K–12 curriculum sequence. Naturally, a considerable amount of overlap exists among the disciplines, which is in a sense the glue for the social studies. All the social sciences must be combined and used to provide the essential information and experiences that will enable young people to understand and participate in a social and world culture.

Teaching and learning social studies should be approached as something that students do and live—not something they just read about. Learning about people can be interesting and provocative for students. This practical approach to the social studies equips students to actively participate in and contribute to the world in which they live. Students need to understand some of the historical, social, geographic, and economic concepts central to the human experience. Most importantly, students need skills for independent inquiry to understand and use the social studies in their everyday lives.

SOCIAL STUDIES GOALS

The social studies have four main goals. First, and probably most importantly, the social studies have the primary responsibility of developing citizens who participate intelligently in a democratic society by making thoughtful decisions and by contributing in efforts to improve the human experience. Second, knowledge of cultural heritage, developed through analysis of the historical problems and events that have contributed to the democratic values that shape and sustain our way of life, builds appreciation for our pluralistic and interdependent world. Third, critical and creative thinking abilities are enhanced as students make decisions and engage in problem-solving activities related to the people, environment, and world around them. Finally, the social studies enhance the development of self-realization, a better understanding of human relationships, and the development of interpersonal skills that will aid individuals in reaching their potential as human beings.

SOCIAL STUDIES SKILLS

Within the social studies, skills are taught as an integral aspect of the field and not as isolated entities. In order to acquire information and become independent learners of more complex and higher-level material in the social studies, students must develop basic communication and thinking skills. These skills will help students learn how to learn as they apply reading, writing, and study skills to social content. Information processing skills involve the internalization of new knowledge to help understand complex phenomena in society. These skills are developed through direct teaching and frequent utilization and application in daily learning experiences. Skill development in both the basic communication and information processing skills, in conjunction with the social studies skills, offers a multitude of cognitive and affective objectives to enrich the instructional experience. For example, gaining access to information in libraries provides more options for students to learn. Knowing how to read a map or interpret a chart provides greater access to information and power in our society. Full participation in an information age is dependent upon the ability of students to access, select, and use information relevant to a specific issue.

Both basic communication skills and those skills identified as the social studies skills are essential for achievement in school. If a student struggles with the mechanics of reading a social studies lesson, then the potential learning or overall comprehension of the content will be affected. Likewise, if a student has no sensitivity to the feelings of others and cannot participate in the group classroom experience, his or her opportunities for learning and achievement will be severely limited. The utilization and attainment of both types of skills are most effective as an integrated process and not as separate goals of the learning experience. As they learn the skills, attitudes, and values of the social studies curriculum, students are more apt to enjoy an attainable challenge but become discouraged with material or skills not appropriate for their developmental levels. Thus, it is especially critical for special students, who may have already experienced a lot of failure in school, to enjoy successful practice of their skills in learning the content.

The skill framework in this book was extracted from a scope and sequence of social studies skills developed by a Task Force of the National

Council for the Social Studies (Jarolimek, 1984). The list of skills is subsumed under three major categories: 1) skills related to acquiring information, 2) skills related to organizing and using information, and 3) skills related to interpersonal relationships and social participation. Although some of the skills may serve as prerequisites to others, this framework is by no means cumulatively developmental in nature. That is, success at one level is not predicated upon mastery of skills at lower levels. These three major categories will be identified with each activity in this book and will be referred to as Strands 1, 2, and 3 respectively. The three strands are outlined in Figure 1.1.

FIGURE 1.1   Social Studies Skills

STRAND 1 Acquiring Information	STRAND 2 Organizing and Using Information	STRAND 3 Participating Socially
• Reading • Study • Information search • Technical	• Classifying • Interpreting • Analyzing • Summarizing • Synthesizing • Evaluating • Decision Making	• Personal skills • Group interaction • Social and political skills

Strand 1: Skills in Acquiring Information

As outlined in Figure 1.2, Strand 1 includes those broad skills related to acquiring information, including reading, study skills, reference and information search skills, and technical skills unique to electronic devices. Students who have not mastered these basic academic skills often will find

FIGURE 1.2   Strand 1: Acquiring Information

READING	STUDY	INFORMATION SEARCH	TECHNICAL
• Comprehension • Vocabulary • Rate of reading	• Find information • Arrange information in usable forms	• Library • Special references • Maps, globes, graphics • Community resources	• Computer • Telephone and television information networks

Note: The skill framework used in this book is adapted and reprinted from *Social Education* (Vol. 48, No. 4, April 1984, pp. 260–261) with permission of the National Council for the Social Studies.

acquisition of information a difficult task. This also means that they will not be able to operate independently to learn new information unless special situations can be designed or the basic skills circumvented.

Reading

Reading is the most basic of the information acquisition skills and also the most frequently used method for acquiring social studies information. It is also, unfortunately, one of the most problematic learning tasks for special students. Because reading is highly symbolic in nature, the skills can be extremely difficult for students to master, making it necessary for teachers to find ways around the reading barrier and use alternative acquisition strategies. In the area of reading comprehension, learners must be able to understand both literal and inferential meanings, differentiate between main and supportive ideas, identify cause-and-effect relationships, and distinguish fact-and-opinion statements. They must be able to read various forms of print material for a variety of purposes in order to stay current with a fast-paced world. In addition, they must learn to adjust their speed of reading to suit the purposes and difficulty of the material.

Vocabulary skills demanded of learners include the ability to use context clues to determine meanings, apply word attack strategies, and use appropriate sources to determine meanings when they are unable to decode the words. Technical, or content-specific, vocabulary terms related to the various social studies areas will increase in number and level of difficulty as students progress. Many of these terms are highly abstract and may be especially problematic for special learners. It is essential that the language of social studies be carefully taught since it is through vocabulary that we designate concepts and give special learners the concreteness they need for discussion and understanding of ideas.

Study Skills

Study skills, such as locating, organizing, and reporting information found in a variety of sources, provides the learner with independence in continued learning. Other activities, such as taking notes, preparing outlines and summaries, writing reports, and preparing bibliographies, are many times included in this skill area also. Important to learners' independence in the study skills are those self-discipline skills required for reviewing information and committing it to memory if necessary so that they may access the information when it is needed.

Reference and Information Search

Knowing where to go to find needed information and how to use the technological forms in which it will be found is more important to all learners than remembering by chance what may or may not have been taught in a classroom. Resources such as the library, the card catalog, almanacs, encyclopedias, and indexes and news sources such as periodicals, TV, and radio contain a wealth of relevant, current, and informative social studies content that may not be available to teachers or students in curriculum materials. Thus, it is important to know how and where it can be located. Again, access to these sources must be gained with a minimum of dependence on reading ability. For example, teaching students in a library who to ask for assistance and that telephone homework hotlines and other information sources can be accessed can be beneficial to low-ability readers.

Maps, Globes, and Graphics

Knowing how to interpret maps, globes, graphs, and charts and how to seek and find information beyond textbook sources empowers students to become life-long learners as well as provides them with alternative ways of acquiring information in social studies when other basic skills are deficient. Alternative skill paths include math to compute distances and scales; visualization of map symbols to interpret relationships and make conclusions; interpretation of cartoons to understand social and political messages; and manipulation of concrete artifacts in the interpretation of history.

Community Resources

Conducting interviews and using community newspapers and other resources are additional activities requiring skills that must be carefully taught in order to insure that these materials can be accessed by learners.

Strand 2: Skills in Organizing and Using Information

Strand 2 skills, outlined in Figure 1.3, relate to organizing and using information and are often referred to or designated as *thinking skills.* Included within this area are those skills required in critical thinking to appraise objects and activities, in creative thinking to synthesize elements in new ways, in problem solving to propose solutions, and in decision making to select desirable alternatives. Classifying, interpreting, analyzing, summarizing, synthesizing, and evaluating information are the primary activities in the development of these skills. Once information has been acquired, organizing and using it becomes the most critical aspect of making any new

FIGURE 1.3 Strand 2: Organizing and Using Information

INTELLECTUAL SKILLS	DECISION-MAKING SKILLS
•Classifying information	•Identifying decision situations
•Interpreting information	•Securing factual information
•Analyzing information	•Recognizing implicit values
•Summarizing information	•Identifying alternatives
•Synthesizing information	•Taking action
•Evaluating information	

learning a part of students' cognitive structures. Unless students do something with information, it is not likely to be retained; and it is through these intellectual skills that information is actively manipulated, making it more available for retrieval at later times. Lack of experience in these types of activities is a primary contributor to many special students' difficulties in this area. Many students with reading and other communication deficits are able to participate and develop skills within this domain and through these types of activities even when they are unable to read or write well. In fact, these become the coping and survival skills for special students when they are severely limited in the academic areas.

Classifying

Identifying relevant factual material, sensing relationships, and grouping data in categories according to criteria are the primary activities involved in classifying. In many instances, data can be grouped by several criteria and students must be able to distinguish characteristics and focus on multiple outcomes. Placing the data in tabular form, charts, graphs, or illustrations is an extension of interpretation and another means for presenting understandings, especially when oral or writing abilities are limited.

Interpreting Information

Interpretive skills require the ability to state relationships between and among categories, note cause-and-effect relationships, draw inferences, and predict outcomes. Interpreting factual material also involves value dimensions, which students must be able to sense when they are not stated and apply broad understandings of people and their motivations to interpret properly.

Analyzing Information

Analysis is a higher-order cognitive skill requiring comparison and contrast, detecting bias in data, separating topics into major components, and examining their relationships. Special students will need careful sequencing of events in developing this skill as well as individual guidance in detecting essential differences and separating parts from wholes.

Summarizing Information

Extracting main ideas from supporting details, making conclusions and forming opinions from data, and stating hypotheses for further study are the primary summarization activities. This skill requires students not only to process the information but also to recode it into responses that demonstrate an understanding of the meaning of what they have read, heard, or seen. These responses often take the form of outlines, charts, tables, or maps.

Synthesizing Information

Bringing parts together into new wholes or developing new products, systems, or plans from elements is a creative process. Students will need opportunities and flexible environments for expressing their creativity. The judgment of their creative efforts must be made in light of the originality of ideas along with the processes involved and connections made between the original information and the new products or ideas.

Evaluating Information

To make a judgment of worth, value, or merit, students must apply some criteria against which to measure; otherwise, the judgment is merely an opinion. Validity, pertinence, and adequacy are the basic criteria for forming evaluative conclusions, and students will need directly focused questions and guidance in applying standards and judging in relation to them.

Decision Making

Many of the above skills are incorporated into the process of making decisions, which involves defining a problem, considering standards, making proposals, considering consequences of the proposals, and choosing an action that best meets the defined standards. In addition, most decisions involve acknowledging differing values and views of a situation. Unless students learn how to appraise these aspects of the decision, little progress can be made.

Strand 3: Skills in Participating Socially

Strand 3 skills, depicted in Figure 1.4, emphasize interpersonal skills and social development and participation of individuals in group living. Although social skills are obviously developed throughout the school curricula, the responsibility for the direct teaching of these skills is given to the social studies curriculum. Because the special student is often characterized by his or her difficulty in becoming accepted as a participant in society,

FIGURE 1.4 Strand 3: Participating Socially

PERSONAL SKILLS	SOCIAL AND POLITICAL GROUP INTERACTION SKILLS	PARTICIPATION SKILLS
• Expressing convictions • Communicating feelings • Adjusting behavior to group • Recognizing mutual relationships	• Contributing to group climate • Participating in making rules • Serving as leader or follower • Participating in group actions • Resolving group conflicts	• Keeping informed on social issues • Identifying social action situations • Working with others to decide actions • Working to influence social powers • Accepting social responsibilities

these skills become equally important with the more academic areas as young students enter into formal educational settings. All these learning experiences are group oriented and will be throughout students' school days and later life unless special circumstances warrant otherwise. These skills also contribute most directly to an individual's personal happiness and sense of worth, giving him or her a sense of accomplishment and the determination to meet the next challenge. All people need to be accepted as members of social groups.

Personal Skills

Included in personal skills are the abilities to express personal ideas, beliefs, feelings, and convictions; to adjust behavior to fit dynamics of various groups; and to recognize the mutual relationship between human beings in satisfying each other's needs. Expressing convictions and communicating with others about beliefs and feelings in ways that are not apologetic, fearful, or guilt laden can be difficult for those who lack a strong sense of self-worth or confidence. These individuals typically withdraw and withhold these feelings, denying themselves the opportunities to build mutual and satisfying relationships. Students such as these may find themselves in repetitive and self-defeating cycles that often have negative consequences. The ability to adjust one's behavior to fit the dynamics of situations is especially difficult for many special students who have under-developed self-controls. The skills required for making these adjustments must be practiced and positively reinforced just as academic skills are.

Group Interaction Skills

Interaction skills include those abilities involved in making and following rules for group life and making decisions, compromising, debating, and negotiating for resolution of conflicts. Serving as a leader or a follower in any group activity requires certain dynamics to be effective. It is often assumed that learning these roles comes as a natural consequence of simply participating in group interactions. This is not the case, however, and direct teaching and learning experiences that instruct about and examine these roles are recommended.

Social and Political Participation Skills

Keeping informed on issues that affect society, identifying social action situations, working individually and in groups to decide on a course of action, and fulfilling social responsibilities associated with citizenship in a free society are the skills and concepts included in this area. Special students can become active participants in all social milieus and exercise their citizenship rights and responsibilities most effectively when they have had appropriate learning experiences throughout their school days.

SUMMARY

The ability to function in a large, technologically and economically complex social world is becoming increasingly more important each day. Students with special learning needs clearly face additional challenges in meeting the demands of a social world.

The content of social studies is diverse and almost limitless; thus, it must be chosen carefully, matching particular students to concepts and skills relevant to their lives presently and in the future. Factors to consider when selecting topics for study include: the abilities and the ages of the target students; practical application to students' lives; enhancing and enriching students' lives; improving students' overall literacy; and increasing students' interest in social studies.

The skills of social studies are grouped into three areas or strands: 1) acquiring information through reading, study, information search, and technical skills; 2) organizing and using information through such activities as classifying, interpreting, analyzing, summarizing, synthesizing, evaluating, and decision making; and 3) participating socially through adequately developed personal skills, group interaction skills, and social and political skills. There is no implied hierarchical nature to the skill framework presented here. Many of these skills are taught and learned concurrently and recursively as needed to understand the particular topic of study. Establishing relevance to students' present lives and predicting the significance of concepts for future use are particularly important concerns when teaching the special students described in the next chapter.

CHAPTER 2 /
THE SPECIAL LEARNER IN THE SOCIAL STUDIES CLASSROOM

All learners have special learning needs. The focus of this chapter is those learners who differ markedly from the regular classroom norm to such an extent that they are problematic for teachers in these settings, at risk of academic failure in these classrooms, or eligible and classified for special education services in other subject areas but could be mainstreamed in the social studies classroom. The characteristics of these special learners and the adjustments in instruction required for effective teaching of social studies skills and concepts for these individuals are discussed below.

The social studies classroom in any school is rarely leveled on the basis of academic learning ability or any other special learning characteristics of students. In fact, this particular content area is often thought of as the ideal environment in which to implement the principles explicitly outlined in the legislation that mandates that students with handicapping conditions shall not be excluded from the mainstream of public education. Most special learners will have deficiencies in collecting or processing information; however, through proper planning, making adjustments, and taking precautions, the mastery of social studies content and skills can become a reality for these students.

NONHANDICAPPED SPECIAL STUDENTS

Although students may be grouped into any number of categories according to a broad range of learning characteristics, this discussion is limited to four nonhandicapped groups that might be anticipated in the regular social studies classroom. Descriptions of nine handicapped groups follow, and academically gifted students are then briefly mentioned.

The Culturally Different Students

The culturally different student is one whose race, social class, or language varies from that of the majority, complicating the learning tasks and contributing directly to low achievement. A culturally different student who is achieving will seldom need any special adjustments in instruction.

Description. Culturally different students are those whose backgrounds are different enough to require special methods of assessment, instruction, intervention, or counseling. They may be different from the majority of students attending their school, or they may share the culture of the majority of their classmates but differ from most of the students for whom the social studies curriculum and textbooks were developed. In some instances, the culture of the teacher may differ from that of the students and result in learning problems. The critical problems for the culturally different usually involve a language difference that results in limited oral and reading fluency and narrow vocabularies. In addition, these students often have not had typical life experiences that constitute the foundation for academic achievement measured by achievement tests and emphasized in textbooks.

Special Problems. The major problems of culturally different students center around their different languages, value systems, and experiential backgrounds. These differences may interfere with students' understanding of the common reference points and examples used to illustrate social concepts. Limited vocabularies and fluency in the teaching language hinder information acquisition skills, such as listening, reading, and studying. And even when information is acquired, these same deficiencies also limit students' abilities to organize and use the information as well as to communicate the true extent of their knowledge. Discrimination, misunderstandings, and stereotypical attitudes toward certain cultural groups often result in a lack of communication in general and can even cause students to be unable to learn and practice skills related to interpersonal relationships and social participation.

Instructional Implications. Culturally different students need extended background concepts and experiences with emphasis on the common reference points. The development of good language and reading patterns is prerequisite to success in school and these basic skills must be given priority. The use of ideas relevant to students' lives and cultures and activities that stress concrete experiences are valuable. Aides, parents, or older children with more developed language may be helpful in translating vocabulary and giving instructions. If speaking and writing abilities are weak, students may need to perform or demonstrate their understandings. Interpretations and value judgments of students' behaviors must be made cautiously, since what is normal and acceptable in some students' cultures may be regarded as unacceptable and abnormal in school, thus increasing the learning and communication difficulties. Sensitivity to language, communication, and value differences is important in working with culturally different students. To accommodate slow learning rates, real-life topics should be emphasized, making them as relevant to students' lives and cultures as possible. If necessary, topics of lesser practical value should be omitted.

Slow Learning Students

Slow learners are those whose learning rate is noticeably slower than the rate of their peers. It is important to note that the individual's rate of learning is often judged in comparison with a particular group of peers and the curriculum they follow. In other circumstances, the slow learner might be judged as excelling, especially when placed with others who also progress slowly.

Description. Slow learners progress at rates that are slower than the rate of their peers, the pace of the teacher, and the pace of the curriculum. They often struggle to keep up and without special provisions fall farther and farther behind. The slow learner often ranks low on general social skills and acceptance among classmates his own age. A short attention span and difficulty attending to relevant stimuli often characterize the slow learner and may interfere with cognitive learning tasks.

Special Problems. The acquisition of information, especially in the areas of vocabulary and reading comprehension, will be especially problematic for the slow learner, whose skills are not congruent with the level of the curriculum materials or the pace of the instruction. Once the information is acquired, more time may also be necessary for these students to classify, interpret, and synthesize than would be required for other students. Behavorial problems may manifest the slow learner's frustration with a curriculum that is beyond his or her learning pace. Interpersonal skills and social relationships with peers are often underdeveloped as a consequence of inability to communicate and interact with others in age-appropriate ways.

Instructional Implications. Slow learners need more time on learning tasks, and instruction must be highly structured and adapted to students' learning capacities, rates, and levels. They require concrete learning experiences, especially with abstract social concepts, and activities that can be finished in one sitting. Extra review, practice, reinforcement, and study time may be required. Plan team-learning activities to gather data, prepare reports, make maps, and so on. Identify and use the special talents of less able students to contribute to these activities. Cooperative learning tasks with peers can do much to improve and provide practice settings for developing group interaction and social participation skills. These tasks can range from peer tutoring to physical assistance and manipulation of learning tools to simple social skills, such as taking turns.

Teacher-Disabled Students

Teacher disabled is a relatively new term used to describe a category of learning problems that result primarily from incorrect or ineffective teaching. Such problems are significant to many of today's students.

Description. Many of these students are described as "trying hard" but simply not reaching their potential, when in reality it is the instruction that has failed to meet their learning needs. As a consequence, students appear to have lost confidence in themselves and display generally depressed, defeated attitudes. As a defense mechanism, these students may also display highly negative and even hostile attitudes toward most teachers and school.

Special Problems. The negative effects of inept or inappropriate teaching may result in a pronounced dislike of the social studies, a condition resulting from experience with teachers who have had limited knowledge and/or who themselves disliked the subject. Social studies instruction that has consisted of rote memorization of facts and dates, with very little application and demonstrated relevance to students' lives, may produce a negative attitude, a limited conceptual knowledge base, as well as little understanding of the basic social studies goals. Teacher-disabled students will have difficulties in organizing and using information primarily because they may never have been required to do so and their teacher did not provide the motivation. Their study skills, especially in the areas of retention and application, will be limited. Low self-concepts and hostility toward the social studies curriculum may result from bad experiences with the subject and previous teachers. Overcoming these problems may represent a monumental motivational task for the new teacher.

Instructional Implications. In all the learning tasks, teachers will need to compensate for previous inappropriate teaching, inspire enthusiasm for social studies, improve the student's general attitude, and find ways for him or her to succeed. Building personal trust in the teacher is essential. Modeling the learning for students can be especially effective when trust has been established. Teaching study strategies, note taking, key vocabulary, mnemonic techniques, and other acquisition and retention skills will have positive influence on students' attitudes and should benefit their learning in the social studies as well as across the curriculum.

Underachieving Students

Underachievement is cited when teachers compare students' typical classroom performance to achievement test scores and find classroom performance lower. Vascillation between excellence and failure can also indicate underachievement, as can wide disparities in performance when two subject areas are compared. Some underachievers may in reality be undetected learning-disabled students.

Description. Underachievers are those students who are capable of performing at higher levels than they typically do. Negative attitudes toward school in general rather than social studies as a particular subject are often characteristic.

Special Problems. A variety of factors can contribute to underachievement, including inept teaching, cultural differences, and peer pressures. Initially, underachievers may have difficulty in any of the social studies skill areas. If the students continue to fall behind in the basic information acquisition skills, such as reading and vocabulary, this will eventually impact on their overall ability to achieve at higher levels.

Instructional Implications. Motivation, reassurance, and a personal interest in these students' progress are the major needs of underachievers. The opportunity to choose for study from an array of subtopics often increases their interest. Such practices as direct instruction with built-in successes and appropriate feedback are important elements for increasing students' achievement in social studies. In addition, establishing personal relevance in the study of social concepts is of key importance. Opportunities to work with normal peers in paired tutoring or other cooperative learning situations can also be beneficial.

SPECIAL EDUCATION STUDENTS

Students whose performance deviates from the norm, either below or above, to such an extent that it is apparent that the regular classroom cannot meet all their needs may be classified as exceptional and become eligible for special educational services. The nature and degree of their handicaps determine the amount of regular classroom instruction that is appropriate to their learning needs. In the social studies classroom, it is expected that, with relatively minor modifications, most disabled students should be able to master the most important concepts and skills that contribute to the attainment of the goals of the social studies curriculum.

This section describes the cross-categorical, or generic, handicapping conditions and proceeds to discussions of the traditional categories of handicapped learners. Academically gifted learners are described later as a separate group, although many states include them in special education services.

Cross-Categorical Handicapped Students

Many school systems classify students for instruction according to the degree of their handicap rather than on the basis of a particular type. Thus, students whose handicap is considered to be mild to moderate degree are grouped together as are those with conditions ranging from severe to profound.

Description. *Cross-categorical handicapped* does not denote a type of learner but rather a description of an instructional services model. Students who are evaluated for special education services must meet specified criteria for a particular category of exceptionality, but it is the degree of handicap that determines their placement and not the categorical label. These students are thereafter taught as a generic group on the basis of their characteristic learning patterns, which usually reflect commonalties such as low academic achievement, especially in reading and other basic skills, short attention spans, memory deficits, distractibility, and inability to generalize from specific information.

Special Problems. A large percentage of these students exhibit disabilities in reading and study skills and will have considerable difficulty acquiring and retaining information that they can later organize for useful purposes. Interpersonal relationships and social participation skills may lack maturity commensurate with chronological age.

Instructional Implications. Mildly to moderately handicapped students are considered to be capable of and are largely expected to master the principles and major concepts of the social studies curriculum. The severely and profoundly handicapped are expected generally to master enough social and personal skills to function in their common social contexts. The social studies curriculum should be analyzed for those concepts and skills that are most practical and contribute most directly to quality of life. The instructional emphasis should be provided accordingly. Handicapped students require a great deal of individualization and often benefit significantly from multisensory instruction. Other suggested techniques for meeting the needs of all exceptional students include direct instruction, extra review and reinforcement, and use of concrete learning materials and direct experiences. Alternatives to reading as a primary means of acquiring information should be sought and practiced whenever possible. Most importantly, the personal and societal relevance of each topic of study should be established for learners. Other specific instructional implications also apply and are cited for each of the exceptional categories presented in the pages that follow.

Behavior-Disordered Students

The characteristics of behavior-disordered students that are most obvious to teachers are acting out and aggression, although excessive passivity and social withdrawal are commonly manifest behaviors at the other extreme. In the classroom, the aggressive behaviors of these students not only impede their own capacity for learning but also that of their classmates.

Description. Among the most often cited classroom behaviors of behavior-disordered students are short attention span and failure to follow directions, complete assignments, or comply with adult commands. Yelling out, hitting and fighting, running around the room, and disturbing peers are other common problems. Persistence of these behaviors despite ordinary attempts to change them is also characteristic. As these students grow older, their aggressiveness often causes conflict in the community, leading to problems with law enforcement officials and criminal arrests.

Special Problems. Social studies classrooms should not be particularly problematic for these students. However, general learning characteristics usually include failure experience in one or more academic areas, with reading being most common. Because of attention deficits, behavior-disordered students may also have difficulty in other information attainment skills, such as observing, listening, and studying. Any interruption or deviation from classroom routines can create negative displays of behavior; thus, classroom presentations must be carefully structured.

Instructional Implications. Stability, structure, and consistency in work standards, daily routines, and behavior expectations are the most important elements in an instructional program for behavior-disordered students. In social studies, activities should be presented that are pleasurable, interesting, and commensurate with attention span and current skill level. Lessons should have a definite beginning and ending and include discrete steps leading to task completion with appropriate and on-task behavior positively and even extrinsically rewarded. Social interaction concepts will need direct and frequent modeling in simulated environments or roleplay.

Hearing-Impaired Students

Hearing-impaired students are those whose auditory acuity and sensitivity are deficient to the point of interfering with educational performance. Many overcompensate for this deficiency by developing strong visual modalities.

Description. Hearing-impaired students have great disadvantages in acquiring receptive and expressive language skills. Their personal (both oral and sign) reading and writing vocabularies are often small and sentence structures limited and rigid. They are less able to learn from the oral facts presented in class and may have limited perceptions of the shades of meaning that add depth to comprehension of study material as well as interpersonal and social interactions.

Special Problems. Hearing problems limit students' abilities to acquire information from oral teaching and discussions. Generally, reading, writing, and speaking skills are also limited and may inhibit students' abilities to express ideas, manipulate concepts, and communicate knowledge. Especially problematic in social studies is students' limited ability to learn abstract vocabulary. Although language problems may require students to expend more effort in attaining information, once gained, the other social studies skills should not be overly difficult problems.

Instructional Implications. Students with hearing deficits should be seated in close proximity to the teacher and the chalkboard where all visual clues can be easily perceived. Clear enunciation to aid speech reading and the use of visual materials to clarify concepts, values, and main ideas are key elements in instruction. New vocabulary as well as all instructions for assignments should be introduced both orally and in writing. Teachers and classmates who want to learn or know how to sign can close large social and emotional gaps by communicating in this medium. All social studies concepts and activities should be evaluated for possible means of visual presentation.

Language-Disabled Students

Students whose expressive and receptive language abilities are so disordered that they draw unfavorable attention to themselves, are unable to communicate effectively, or have social and interpersonal problems as a consequence of being unable to communicate are generally described as language disabled. Because the social studies classroom is so heavily reliant upon language for instruction, these students are unduly penalized.

Description. Language disorders are classified as either *receptive* or *expressive*. Receptive disorders cause students to misunderstand what they read or hear while expressive disorders interfere with the production of language. Students may have severely limited vocabularies, may use words and phrases incorrectly, or may not speak at all, communicating only through gestures. Language disorders can take a variety of forms, but all can interfere with the mastery of concepts and skills.

Special Problems. Language is a critical element in social studies learning and without strong language foundations, students are going to be at particular disadvantage. However, many skills and concepts in the field can be mastered without strong reliance on language and, depending upon the particular problems of students, can be manipulated to demand less language. Demonstrations, visual presentations, and nonverbal communication activities can be utilized to present information that students can then organize and use through classifying, interpreting, and evaluating for decision making. Nonverbal communication can often be as powerful as verbal in the development of interpersonal relationships.

Instructional Implications. All activities and tasks required of language-disabled students should be concrete, hands-on, and visually aided when possible. Particular assistance will be needed in developing abstract social studies vocabulary and in modeling appropriate communication techniques. Drawing, gesturing, or signing can be beneficial alternative forms of communication. Sincere teacher and peer encouragement will be helpful as well as arrangements for functional social interactions occurring in natural environments.

Learning-Disabled Students

Learning-disabled students present the greatest variety of learning characteristics of all groups of special learners. Their most commonly cited quality is a significant achievement deficit in the presence of adequate overall intelligence.

Description. Learning disabilities are typically manifested in significantly poor performance in one or more areas that include reading, writing, spelling, oral expression, and comprehension or even math and basic thinking skills. Many times a specific academic weakness is balanced by a strength in another of these areas. Other characteristics often associated with the learning disabled include hyperactivity, perceptual/motor impairments, attention disorders, impulsivity, extreme mood swings, and disorders of memory and thinking.

Special Problems. Because of the diversity of learning problems exhibited by these students, it is difficult to pinpoint specific problem areas in teaching social studies. Generally, it can be expected that learning-disabled students may have difficulties in any one or all of the language areas, making information acquisition skills difficult to master. Math deficits will impact learning from graphs, tables, and other quantitative material, and perceptual problems may make reading maps difficult for some. Organization and use of information are also likely to trouble many of these students. Social and interpersonal skills need not necessarily be a problem for learning-disabled students, although they can be for those who have experienced extensive failure and frustration or those whose problems are readily apparent in most contexts.

Instructional Implications. Reading, writing, and other language activities in social studies will need adaptations to the particular learning problems of individuals. Precise directions, clear work standards, and short assignment segments will also be beneficial. Tape recordings and visual and talking computer software can help to overcome some language processing problems. Unit-related computer software that the student can use alone or with a partner can be used to support reading, interpreting maps, and other skills. Careful attention may need to be given to the control of extraneous stimuli and/or distractions in the classroom.

Mentally Retarded Students

Mental retardation refers to below-average general intellectual functioning accompanied by impairment in adaptive behavior. Unfortunately, it is one of the largest categories of exceptionality.

Description. Mental retardation can range from mild to profound and the degree largely determines what is appropriate placement for educational services. Because social functioning is also depressed below chronological age, it is sometimes difficult to integrate these students with nonhandicapped peers. Their learning rate is exceedingly slow and language-processing skills are noticeably weak for the chronological age.

Special Problems. Social studies skills can be difficult for these students, even the mildly retarded, to master. They will need extensive and intensive instruction to understand key concepts and vocabulary. Reading, studying, writing, and communication in general often will be difficult but learning is possible with constant review and reinforcement.

Instructional Implications. Because of mentally retarded students' slow learning rates, it is necessary to select judiciously from the social studies concepts and present only those deemed most essential to life skills. Most students will need to overlearn the skills through constant practice and review. Adaptations should be made and alternatives to common learning practices and activities found that will substitute for those requiring higher cognitive processing. Concrete examples and rote memory exercises should be used when possible. Peer tutoring by other sensitive and responsible students can benefit retarded students in social adaptations and participation.

Physically and Medically Handicapped Students

Physically and medically handicapped students probably will not experience particular problems in the area of social studies unless their specific condition adversely impacts on their academic progress in some direct manner.

Description. Physical and medical handicaps can sometimes interfere with the acquisition of basic skills, such as reading and math, especially when conditions have caused students to be absent during critical learning times or when prescribed medicines have affected general intellectual functioning. The physically handicapped may also tire more easily from physical strain, which can cause fluctuations in performance.

Special Problems. The problems of these students are mostly physical and are generally exhibited only in decreased opportunities for developing the wide range of experiences needed to understand and interpret the content of social studies lessons. Some students have fine- or gross-motor coordination problems that interfere with writing- or hands-on-type activities. Socially, many disabled students suffer from overprotection, excessive pity, and even cruel rejection or exclusion from activities of the nonhandicapped. These attitude problems can in turn adversely affect academic functioning when self-concept is involved.

Instructional Implications. The classroom adaptations most helpful to the medically and physically handicapped are specific changes to the physical environment to accommodate the handicapping conditions, adjustments to the stimulus/response format, and lesson length. Just like everyone else, students with physical and health disabilities need to have successful experiences in learning. Social participation and interaction skills will not necessarily be problematic for students; however, it is not uncommon for nonhandicapped students to be uncomfortable in the presence of a person with a visible handicap, and they may withdraw or be noticeably tense, thereby limiting opportunities for social interactions to occur normally. The classroom needs to be a place where disabilities can be discussed openly and other students are encouraged to accept and understand the nature of the handicapping conditions.

Speech-Disordered Students

Speech disorders are high-incidence handicapping conditions. However, they do not directly interfere with mastery of social studies concepts.

Description. Speech disorders are usually of three primary types: articulation, fluency, and voice. Articulation disorders, or mispronunciations of certain sounds and words, are the most common. The most common fluency problem is stuttering. Voice disorders are characterized by inappropriate pitch, intensity, or quality.

Special Problems. Auditory discrimination difficulties often accompany speech disorders and can also interfere with acquisition of information presented as a listening experience. Some students may prefer to communicate their knowledge in writing and will often avoid speaking activities and class discussions.

Instructional Implications. The primary adjustment required in social studies for speech-disordered students is to offer alternatives to communicating knowledge orally. Alternative methods are usually readily available and should be used when students express tension or insecurity in presenting orally. When these students do volunteer to contribute, it is important to give them time to respond without pressure or interruption.

Visually Impaired Students

Experiences in social studies that are primarily visual will quite naturally penalize the blind or visually impaired student. However, substitute experiences can easily be provided by teachers and students.

Description. Visual impairments include being partially sighted (despite maximum correction) to being totally blind. The adjustments in instruction needed are determined by the degree of impairment.

Special Problems. Social studies instruction need not present particular difficulty to the visually impaired if appropriate adjustments are made. Information that cannot be presented orally in the classroom should be made available to students in Braille or through an aide or parent. Even then it should be expected that these students will read more slowly and take extra time to accomplish their learning tasks. The partially sighted student may tire easily with the strain of trying to read or see demonstrations.

Instructional Implications. Visually impaired students should be seated for ease of seeing and hearing the teacher. Hard-to-read worksheets with extensive details and intricate map work should be avoided. When possible, materials should be adjusted to include large type, raised relief maps and globes, and magnifiers. The opportunity to touch all visual and concrete objects should be provided and encouraged for these students. Assignments of peers as buddies to help verbalize all experiences can also be helpful and can aid in the development of social interaction skills.

THE ACADEMICALLY GIFTED STUDENTS

Students classified as *gifted* are handled differently in various regions of the country. In some instances, they are part of special education, but in others, they are considered a special group outside of special education.

Description. Academically gifted students excel in learning significantly beyond their chronological ages. They are noted for their intellectual superiority, creativity, leadership, and high-verbal abilities. Although most gifted students have little difficulty with social studies, others sometimes achieve far below their potential.

Special Problems. Low achievement in social studies is often the consequence of inappropriate levels of reading materials, the pace of the curriculum, and the teaching. Boredom and limited opportunities to be creative can stifle the curious and result in underachievement. Social interactions with peers can sometimes be a problem if gifted students perceive themselves intellectually superior and adopt offensive attitudes.

Instructional Implications. The variety of abilities and talents of these students should be capitalized on in all activities. Extended opportunities for learning through hypothesizing, drawing inferences, stating generalizations, synthesizing main ideas, and evaluating ideas should be provided. Every lesson should provide some opportunity for extension of the concepts and skills into future societal relevance. Social studies can be one of the richest areas of the curriculum for exploring provocative and challenging ideas.

SUMMARY

Social studies can be the most ideally suited curriculum area for special students to learn life skills and to experience fundamental social principles.

Certain topics and subtopics are more relevant to functioning in real life than others; the greater the degree of handicap and the older the student, the more important the need to select carefully from among possibilities.

Some social studies skills are rendered particularly difficult to achieve due to the learning characteristics of certain special learners. Reading is the most difficult of the information acquisition skills for most special learners. Once the information is attained, the skills involved in organizing and using the information can be considerably less difficult. Also, in most instances, skills related to interpersonal relationships and social participation often are closely correlated with the difficulties involved in the other two skill areas. Although academically gifted students typically master the social studies skills with little difficulty, they, too, need special consideration to realize their potential.

When instruction is adjusted to meet individual learning needs, the problem areas can often be bypassed. Some suggestions for accommodating special needs in social studies are described in the next chapter.

CHAPTER 3 /
DETECTING AND CORRECTING
SPECIAL SOCIAL STUDIES NEEDS

Chapter 1 focused on the content and processing skills associated with social studies education. Chapter 2 described special groups of learners. The purpose of this chapter is to synthesize and extend the content of the first two by answering two questions: 1) How can special needs for social studies information and concepts be detected? and 2) How can these special needs in social studies be corrected?

Planning social studies instruction for the special learner involves: 1) identifying the social studies skills and concepts appropriate to the curriculum and grade; 2) determining students' levels of development in these skills, including those handicapping conditions that contribute to development; and 3) applying principles of corrective and effective instruction, along with the necessary adjustments for handicapping conditions, in a plan designed to improve those skills and concepts. Twelve principles are suggested to help special learners master both the appropriate content information and the learning strategies and skills.

DETECTION

The social studies skills and concepts that need to be taught at each grade are generally available in curriculum guides, adopted textbooks, and guidelines developed by professional organizations, such as the National Council for the Social Studies. Determining which students have deficiencies in these skills, the levels at which these skills need to be taught, and identifying the specific handicapping conditions can be accomplished by: 1) synthesizing available data; 2) acquiring data through direct testing by both formal and informal means; 3) observing students' inside and outside classroom behavior; and 4) interviewing students and resource people who have pertinent knowledge regarding students' performance levels.

Synthesizing Available Data

Previous achievements in social studies should be reviewed by examining cumulative records, past report cards, standardized test results, and, if available, former teachers of special students. Identifying a performance pattern can yield implications for instruction. In particular, comparing students' progress in all subjects and with various teachers can be revealing. Questions to guide the review should include: What social studies classes has the student experienced? How does the student's achievement in social studies compare to that in other subjects? How does the target student's performance in social studies compare with that of peers? Does low achievement in social studies coincide with low achievement in the basic skills? How do scores on the social studies portions of standardized tests compare, especially with grades and classroom performance? Do teachers' comments reveal any particular strengths or weaknesses in social studies or any particular interests?

The nature and possible cause of social studies problems may be suggested in the answers to these questions. If performance in all subject areas is weak, then it is likely that inadequate basic skills, especially in reading, are preventing the student from acquiring the social studies information needed to understand the content. When both social studies and science areas indicate low performance, the demand for independence in acquiring information is probably high, forcing students to rely on their reading and study skills. If social studies is a specific weakness, it is possible that students' performances are a reflection of motivation to study the specific topics or possibly a weakness in instructional approaches. If there are patterns of more positive performance with certain teachers, then those teachers should be interviewed to determine what variables increased progress. In many cases, the synthesis of available information will reveal a composite picture of target students with some implications for instruction in social studies.

Direct Testing

Performance in social studies can be measured to some degree by both formal and informal tests. The level of achievement revealed by testing is not as important as the strengths and weaknesses in performance on specific tasks and content objectives in social studies. This information provides the basis for developing appropriate intervention strategies.

Formal Testing. Formal tests of achievement in social studies are provided on some standardized achievement batteries and are useful for making comparisons of students' performance on a national or regional basis and for identifying students in need of more thorough analysis. Typically, these tests measure skills primarily related to acquiring information, such as reading comprehension of expository text in social studies subjects and map, globe, and graphics skills. Few if any of the skills related to organizing and using information—such as classifying, interpreting, summarizing, synthesizing, and evaluating—are incorporated into these tests. In addition, the skills related to interpersonal relationships and social participation are almost never a part of formal testing.

Other factors also enter into the performance of special students on these tests. Time limits, difficult test formats, and a lack of test wiseness may falsely deflate scores. One major problem often encountered is that the content of the test does not match what the students have studied in their respective social studies classes. Apart from indicating a general level and rate of performance, these scores are limited in usefulness to the teacher, shedding little light on the skills, abilities, or content that needs to be taught. Measures of the student's information-processing system and how readily he or she can integrate newly acquired information with material that was previously learned are not indicated. Performance guaged over time and in comparison with peers are more informal approaches to assessment and have more utility for the teacher concerned with designing an appropriate instructional program for the special learner.

Informal Testing. Some social studies textbooks supply informal tests that can assess both content covered as well as some of the important social studies skills in need of direct instruction. Informal testing techniques, such as the Group Reading Inventory (GRI) and cloze procedure, are recommended for assessing strengths and weaknesses of students' abilities to use their assigned textbooks and silent reading comprehension of social studies text material. These assessment instruments can be constructed, administered, and interpreted by the classroom teacher using the material that will be used for teaching.

The GRI requires the teacher to choose an unread section from the social studies textbook, construct comprehension questions over the material, and have students answer these after they have completed reading the material silently. The level of comprehension of the material is determined and an analysis of types of questions most often missed will indicate the degree to which the textbook will be useful as a teaching tool as well as how able each student will be in using it to gain information.

A cloze inventory will yield similar information. A cloze test is constructed by selecting an unread section from the textbook and typing it with every fifth or seventh word deleted. The ability of the student to reconstruct the text by filling in the blanks with words that help the text material make sense will reveal to a large extent students' information-processing abilities with social studies text material. Instructions for constructing, administering, and interpreting these types of assessment tools can be attained from most reading methods textbooks.

Other types of informal testing can be constructed by the classroom teacher using criterion-referenced formats from a curriculum base. Data collected from these assessments can be compiled into student profiles that yield information on individuals' strengths and weaknesses, mastery of specific skills, evaluation of progress, and appropriate instructional grouping placements. This information should be used to devise plans for instruction that lead to development of proficiency in identified skills and allow students to meet the requirements and expectations for the social studies program. The more systematic and ongoing this type of assessment is, the more useful it is for teachers for making instructional decisions.

Interviews. New approaches to assessment emphasize seeking student perceptions of learning tasks. Student self-analysis of the difficulty of the social studies material can reveal specific kinds of problems they may be having. Another format is to have students recite what they have learned, which often reveals what remains to be learned. Testing formats for these assessment approaches place considerable emphasis on personal, one-to-one or small-group interviews. Open-ended questions that encourage students to elaborate are a most effective interview technique. One technique is to construct a short interview (6-10 questions) over a specific topic in social studies. For example: Do you know anyone who is from Japan? Can you show me where

Japan is on the map? How are the Japanese people like or different from us? Have you ever been to another country? Would you like to go to Japan? Why would anyone need to know about Japan? What would you like to learn about Japan? Content-specific questions such as these can reveal which students have some background knowledge and the extent of interest students have in a particular topic.

Interviews can be used early in the year or prior to the planning of a unit of work to determine students' backgrounds of experience and to give some insight into their learning interests and modalities. Questions such as these might be used: What kinds of lessons did you like most in social studies last year? Why? Which did you like least? Describe what helps you to learn social studies. What kinds of activities do you like most and which do you like least? Why? If students have difficulty verbalizing their responses, alternative study approaches might be presented from which they could choose. For example: If you had to learn about a particular country, would you prefer to have the teacher tell you about it, read about it for yourself, have someone from that country come to class and talk about it, or see a film and hear a narrator talk about it? An interest inventory can be constructed by using the table of contents of the assigned textbook to compile a list of topics and ask students to rank them in order of their interest or to choose the five most interesting and the five least interesting.

Collaborative discussions with other teachers who have or have had interactions with students are also often insightful. Ask questions such as: What lesson format seems to be most effective for students? How much time can students be expected to attend to learning tasks? Describe the typical performance of a student(s). Which of the information acquisition skills are the strongest? What particular content and social skills problems have been noted? In addition, parents, siblings, friends, and other resource people who know students well can provide information relative to social dynamics within and outside of the classroom. Knowledge of students' prior experiences and familiarity with their immediate environments can provide helpful information about what has shaped the social development of the learner.

Observing Behavior

Teacher observation of behavior and performance under specified conditions can provide a broader view of what elements contribute to students' progress in social studies. Measures of this type should be designed as profiles or checklists that permit a more holistic look at how students are developing in the social studies, areas of interest, types of grouping, various learning and teaching styles, and other factors within the learning environment. Informal observations of students as they interact in settings outside the formal classroom—such as before and after school, at lunch, and on the playground—also provide valuable information. Special attention should be given to the development of social participation with observation focused on leadership and followership in groups.

The most convenient and reliable means of conducting observations is to utilize a checklist of behaviors and skills while observing. Figure 3.1 is

FIGURE 3.1   Checklist for Detecting Special Needs in Social Studies

Student's Name —————————————— Observer —————————————— Date(s) ——

SKILLS	STUDENT BEHAVIORS	OBSERVED	REPORTED	COMMENTS
I. Acquiring Information				
Reading	• Recognizes and understands word meanings • Comprehends details • Makes inferences • Reads critically • Other:			
Study	• Locates information in text and other resources • Outlines and/or summarizes • Takes notes • Organizes for study • Works independently • Other:			
Information Search	• Uses card catalog • Uses special reference sources • Interprets maps, graphics, and charts • Uses community resources • Other:			
Technical Skills	• Operates a computer to enter and retrieve information • Accesses information through telephone and television • Other:			
II. Organizing and Using Information				
Classifying	• Identifies most salient features • Groups by criteria • Places data in tabular form • Other:			
Interpreting	• States relationships • Notes causes and effects • Draws inferences • Predicts outcomes • Recognizes value dimensions • Other:			
Analyzing	• Identifies unique features • Identifies relationships and patterns • Detects bias • Questions credibility of sources • Other:			

SKILLS	STUDENT BEHAVIORS	OBSERVED	REPORTED	COMMENTS
Summarizing	• Extracts significant ideas • Combines concepts to form conclusions • Restates ideas in concise form • Other:			
Synthesizing	• Creates new ideas from details • Reinterprets events by what might have happened • Finds new solutions to problems • Other:			
Evaluating	• Selects pertinent ideas • Estimates the adequacy of information • Tests the validity • Describes personal relevance • Describes societal relevance • Other:			
Decision Making	• Identifies decision-making situations • Recognizes relevant facts • Recognizes implicit values • Identifies alternative courses • Takes actions • Other:			
III. Relating Interpersonally and Participating Socially				
Personalizing	• Expresses convictions • Communicates feelings • Adjusts behavior to fit groups • Recognizes mutual relationships • Other:			
Interacting in Groups	• Contributes to group interactions • Participates in making rules • Participates in group activities • Other:			
Participates in Political Events	• Keeps informed on issues • Identifies social action situations • Works to influence social decisions • Accepts citizenship responsibilities • Other:			

ADDITIONAL COMMENTS:

SUMMARY OF OBSERVATIONS:

an example of such a checklist. Such instruments not only focus the observation but also provide a format and written record of behaviors. They can be used by teachers during social studies lessons, by outside observers in the classroom, or by interviewers for structuring individual interviews.

Although there are numerous types of assessment approaches and formats, the most complete picture of the special student's performance emerges when all of the accumulated diagnostic information is synthesized. When that profile is in hand, teachers may begin to select strategies that are most likely to correct individual students' special needs in social studies.

CORRECTION

Corrective instruction is most effective when it is designed around individual students' needs and previous learning. Instructionally, all students, including special students, require the same skills for learning social studies. Adaptations, variations, and more individualized instruction may be necessary in some circumstances to make learning more effective for special students. Research relative to the teaching of special learners and a compilation of publications containing good teaching practices can be found at the end of this chapter. The following discussion is an outline of 12 basic principles suggested for achieving mastery of social studies content and skills.   These principles are appropriate for all learners, but they are particularly important for teaching social studies to special learners.

FIGURE 3.2 Twelve Principles for Teaching Social Studies to Special Learners

---

1. Choose topics that have personal relevance
2. Build on what students already know
3. Directly teach the skills needed for the task
4. Establish safe learning environments
5. Develop activity-centered lessons
6. Promote inquiry learning
7. Teach to learning styles
8. Provide positive and informative feedback
9. Encourage parental involvement
10. Stay knowledgeable of current events
11. Promote effective social interaction
12. Both teach and adjust for specific skill needs

---

1. Choose Topics That Have Personal Relevance

Students must see the relevance of what they are studying to their personal social realities. Unless connections are made between classroom study and their own world, students are not likely to retain the learning, internalize the concepts, and make practical applications. Two guiding questions for teachers in selecting content should be: 1) How are students going to function better in society as a result of studying this topic? and, 2) Is the time spent learning this content congruent with its importance to them later? This is especially important for the special learner, who often cannot or does not transfer the specific bits of information of a subject and thus needs principles or procedures for generalizing, deducing, relating, and expressing ideas. Strength of learning and knowledge is grounded in each individual's acceptance of the personal relevance of information and is increased by building on what then becomes prior knowledge.

For the special learner, who takes more time to learn skills and concepts in social studies, teachers must decide to delete nonessential topics, teach only the major concepts of other less practical topics, and teach the most practical topics in some depth. These decisions are best made when the criteria for which topics to teach and for how long are based on a realistic judgment of the importance of the topic to special students' need for survival and day-to-day functioning. Selections can be made on the basis of currency in newspapers and television newscasts, practicality in everyday life, and students' personal interests in learning. When students have learned the basic and practical application of the concepts, it is possible to go back and extend the learning to more abstract levels.

Certain topics in social studies are inherently more oriented toward real life than others. Of the activities that follow in later pages of this book, younger special students should probably be taught Topics 6, Respect for Others, and 8, Social Participation, in Chapter 4 first. Older students would probably benefit from Topic 9, Social Interaction (Ch. 4), and Topic 40, Law and Society (Ch. 8). Topics which are less practical, such as 20, Shopping Centers (Ch. 6), and 35, Life in Colonial America (Ch. 8), may be skimmed with only the major concepts stressed. Topics that are non-essential, such as Canada (49), Mexico (50), Russia (51), and Japan (52), should probably be saved for the end of the year or omitted completely to allow for in-depth treatment of the more practical concepts.

2. Build on What Students Already Know

The most current and interactive models of learning and teaching emphasize the process of applying prior knowledge to develop and add to the conceptual and knowledge base of all learners. Indeed, many learning deficiencies of special students are directly related to having limited experiential bases, as they often have been shielded by overprotective parents or excluded from certain types of activities. When experiences have been limited, students do not have the core of knowledge needed for connecting and providing meaning for new ideas. This principle of learning applies not only to the broad, social experiences of students but also to the curriculum-based experiences students have had in other grades and in other subjects. If students do not have the prior knowledge needed for learning new concepts, teachers must design appropriate experiences that will foster learning on the students' level. This often means providing firsthand experiences through such activities as fieldtrips or vicarious ones through videotape productions or simulations. Teachers may then build on these common or core learnings through direct teaching.

3. Directly Teach the Skills Needed for the Task

Academic as well as social skills are complicated tasks even for the best of students. Breaking these skills into smaller units of instruction and then teaching them sequentially and concretely to accomplish a learning objective provides the teacher more opportunity to observe and identify precisely where students are having problems.

Basic skills in reading are the most fundamental tools for learning social studies concepts. Without the ability to read and comprehend what is written, students will always struggle to achieve; thus, it is extremely critical that the special learner be equipped to apply word recognition skills that will assist him with specific vocabulary in the study and comprehension of a particular concept. Social studies vocabulary is often abstract, and special students will need concrete and practical examples to master concepts. Functional language should be used whenever possible. For example, it is possible to teach about citizenship by talking about helping others, obeying rules and not fighting. Provision for overlearning essential vocabulary and an emphasis on multisensory input are recommended techniques for the special learner. Games and computer activities are also good techniques for practicing and reinforcing word recognition skills that contribute to students' overall comprehension ability and long-term academic progress. Words selected for study should be those most personally relevant to the student and most critical to the basic comprehension of the concept.

Similarly, other social studies skills, such as map reading, referencing, and organizing and using information, must be analyzed for prerequisite abilities and activities designed to master these skills before proficiency in others can be expected. Constant monitoring of students' quality of achievement at each step will help ensure they experience success and thus feel safe in risking an attempt at the next higher-level task.

4. Establish Safe Learning Environments

Classrooms that are chaotic, where students feel anxious or alienated, are not going to produce students who are motivated to learn social studies content and skills. Risk-free learning environments are especially important for special learners. Teachers must maintain classroom control, encourage students, patiently support their efforts, and make them feel comfortable in taking intellectual risks without fear of being criticized for making mistakes.

Values teaching and clarification experiences, which are primary goals in social studies education, cannot satisfactorily develop unless students feel comfortable to share their personal views and express their feelings. The social/emotional context of the classroom, including the students' perception of the teacher, is a strong force in determining level of involvement and strength of learning in all students. Learners who have experienced failure or who lack personal acceptance from environments that have not been altogether supportive will be unlikely to act on their values and put their basic thinking and decision-making skills to use if they do not perceive themselves to be safe in doing so.

Special students who are particularly distractible or hyperactive or who display frequent and significant mood swings need environments that are highly organized with specific tasks clearly delineated. Consistency in format of lessons and fair and consistent dispensation of discipline give comfort to students who need to know what to expect and the manner in which they are expected to respond.

5. Develop Activity-Centered Lessons

Because special learners' reading abilities often do not match the readability levels of the books assigned for their grades, it becomes essential that social studies lessons be activity-centered, providing as many concrete experiences as possible. The content should be presented in language-rich environments that enhance and allow the processes of thinking, reading, speaking, and writing to be acquired together with the products or facts of the social studies curriculum.

Activity-centered lessons provide more opportunity to involve several learning modalities. The memory traces of what is seen, heard, felt, smelled, and tasted are often stronger than what is only read and can provide a solid basis for understanding. A variety of materials, strategies, and techniques that are motivating and interesting make the message stronger when more than one sensory system is involved. Activities such as dramatic play, roleplaying, simulations, and social action projects are ways of combining the teaching of skills, values, and content outcomes into holistic lessons with multiple outcomes for achieving a balanced emphasis and a more well-rounded program.

6. Promote Inquiry Learning

Inquiry learning is a strongly supported strategy for teaching many social studies objectives. This approach focuses on making students primarily responsible for processing information to answer or solve a problem. The students' behavior occurs in several phases, including becoming aware of a discrepant event or problem to be solved; identifying tentative solutions; testing the hypotheses or solutions with supporting information or data; and accepting, modifying, or rejecting the hypotheses.

Research indicates that students' critical thinking and deductive reasoning skills are enhanced through this approach and that students enjoy increased benefits from group experiences in which they communicate, share responsibilities, and jointly seek knowledge. Underlying the strength of this approach are the questions the teacher asks and the purpose for asking them. It is also critical that the inquiry process for special learners be structured, modeled, and guided by the teacher to ensure that the inquiry remains focused. Cognitive modeling by the teacher, where he or she shows the students what to do and how to think out loud, is also helpful to learners as they model and participate in the problem-solving strategies.

7. Teach to Learning Styles

All learners have individual preferences for how they best assimilate information, which are generally referred to as learning styles. Factors that contribute to individual learning styles include instructional modes, tolerance for structure, need for praise/reward, and goal preferences. Some individuals work better when information is presented through verbal presentations. Others learn best through reading or observation. These styles can also vary depending upon the kind of information; for instance, some students prefer to read social studies material but would rather listen to math explanations.

Students also vary in the amount of structure they need from the teacher and the organizing they can do on their own. Other variance in learning styles can be accounted for in the needs students have for praise and rewards. Some students demand constant attention and feedback, while others are reliant on internal praise and/or self-satisfaction. In addition, some learners are more efficient when tasks are short range and within their immediate grasp, whereas others can work toward longer-range objectives that cover more time. Other conditions that sometimes affect learning styles include light, degree of sound before distraction occurs, time of day, room temperature, and grouping patterns. Determining learning styles through systematic observation, and/or questioning or through formal published learning-style inventories can be effective in helping a teacher identify and establish appropriate learning conditions for students.

8. Provide Positive and Informative Feedback

The reporting of results, or feedback, is a widely accepted learning principle. Quick, appropriate, and specific responses given to students to let them know how they are doing is often critical in sustaining their continued learning and preventing their internalizing incorrect procedures and information.

Feedback can be provided in numerous ways, such as questions and answers, spot checking, correcting papers, and corrective comments that prevent incorrect behaviors from being perpetuated as the teacher moves around the room. The tone used by the teacher to convey the feedback can sometimes be important as students become sensitive to sincerity and negative information. In addition, feedback that specifies behavior that can be modified is more helpful than comments that are evaluative but do not represent something students can do anything about. Consistent and thorough application of this principle of learning can significantly improve students' attitudes and achievement

9. Encourage Parental Involvement

Informed and involved parents can be a significant asset in the teaching and learning situation. It is not unusual for parents of special children to be more involved in their children's education than other students' parents because their participation is often required in order to receive some of the special services; regardless, most usually welcome and appreciate the opportunity to participate. Sending home brief descriptions of the learning objectives and suggestions for specific ways in which the parents can be helpful provides another means of reinforcing and extending the social studies concepts, establishing relevance, and broadening the experiential base.

10. Stay knowledgeable of Current Events

There is always the risk in the social studies program that the most current happenings in the world will escape classroom investigation because there are no guidebooks for the study and it is often problematic to collect all of the background information and materials needed. However, it is the study of those things students see on television and hear about in their everyday lives that gives relevance, reality, and immediacy to the other concepts chosen for study in the social studies program. Current affairs are the bridges to the past and the connections between in- and out-of school experiences. Choosing events to study and discuss requires careful selection based upon criteria such as educational value of the event, appropriateness for maturity and ability of students, and relationship of the present event to past and future units of study.

11. Promote Effective Social Interaction

One of the major goals of social studies education is to promote and enhance social interaction skills among people. The classroom can be the most natural setting for reflecting the real world and providing opportunities for students to develop and refine social interaction, social contact, and social action skills. This implies that a teacher must be flexible in allowing students to interact socially within the classroom and to refrain from being so rigid in expectations of behavior that students are not allowed to talk informally and interact naturally. It also means that specific learning opportunities should be planned for students to practice modeling some of the more basic social interaction tasks. Social participation and interaction activities, such as those presented in Chapter 4 (especially Topics 8, Social Participation, and 9, Social Interaction), are examples of ways of incorporating this learning into the classroom.

Recent research indicates that cooperative learning is not only a positive achievement variable in all content areas but is also a powerful means of promoting and developing social skills among peers. This instructional approach is characterized by students working in small, mixed ability learning groups with each member having the responsibility for helping the others learn. The approach is based on the premise that working together to achieve a common goal is motivational, much like a sports team trying to win a game. Other benefits include talking about things with other people, helping everyone understand and remember them much better.

Cooperative learning also has potential for influencing and minimizing negative peer pressure, which sometimes severely limits students' achievement. The opportunity to teach, for example, in peer-tutoring situations, is available to students as they explain ideas to their teammates and engage in cognitive elaboration, enhancing their own understanding. For the special student, the risk of speaking out in class and being criticized is minimized. It also becomes legitimate for students to ask for help from their peers when they are working toward the same goal. Positive learning effects have been found on such social outcomes as race relations, acceptance of mainstreamed academically handicapped students, and student self-esteem and liking of class. This particular approach to learning seems especially suited to the goals and objectives of the social studies curriculum and most beneficial to special students, who lack peer acceptance and often have major problems in social skills.

12. Both Teach and Adjust for Specific Skill Needs

Several strategies are suggested for both teaching and adjusting for particular needs in the three skill areas: 1) acquiring information; 2) organizing and using information; and 3) relating interpersonally and participating socially. Charts of the skills with which particular groups of special learners may have problems are presented with each discussion. The skill needs marked for each special group were selected as likely correlates with the learning characteristics of that category. These needs are not necessarily representative of the categories or exclusive to them.

Strand 1: Acquiring Information Skills

Figure 3.3 is a summary of the learner groups and the degree of difficulty they are likely to have with Strand 1 skills, which are reading, study, information search, and technical skills.

Reading. Reading is one of the most essential communication skills used in learning social studies. Unfortunately, it is also one of the primary difficulties experienced by most special students. Key principles of instruction for teaching reading to special students include: 1) preparing students for reading by building interest, connecting with their past experiences and setting purposes; 2) teaching key vocabulary prior to reading; 3) teaching the comprehension skills and practicing them; and 4) applying the reading to other materials and contexts.

The most critical aspect of reading in social studies is the development of vocabulary that expresses the concepts studied. Words central to the core of instruction and technical to the areas of study—such as *democracy, values, culture, peninsula, globe, urban, illegal,* and *population*—must be taught in meaningful ways, appealing to as many senses as possible, and in a concrete manner. Firsthand and visual activities, such as the use of pictures, models, realia, films, or demonstrations, are especially useful. When teaching a concept such as water bodies, label and catagorize for students by grouping terms such as *river, lake, gulf,* and *ocean.* State behaviors of people to define roles: A policeman watches for people who break the law and takes them to jail or court. Describe a new concept in terms of its salient features and then provide as many examples of the concept as possible. Ask students to distinguish examples from nonex-

FIGURE 3.3 Strand 1: Information Acquisition Skills with which Traditional Categories of Special Learners Might Have Difficulty

SPECIAL LEARNER GROUP	READING	STUDY	INFORMATION SEARCH	TECHNICAL SKILLS
REGULAR/REMEDIAL STUDENTS				
Culturally Different	S	S	S	
Slow Learners	S	S	S	S
SPECIAL EDUCATION STUDENTS				
Behavior Disordered	S	S	S	S
Hearing Impaired	S	S	S	S
Language Disabled	S	S	S	S
Learning Disabled	M	M	S	S
Mentally Retarded	M	M	M	S
Physically Handicapped	S			S
Speech Disordered				
Visually Impaired	S		M	M
Generic Handicaps	S	S	S	S

S = SOME of these students might have difficulty
M = MANY of these students are likely to have difficulty

amples: Which are examples of things found in an urban area and which are not? *(horses, suburbs, farmland, skyscrapers, airport)* Relate new terms to known terms as in analogies: A governor is like a president except he or she rules only one state instead of all the states. Discuss the most useful prefixes, suffixes, and root words commonly found in social studies: *cooperate, coexist, coworker.*

Other strategies that are useful include: giving students study guides that focus on the important information in the text; dictating oral summaries or writing summary notations on the overhead projector for students to write in their notes; reading the material orally to the students or preparing an audiotape of the most important sections of the text; rewriting the most important ideas at a lower reading level. Alternate forms of acquiring information should be considered when students are having extreme difficulties. Listening, observation of video and roleplays, and fieldtrips or other direct experimentations are useful in circumventing reading as the primary means of acquiring information.

Study. Study skills are usually an extension of reading skills and generally an independent activity. Special students need to know some basic sources for locating information, such as the textbook itself, encyclopedias, and the library. They will also need rudimentary skills, such as alphabetizing and scanning for specific dates and topics, in order to make study a useful and productive activity. Learning the parts of the social studies textbook through such activities as examining the table of contents, and using the glossary, list of maps, and index will equip students to use their most readily available resource. Mnemonic techniques (such as HOMES to remember the Great

Lakes) or visualizations and funny rhymes can sometimes be useful in keying memory of details and facts that students will be expected to know.

Information Search. A further extension of study skills is the ability to find information through such sources as the card catalog, yellow pages of the phone book, library, and other community telephone information services. Interpreting maps, graphics, and charts are also primary sources of information in the social studies. When students have difficulty with these tasks, it is helpful to walk and talk them through finding information and then provide activities that will reinforce the skills. Knowing alternative sources for information is also important for students with handicaps that prevent them from using a particular source. For example, hearing-impaired students will be unable to use a library telephone information service but will be able to use a computer data base to search for information. The fundamentals of reading maps and charts can be taught by using models, pictures, and blocks to stand for real things on floor maps. Semipictorial symbols to represent houses, schools, and other objects and concepts can then be added, as can colors to represent water, land, forest, and other geographical features. Direction concepts will need to be taught in relation to the students' physical selves and classroom orientation. Concepts should be expanded outside the classroom into the immediate community and beyond. Scale and distance are measurement concepts that also are best taught by beginning with the students' immediate surroundings. Relief maps provide concrete examples of a number of concepts, such as why some areas receive more rainfall and others are dry, how climate is affected by terrain, and other questions related to distance and geography. The tactile manipulation of the clay or papier-maché and the enabled visualization are especially helpful for the special student.

Technical Skills. The advent of microcomputers and quality social studies software has provided many options and learning advantages for the special student. Programs include drill and practice on skills, tutorials, creative expression opportunities, and simulations. Among the advantages are individualization, immediate feedback, self-pacing, and development of problem-solving and decision-making skills. Learning to use the computer itself should not represent a problem for special students, as the teacher can prepare the computer for instruction if necessary. The quality of the software and how user friendly it is will determine what learning benefits can be had. Generally, computer skills needed can range from pressing a single key to input a certain response to typing creative text for stories, maps, charts, drawings, and puzzles. Accessing data bases for social studies information to solve puzzles and make decisions can be extremely simple operationally. Cooperative learning, with students of greater ability paired with students of lesser ability, has been demonstrated as an effective approach in computer-assisted instruction and will also be helpful for those students who have physical disabilities related to the hands.

Strand 2: Organizing and Using Information Skills

The skills involved in processing social studies information are especially critical for building knowledge. As can be seen in Figure 3.4, students with speech disorders and physical handicaps are least likely to have weaknesses in these skills.

Classifying. Classifying is an essential component of concept development and involves grouping and organizing items or ideas by relevant characteristics, uses, or relationships. Development of this skill requires beginning with concrete objects and asking questions that guide students' thinking until they can become independent in the process. Questions such as these—"How are these items alike? How are they different? What are the most important likenesses? Most important differences?—can aid students in perceiving distinguishing features. Depending upon the skills of the students, important terms and even the designation of the categories may have to be supplied until students become efficient at making decisions based upon criteria. It may also be helpful to insist that students defend their answers orally or if needed have a peer defend the answers for them. Many times, the defense process will reveal erroneous patterns of thinking or the stimuli that prompted the decision, giving the teacher insight into where to begin helping students make better decisions.

Interpreting. Interpreting relies heavily upon students' prior experiences with the target elements, events, and objects. It is important to monitor special students closely to prevent them from misinterpreting information and operating upon these misconceptions for any period of time. This is especially important if students have been asked to predict outcomes and never realize after their predictions what the outcomes actually were or why or how their predictions were incorrect. Recognizing and explaining the meanings of important ideas and relationships are key factors in interpretation skills. Students may have to begin by stating their wild guesses about relationships, what they think will happen next, or main ideas and, through

FIGURE 3.4 Strand 2: Information-Organizing Skills with which Traditional Categories of Special Learners Might Have Difficulty

SPECIAL LEARNER GROUP	CLASSIFICATION	INTERPRETATION	ANALYSIS	SUMMARIZING	SYNTHESIZING	EVALUATING	DECISION MAKING
REGULAR/REMEDIAL STUDENTS							
Culturally Different		S		S		S	S
Slow Learners	S	S	S	S	S	S	
SPECIAL EDUCATION STUDENTS							S
Behavior Disordered	S	S				S	
Hearing Impaired		S	S		S		
Language Disabled	S		S	S		S	
Learning Disabled	S	S	S	S	S	S	
Mentally Retarded	M	M	M	M	M	M	M
Physically Handicapped							
Speech Disordered							
Visually Impaired	S		S			S	S
Generic Handicaps	S	S	S	S	S	S	S

S = SOME of these students might have difficulty
M = MANY of these students are likely to have difficulty

produced the outcome. Providing several options from which students may choose is also helpful until students become better able to structure their own options and describe relationships.

Analyzing. To analyze is to form simple organizations of key ideas, to separate topics into major components according to criteria, to compare and contrast differing accounts of the same events, and to make conclusions based upon the analysis. This is a higher-order intellectual process that requires prerequisite skills in categorizing and interpreting. The use of charts and pictorial presentations of information, with questions to help students see how the problem can be broken down in useful ways, can benefit students who have difficulty with this skill. Hearing the teacher think outloud in an analysis process as well as the use of such questions as these—What are the main parts of this story (map, picture)? What is the central idea? How is the material organized? How can we know which idea is better? True?—can be useful in guiding students through analysis. Asking experts to present different sides of a local community issue, discussing and drawing conclusions from what was heard, and evaluating what swayed the most opinion is one way of developing critical analysis skills.

Summarizing. The ability to extract ideas and restate them in concise form will be difficult for special students who have significant deficiencies in oral and written language, primarily because of the reliance on these avenues of communication for summarization. Suggestions for helping students in this area include giving them a partial outline of information to complete or having them complete a sentence that summarizes the main idea: How industries decide to locate in a particular area depends on _____. Use charts and tables to present information and provide an opportunity for students to make conclusions: Write down three things you know from looking at this map. Before beginning a unit, give students a study guide with a summary of the main points and have them check which one was the main idea after study and discussion. When writing is problematic, use the overhead projector or chalkboard to write down for students, summaries of information they help to formulate after short intervals of study and discussion; present a selection of answers from which students choose; or ask oral questions that require one- or two-word responses. After discussing a topic or making an important point, ask someone, "What did I just say?" and have them retell the point in their own words. At the end of a lesson, ask students to write in their journals or on a piece of paper to hand in (or tell in their own words as they leave the classroom) one thing they learned in social studies today. Providing many opportunities for students to practice summarizing in a variety of formats will enhance the development of this skill.

Synthesizing. Synthesis is the process of reorganizing social studies information to form new ideas and concepts or to present information in new forms. Models, reports, maps, charts, stories, displays, songs, artwork, or dramatic presentations can bring together the parts of something into a creative and new whole. Because this skill is rooted in a high-level intellectual process, it is often overlooked in the social studies classroom as a process that can reflect not only students' creative and artistic abilities but also the depth of their thinking and knowledge.

Evaluating. Distinguishing the veracity of ideas and information is of vital importance in developing students' abilities to make wise decisions and, ultimately, for becoming informed consumers and citizens. Activities for developing this skill include teaching the basic propaganda devices and applying the principles to television ads and even political rhetoric that may be relevant to the local community or school organizations. Choosing among fact-or-opinion statements, checking the accuracy of sources and information, and answering "why" questions with supporting information and facts are several ways to develop this skill.

Decision Making. Decision making in social studies involves identifying and choosing from among alternatives based upon the clarification of values and evidence available. Simple charts of pros and cons or "the best that could happen" and "the worst that could happen" from a listing of alternatives are good beginnings for helping students make decisions. When brainstorming ideas for possible resolution of a problem, students should be encouraged to accept all suggestions for consideration, no matter how unorthodox they may sound, and to rule out ideas only for substantiated reasons. Recognizing key values that play a part in a decision is also important and a more abstract approach to understanding people's choices. Students should be encouraged not only to identify the alternatives but also to ask questions such as: How would this decision help the individual or group and in what ways? What would be the negative consequences? Once alternatives have been analyzed, prioritizing the alternatives in terms of optimum desirable consequences and minimum undesirable consequences can lead to making decisions that are informed and well thought out. Demonstrating this process of carefully analyzing each option can be done with a large group until students internalize the process, transfer it to their personal lives and apply it as a useful personal skill.

Strand 3: Interpersonal and Social Participation

Skills related to interpersonal relationships and social participation are especially problematic for behavior-disordered students, who have particular difficulty adjusting their behavior to fit the dynamics of various groups and situations. Other special students, too, often have problems in this personal dimension of social behavior, as can be seen in Figure 3.5.

Personal Skills. The social studies program is concerned with developing the personal interests, attitudes, appreciations, values, and democratic behavior of all students. Special students will need supportive environments, with teachers and students who are sensitive to the particular personal problems found in the classroom. Opportunities to express personal convictions in socially acceptable forms can be a part of every activity in the classroom. It is through these naturally occurring events that appropriate social behaviors can be modeled for students by both their peers and teachers. Often it is not enough, however, to simply model behaviors. Many special students will need specific, planned, and sequenced activities, designed to teach

FIGURE 3.5 Strand 3: Interpersonal and Social Participation Skills with which Traditional Categories of Special Learners Might Have Difficulty

SPECIAL LEARNER GROUP	PERSONAL SKILLS	GROUP INTERACTION	SOCIAL AND POLITICAL PARTICIPATION
REGULAR/REMEDIAL STUDENTS			
Culturally Different	S		S
Slow Learners	S	S	S
SPECIAL EDUCATION STUDENTS			
Behavior Disordered	M	M	M
Hearing Impaired	S	S	S
Language Disabled	S		S
Learning Disabled	S	S	S
Mentally Retarded	M	M	M
Physically Handicapped		S	
Speech Disordered			
Visually Impaired	S	S	S
Generic Handicaps	S	S	S

S = SOME of these students might have difficulty
M = MANY of these students are likely to have difficulty

social behaviors and skills such as making friends, expressing feelings, and finding alternatives to aggressive acts when they are stressed or frustrated. Teachers will find it helpful in planning activities to task analyze each target behavior to determine the sequence of behavioral steps required for successful performance. When modeling the behavior, all steps and activities that are a part of it should be shown and talked through so that students are aware of what should be happening or what they should be doing when the behavior is performed successfully. Roleplaying is an especially useful technique for teaching appropriate social behaviors; the debriefing that should occur when the roleplaying is finished is probably the most critical aspect of teaching through this technique. Other techniques for teaching positive social behavior include contingency contracting, self-monitoring and evaluating with charts and journals, and behavior modification techniques using both social and material reinforcement. For the special student, appropriate social behaviors may be one of their most difficult learning challenges, but without these skills, it is unlikely that many of the academic learning skills can be mastered.

Group Interaction Skills. Teaching strategies for promoting positive group interaction skills include detailed organization of group work, such as designating leaders and their specific responsibilities; creating smooth transitions from one activity to another; avoiding boredom by not overextending an activity; and teaching potential student leaders such leadership skills as being sensitive to the group (e.g., sensing when they are losing others' attention so that they can make changes and shifts as necessary to bring the group back to focus). As students grow older, skill-competent peers can be even more effective than teachers in modeling and discussing appropriate behaviors.

Social and Political Participation Skills. Keeping students informed of events and issues within their school and local community and demonstrating how they can effect changes with their actions help promote students' sense of confidence in participating in social and political events. Writing letters to the editor of the local newspaper, voting in class and school elections, and comparing individual or regional varieties of solving problems are possible activities that can begin to move students to accepting and fulfilling social responsibilities required of citizens in a free society. Before these kinds of skills and attitudes can be built, however, students will need to see how even small changes can be brought about through their efforts in their own local environments.

SUMMARY

To detect students' special needs in social studies, it is useful to observe them in their classroom environments; a checklist of skills is a structured means for doing this. Other diagnostic data from school records, testing, and interviews with students and past teachers can add information to student profiles and aid in selecting effective corrective strategies.

To correct special needs in social studies, base teaching upon principles of corrective instruction such as these: Choose teaching topics that are personally relevant; build upon students' experiences; emphasize social studies vocabulary; establish emotionally safe environments; use activity-based lessons; promote inquiry learning; adapt teaching to learning styles; provide positive and informative feedback; involve parents; stay current; and directly teach appropriate social behaviors.

The instructional practices discussed above are those identified in effective teaching research as well as recommended by teachers experienced in promoting academic and social growth of students with special learning problems. Perhaps the most important practices for developing the goals of social studies education are: 1) establishing personal relevance for ideas and concepts that are abstract and somewhat removed from many students' backgrounds of experience and 2) developing cooperative and supportive learning environments where students can apply social skills in the context of learning the academic discipline.

Teaching and adjusting for special skill needs, the final corrective principle, is particularly important for accommodating the needs of special students. Several corrective strategies are outlined for making needed adjustments. The underlying theme of the strategies for corrective instruction in acquiring information is interchanging stimulus/response formats. Questions, modeling, and guided thinking are the primary suggestions for corrective instruction in the organizing and using information skill area. Roleplaying and modeling are especially important in the development of personal and social skills.

It is expected that teachers will find many other ways of enhancing instruction for the special student. The suggestions here are not intended to be exhaustive but are provided as a framework for correcting special needs in social studies and for selecting topics and activities from the chapters that follow. Other sources are listed at the end of Part I.

REFLECTIONS

1. The most accepted way of organizing social studies is through the expanding communities approach, developing concepts about self, home, community, nation, and the world. Examine curricular guides or textbooks to identify other conceptual approaches. Discuss with several teachers the rationale for various curricular approaches.

2. One of the primary goals of the social studies is to develop good citizens. How is *citizenship* defined in journals and books? Compare and contrast these definitions and develop one of your own. Discuss your ideas with several teachers.

3. Social studies and other subjects are very dependent on a student's reading level to comprehend information in books and other sources. Many at-risk students have difficulties with reading. Discuss with or observe teachers to determine how they teach social studies to students having difficulties with reading.

4. Special-interest groups impact the content and teaching strategies of social studies teachers. Examine the literature to note the areas of concern for special-interest groups. Can you identify topics that would be provocative to the community where you teach or will teach? Discuss with teachers how this impacts the teaching of social studies.

5. Three strands, or groupings of social studies skills are described in Chapter 1. In each grouping, decide which one skill you want to emphasize in your class and justify each choice. Then identify the one skill in each group that you think should receive the least emphasis, and again justify your choice. Compare your choices with the social studies skills that are emphasized in most social studies classrooms in the schools in your area.

6. In Chapter 2, the social studies needs of special categories of students are described. Contrast the special problems of nonhandicapped special students and special education students. Which categories cite the most dissimilar problems? Which are the most similar? Are specific problems common to most groups? Why or why not?

7. One of the special categories of learners is labeled *teacher disabled*. Discuss with your peers how often you think this happens in social studies classes. Make a list of suggestions for alleviating this problem when it is perceived.

8. The debate as to the selection of content—What is important to teach?—in the social studies varies with each school system or state curriculum. Develop a list of concepts and generalizations that you believe are important for all students and then for special students. Compare your list with the adopted textbook series or a local curriculum guide.

9. Action research (i.e., the formulation of a research question and the investigation of it within a regular classroom setting) is a valuable means of validating research and exploring new ideas. Examine the social studies research available and devise an action research study to be completed, submitted, and presented at a state or national conference. Submit a proposal to present your findings at one of these conferences.

10. A number of texts address the needs of special students and the social studies. Compare and contrast discussions in these sources with the information in Part I.

Adams, A. H., Coble, C. R., & Hounshell, P. B. (1977). *Mainstreaming language arts and social studies: Special ideas and activities for the whole class.* Santa Monica, CA: Goodyear.

Ally, G., & Deshler, D. (1979). *Teaching the learning disabled adolescent: Strategies and methods.* Denver, CO: Love.

Clarke, J. H. (1990). *Patterns of thinking: Integrating learning skills in content teaching.* Boston: Allyn and Bacon.

Banks, J. A., & Clegg, A. A., Jr. (1985). *Teaching strategies for the social studies: Inquiry, valuing, and decision making.* White Plains, NY: Longman.

Evans, J. M., & Brueckner, M. M. (1990). *Elementary social studies: Teaching for today and tomorrow.* Boston: Allyn and Bacon.

Gearhart, B. R., Weishahn, M., & Gearhart, C. J. (1988). *The exceptional student in the regular classroom* (4th ed.). Columbus, OH: Charles E. Merrill.

Gloeckler, T., & Simpson, C. (1988). *Exceptional students in regular classrooms: Challenges, services, and methods.* Mountain View, CA: Mayfield.

Heilman, A. W., Blair, T. R., & Rupley, W. H. (1986). *Principles and practices of teaching reading* (6th ed.). Columbus, OH: Charles E. Merrill.

Jarolimek, J. (1984). In search of a scope and sequence for social studies, *Social Education, 48,* 249–261.

Kameenui, E. J., & Simmons, D. C. (1990). *Designing instructional strategies: The prevention of academic learning problems.* Columbus, OH: Charles E. Merrill.

Manzo, A. V., & Manzo, U. C. (1990). *Content area reading: A Heuristic approach.* Columbus, OH: Charles E. Merrill.

Marozas, D. S., & May, D. C. (1988). *Issues and practices in special education.* White Plains, NY: Longman.

Michaelis, J. U. (1988). *Social studies for children.* (9th ed.). Englewood Cliffs, NJ: Prentice-Hall.

Morrissett, I. (1983). *Social studies in the 1980's.* Alexandria, VA: Association for Supervision and Curriculum Development.

Ochoa, A. S., & Shuster, S. K. (1980). *Social studies in the mainstreamed classroom, K-6.* Boulder, CO: Social Science Education Consortium.

Polloway, E. A., Patton, J. R., Payne, J. S., & Payne, R. A. (1989). *Strategies for teaching learners with special needs* (4th ed.). Columbus, OH: Charles E. Merrill.

Schulz, J. B., Carpenter, C. D., & Turnbull, A. P. (1990). *Mainstreaming handicapped students: A guide for classroom teachers.* (3rd ed.). Boston: Allyn and Bacon.

Selakovich, D. (1970). *Social studies for the disadvantaged.* New York: Holt, Rinehart and Winston.

Siegel, E., & Gold, R. (1982). *Educating the learning disabled.* New York: Macmillan.

Welton, D. A., & Mallan, J. T. (1981). *Children and their world: Strategies for teaching social studies.* Boston: Houghton Mifflin.

Wood, J. W. (1989). *Mainstreaming: A practical approach for teachers.* Columbus, OH: Charles E. Merrill.

PART II

PERSONAL GROWTH

The social studies strategies for special learners presented in Parts II, III, and IV are organized around the expanding communities approach used in many curricula and textbooks. This approach was selected to insure that special learners have opportunties to learn concepts and content similar to those studied by other students. Strategies that are based on this approach activate special learners through concrete experiences and interactions as they learn about themselves and the world around them. With minor adaptations by the teacher, many of the strategies are appropriate for developing important social studies concepts for all learners.

Each chapter in Parts II, III, and IV represents a major social studies topic selected from an array of textbooks and curriculum guides. Each topic within the chapters is introduced with a DETECTION section, identifying specific behaviors that may indicate special problems in mastering the topic. In DESCRIPTION, the major concepts and content related to the chapter topic are identified. In CAUSATION, etiological factors that contribute to the learning and knowledge deficiencies of special learners are discussed. Finally, in IMPLICATIONS, a rationale for the need and contribution of this topic to the intellectual and social development of special students is presented.

The second part of each topic, CORRECTION, presents several learning strategies related to the topic and suggested for correcting and practicing a specific social studies skill. Each strategy is prefaced with a short title, followed by an identification of the major skill strands and specific area of emphasis within each strand. However, it is obvious that many of the strategies include other skills not designated. As discussed in Part I, the three major strands include: 1) acquiring information, 2) organizing and using information, and 3) participating socially. Although an attempt was made to include all the strands throughout the book, some topics reflect stronger emphasis in a particular area due to the nature of the topic.

The expanding communities approach is based on the premise that students learn about those ideas most familiar and most concrete before learning about more abstract and distant ideas. As students learn basic concepts about their immediate environment, such as their home and community, they are able to apply these concepts to more complex global topics.

Part II topics and strategies are related to the personal growth of the individual and are initially developed to establish a base for future learning. These topics are considered of high priority for special students to facilitate their quality participation and living in the real world. Thus, it is assumed that learning about self is more important for the younger and lower-ability students than learning about world cultures or the legal system and other topics that follow in Parts III and IV. The wide range of strategies enables teachers to match those most appropriate to the content they are expected to teach with the needs of special learners.

Because many special learners have particular difficulty with reading and information-processing skills, many of the strategies emphasize concrete and project-oriented learning. The corrective principles described in Chapter 3 should be utilized to structure and implement each learning activity. Roleplaying and simulations are emphasized in many of the activities to connect the learning with real-world experiences. Since the development of personal social skills is of utmost importance for special learners, specific strategies have been incorporated to meet this need. However, teachers will still need to select and adapt these activities carefully to match the individual learning styles and abilities of their students.

Part III will expand and enlarge upon the personal and social skills of the students with content that is appropriate for higher grades and more advanced special learners.

CHAPTER 4 /
LEARNING ABOUT ME AND OTHERS

1. SELF

DETECTION Students may have difficulty mastering key concepts if they:

- Are not aware of their own personal characteristics
- Do not value their own individuality and uniqueness
- Have difficulty understanding their personal histories
- Have difficulty in comparing and contrasting
- Do not understand their strengths and weaknesses

Description. One of the values instilled in the American way of life is the idea of individual differences. Understanding that there are both similarities and differences among people helps students value, accept, and have basic appreciation for the differences that exist. Classrooms, like the United States, are made up of people who have different customs, languages, and personal characteristics. People have a variety of skills that are needed to make contributions to society. Each individual can make a contribution to society if given the opportunity to capitalize on his or her strengths. Respect of these differences and knowledge of the individual contributions people make are important for mutual understanding and cooperation among people.

Causation. Students who have had limited opportunities for introspection or thinking about themselves as unique individuals may have difficulty with this topic. Often special-needs students have been caught in failure syndromes which have focused on their weaknesses, while suppressing perceptions of their strengths. Due to labeling or other social stratifications, students may have developed negative views of themselves, their worth, and their contributions.

Implications. When students perceive themselves negatively, they are unable to achieve. These negative perceptions also affect their quality of life, making themselves as well as people around them unhappy. Individuals who understand themselves are able to set and achieve realistic goals and manage personal weaknesses. Most importantly, students who have positive views about their lives tend to be more motivated to set and then accomplish their goals.

CORRECTION Modify strategies for topical and learning needs.

1. *Body Pictures* (Strand 1, *Skill:* Analyzing Information)
   Using large sheets of newsprint, make an outline of students by having them lay on the paper. Use large markers with a variety of colors. Students can then complete the body prints by adding a shirt or dress with their favorite colors and designs. Complete other details on the body prints by designing belt buckles with students' names. T-shirt design and jewelry could become part of the overall design. Place the Body Pictures on the wall and guide students to make observations about the individuality seen in each picture.

2. *Personal Data* (Strand 2, *Skill:* Classifying Information)
   Give each student a personal data sheet listing height, weight, hair color, eye color, and skin color. Provide a scale for students to weigh and measure themselves and have them record information on their data sheets. Students may help each other complete this activity, and the overall results may be shared in group discussion. Students will obviously note individual differences as well as similarities among their peers. Place the sheets on a bulletin board.

3. *Strengths and Weaknesses.* (Strand 2, *Skill:* Decision Making)
   Make a list of characteristics on cards to include such things as reading, writing, football, soccer, running, helping parents, helping teacher, skating, coloring, drawing, riding a bicycle, swinging, baseball, and so on. Ask students to select 2 things that reflect their strengths. Encourage students to help each other complete this task and emphasize during discussion that people have different strengths and abilities. Ask students to choose a strength they would like to have and work toward it. Students could also select a secret weakness and discuss it privately with the teacher.

4. *Detective Prints.* (Strand 2, *Skill:* Analyzing Information)
   Using an ink pad, make 2 sets of the forefinger and thumb prints of each student. Place the prints on a bulletin board for the class to analyze and compare. Each day, have students select a set of prints and try to find the owners.

5. *Self-History.* (Strand 1, *Skill:* Arranging Information)
   Have students draw a series of pictures on a sheet of paper divided into 6 sections, noting their history from birth to the present. Emphasize that the pictures represent the places and people in their lives. Students may need some help from their parents to complete their drawings. When finished, ask students to explain.

6. *Family History.* (Strand 1, *Skill:* Acquiring Information)
   Encourage students to interview the oldest member in their family by telephone or in person. Sample questions could include such things as: What were some things you did when you were my age? What was school like? What kind of work did your parents do? Where did you live? Ask students to bring back their ideas to be recorded on sheets of newsprint. Extension: Ask students to think about their future and what they might tell someone their age in seventy years.

2. GROWTH AND CHANGE

DETECTION Students may have difficulty mastering key concepts if they:

- Are not aware of their personal growth and development
- Do not understand that changes occur constantly
- Do not know their ages or birthdays
- Have difficulty in differentiating between child and adult events
- Have little understanding of time

Description. Growth and change are constant. Change occurs at even a faster rate today than in the past due to advances in new technology. With people, growth and change occur at a rate that is difficult to identify, especially at early ages. One indication of growth and development is the number of years that someone has lived. There are certain common elements of growth that almost everyone experiences, such as learning to walk and talk, going to school, getting married, having a family, and eventually dying. Birth begins and death ends the growth cycle. It is important for students to begin at an early age to understand and accept the changes occurring in their lives. In order to adapt to a modern culture, people learn to adapt and to anticipate changes that are inevitable. This will help children assume their roles as they progress from childhood to adulthood.

Causation. Although students have obviously experienced growth and change, this does not mean that sufficient attention has been given to these phenomena for conceptual understanding of the processes to have occurred. Attention must be focused on becoming part of the growth and change cycle. The abstract nature of the concepts demands development at a very concrete level for young people. In fact, some families still explain birth and death by using myths; teachers must be cautious when parental teachings may be in conflict. A certain amount of unlearning may need to occur to capture some but certainly not all of the reality of inevitable events. Also, some students have little understanding of time and how it affects all things. The past, present, and future are abstract quantities, requiring concrete examples for development of concepts.

Implications. As students begin to develop an initial concept of growth and change, they will begin to understand many of the events that are inevitable. Discussing some of the realities of growth and change will enable students to understand themselves, their environments, and the behaviors of other people. Most importantly, students can begin to observe and anticipate certain changes and plan for them.

CORRECTION Modify strategies for topical and learning needs.

1. *Vocabulary Shuffle.* (Strand 1, *Skill:* Vocabulary)

   Place the following words on the chalkboard and on 3" x 5" cards: *growth, change, year, month, young, old, child* and *adult.* Define each word and model how it can be used in a sentence. Distribute the cards among students and start a timer or music. While the music is playing, students should pass their cards around. When the music or timer is stopped, ask students to use the word on their card in a sentence. Repeat the process until the words are learned.

2. *Growth Ruler.* (Strand 2, *Skill:* Analyzing Information)

   Using a strip of adding machine paper with the student's name printed on one end, note the student's height with a mark and date. Each month, measure the student again and note the date. Students can make comparisons with other students, determine the average student height, compare theirs to it, and determine differences among boys and girls.

3. *Baby Challenge.* (Strand 2, *Skill:* Classifying Information)

   Ask students to bring in a baby picture and keep it a secret from the rest of the class. Mix up 3 pictures with the 3 students' names and challenge the rest of the class to match them. Ask students to share the characteristics that were used to match the pictures with the names. This information should include facial features of eyes, ears, hair, and the like.

4. *Growth Line.* (Strand 2, *Skill:* Classifying Information)

   Draw a timeline on the chalkboard starting at 0 years and ending at 100 years. Collect pictures from magazines, noting events that could be placed on the timeline ranging from birth to death. Ask students to explain important events and mark them on the timeline. For example, birth, talking, walking, starting school, playing soccer, learning to read, college, marriage, having children, and death.

5. *Birthday Calendar.* (Strand 1, *Skill:* Study Skills)

   Using a large calendar, post each student's picture and birthday on the appropriate day and month. During the year, students can be spotlighted on their birthdays.

6. *Headlines.* (Strand 1, *Skill:* Arranging Information)

   At the end of the school day, ask students to explain important events or activities that occurred during the day in the classroom, school, community, or world. Develop with an appropriate headline. At the end of the month, challenge students to develop a headline for the month. At the end of the year, the headlines can be reviewed.

7. *Strangers Beware.* (Strand 3, *Skill:* Personal Skills)

   Organize a roleplaying activity, asking a student to enact the parent role for explaining to a child the importance of not talking to strangers or taking something from strangers at any time, especially walking to and from school. Teachers may want to coach students to help with the dialogue. The roleplaying could be extended by having a stranger try to give one of the students a ride home in his new car.

3. SELF-CONCEPT

DETECTION Students may have difficulty mastering key concepts if they:

- Cannot identify their strengths and weaknesses
- Do not demonstrate any positive views of themselves
- Cannot tell any personal success stories
- Often put themselves down
- Are constantly saying, "I can't do that!"

Description. Individuals develop either positive or negative self concepts through family, school, and other life experiences. A positive self-concept gives students a healthy outlook for learning and interacting with peers. Students must have a realistic view of their strengths and weaknesses in order to get to know themselves and in the long run develop a positive self-concept. Positive self-concepts are established through a variety of successes with a realistic understanding of one's limitations.

Causation. A poor self-concept can be developed through a variety of experiences involving failure. Whether in school or at home, once students are captured in the failure syndrome, it is difficult to move toward success. For example, a student who fails to learn to read or do math during the early years in school will continue to have a difficult time. It is not uncommon for special students to have experienced many put-downs in their family or school lives over time, thus contributing to a poor self-concept. The individual personality also emerges as a factor in determining self-concept, resulting in students who believe their lives are determined by an external locus of control (i.e., they are not in control of their own destiny but rather are victims of chance, luck, or circumstances over which they have no control). It is not unusual, too, for students to reflect attitudes of family members who have not aspired or experienced success in society.

Implications. The school environment can help to establish the necessary experiences upon which to build a positive self-concept. It is important that students work on learning materials that challenge them, but most importantly, the materials must be within their abilities and skills. A supportive learning environment, where the teachers and other students are sensitive to students having difficulties, is essential in establishing positive self-concepts. Motivation, work ethic, and interaction with others are impacted by one's self-concept, contributing in significant ways to students' ability and willingness to learn.

CORRECTION   Modify strategies for topical and learning needs.

1. *Me Box.* (Strand 3, *Skill:* Personal Skills)
    Ask students to select pictures from magazines that describe themselves and paste them on the sides of small boxes. Encourage students to select a variety of pictures that describe things they like to do or would like to have. Provide an opportunity for students to explain their choices to the rest of the class. Students may also guess which boxes belong to which classmates.

2. *Strength Drawing.* (Strand 3, *Skill:* Personal Skills)
    Make a list of activities on the chalkboard, such as drawing, writing, singing, playing soccer, coloring, helping, jumping, playing ball, flying kites, swimming, kick ball, and cheering. Provide a large sheet of drawing paper for students to select 1 of the activities and develop a scene. Make sure that students select activities that they are good at. Post the pictures on the wall for students to later explain their choices.

3. *When I Grow Up . . .* (Strand 3, *Skill:* Personal Skills)
    Write "When I grow up" on the chalkboard and have students complete the sentence with a drawing. Provide time for students to share their sentences. VARIATION: Have students show their drawings and ask peers to guess what they said.

4. *Group Drawing.* (Strand 3, *Skill:* Group Interaction Skills)
    Organize students into groups of 4–5. Explain to the groups that they will be given the task of drawing a picture of a house. They will complete the drawing by having 1 student draw 1 part and then pass the crayon to the next student for a turn. Guidelines may be needed: Draw what you would want in or on your house. A time limit of 3 minutes will be used to draw the house. The teacher may want to give signals for students to pass the crayon during the beginning of this activity. Provide time for students to show their house and discuss how each member contributed to the drawing.

5. *My Special Day.* (Strand 3, *Skill:* Personal Skills)
    Establish a time when each student is spotlighted. Each student should bring in 3–5 objects about himself or herself to show and explain to the class. Encourage the class to ask questions about the objects; this gives the student an opportunity to express himself or herself further. The teacher should compliment the child by telling something he or she has done well.

6. *Stand Up for Adjectives.* (Strand 3, *Skill:* Personal Skills)
    Make a list of positive adjectives *(smart, pretty, likeable, happy, bright, funny, kind, strong, athletic, fun,* etc.) to be read out loud. Have students stand when they hear an adjective they think describes them.

7. *Spotlight.* (Strand 3, *Skill:* Personal Skills)
    Choose a student to spotlight and have him or her tell the class 1 thing he or she is really good at. Ask the class to tell 1 thing he is really good at. The teacher should also tell 1 thing.

4. FEELINGS AND EMOTIONS

DETECTION Students may have difficulty mastering key concepts if they:

- Do not demonstrate feelings in their behavior and communications
- Cannot recognize the feelings of others
- Have difficulty controlling emotions and feelings
- Do not empathize with the feelings of others

Description. Feelings are the emotions produced within an individual as a result of a thought, a physical experience, or some type of interaction with others. Feelings are difficult to define specifically but can be explained with examples or through actions. Anthropologists suggest that human beings' ability to express a wide range of emotions is one of the major factors that contributes to humanness. People have feelings at all times, from when they awaken until they sleep, with some support for dreams provoking and reflecting certain feelings. Feelings are very natural expressions that are suppressed to some degree as we develop from childhood to adulthood. Children more openly express their emotions, whereas adults learn to control their emotions to acceptable degrees. Women are able to express their feelings more openly in our society. "Big boys don't cry" is a good example of the values associated with feelings. Feelings are expressed and evident in all communication; more precise meanings are conveyed when emotions are evident and expressed.

Causation. Children are primarily influenced by their families in their expression of emotions and feelings. Students may be taught not to express their feelings and to hold their emotions inside. On the other hand, students may use their emotions in excess to express themselves or to influence others. A void of emotional experiences, either high or low, would certainly determine the way students' emotions are used and interpreted. A child who has not experienced a lot of happiness or even death is not prepared to deal with the natural things that occur in the life cycle.

Implications. Students need to learn to express their emotions appropriately and to share experiences with others. The experience of exhilaration or a good laugh with a group of people creates a good feeling. If students understand the wide range of emotions in human interaction and communication, they will have more information available to interpret messages. Functioning groups of individuals are bonded through common experiences that have a variety of emotions. The classroom should be a safe place for students to experience a wide range of emotions under the direction of a sensitive teacher. The proper balance of emotions and feelings in everyday life varies from culture to culture. Students need to learn to function appropriately in their most common social environments.

CORRECTION Modify strategies for topical and learning needs.

1. *Feeling Words.* (Strand 1, *Skill:* Vocabulary)

    Write the following feeling and emotion words on the chalkboard: *happy, angry, sad, kind, loving,* and *tired.* Pronounce each word and use it in a sentence. Use the following open-ended stem for students to complete: I feel happy when . . . or I feel angry when . . . or I feel sad when . . . (Activity may be written or oral.) VARIATION: Cut out pictures and ask students to describe how the people in pictures seem to feel. Share the descriptions with the class.

2. *Puppet Talk.* (Strand 3, *Skill:* Personal Skills)

    Find or make a puppet and use it to carry on a conversation with a small group of students. Ask the students to give the puppet a name, such as Scat. Explain that Scat expresses a lot of feelings when things happen to him. Give some specific examples and then have Scat ask students how they feel when these things happen to them. Continue the conversation until students have an opportunity to express their feelings about a variety of situations.

3. *Cartoon Emotions.* (Strand 2, *Skill:* Interpreting Information)

    Cut out comic strips from the newspaper, post them on a bulletin board, and ask students to note the emotions of the various characters. The teacher should point out that the artist uses various techniques to show emotions, especially the mouth and eyes. List emotion words such as *happy, sad, angry, sleepy, tired, joyful, kind* and *loving.* Ask the students to explain their choices to the rest of the class.

4. *Feeling Drama.* (Strand 2, *Skill:* Interpreting Information)

    Write feeling words on index cards, distribute them to students, and ask them to act out the feeling. Other students try to guess the emotion. Students could do this in teams and make up other emotions.

5. *Color Me Yellow.* (Strand 2, *Skill:* Interpreting Information)

    Provide a number of different colors of paper disks and discuss their implied emotions (blue = sad, depressed, lonely; green = calm, neutral, smooth, rested, nature's color; yellow = happy, gay, bright, sunny, excited; red = angry, upset). Ask students to select a color that reflects their feelings at the moment and tell why. This can be done each morning for a week or more by having students place colored disks on pictures of themselves on the bulletin board. Set aside time each day to discuss their selections. Students can also change colors appropriately throughout the day and explain why. The teacher might also use this technique to warn students on bad days or to reflect pleasure with their performance.

5.   WORK AND PLAY

DETECTION Students may have difficulty mastering key concepts if they:

- Cannot distinquish between work and play activities
- Have not developed good work habits in school
- Do not recognize that people earn a living by working
- Have difficulty recognizing various forms of work
- Do not know that through good work one can experience self-actualization and personal fulfillment

Description. In order to exchange goods and services, people have to work, performing various tasks. People earn money by performing work in large corporations, through businesses or institutions with which they are associated, or even as owners and operators of their own businesses. The money earned can be used to purchase other goods and services and to provide for shelter, food, or other needs. People of all ages work and all have various forms of play. Usually young people have more time to play by themselves or with others. Many socialization skills are learned through play, such as teamwork, leadership, and communication. As people grow older, they use play or leisure to relax and provide an avenue for the release of the emotions associated with work. Many people associate work with those things that they don't like to do and play with those things that they do like to do. In reality, many people truly enjoy their work, making it difficult at times to distinguish between work and play. Work also is an important means of developing the individual's sense of self-actualization and fulfillment in a job well done.

Causation. Students may have had limited opportunities to accept responsibilities in their home or school lives for work-related activity. Some students have only limited play opportunities, especially with other students. Motivational factors may be keeping students from experimenting with new forms of play or work. If students have been told that they play too much, they may hide the play activities or withdraw from activities. Or if they are overburdened with work, they avoid it when possible. Exposure to role models in the home and community develops values toward certain forms of work.

Implications. Students should see the value in both work and play activities and understand the purpose of each. The development of a work ethic begins with understanding the need to contribute to the economic system and experiencing personal satisfaction and worth after performing a task well. Work earns money that can be exchanged for other services in society. In fact, a person earns time to play or to participate in leisure activities through their work activities. A balance of work and play activities will help to balance the ups and downs of living in a complex society.

CORRECTION Modify strategies for topical and learning needs.

1. *Vocabulary.* (Strand 1, *Skill:* Vocabulary)
    Write the following words on large sheets of paper: *work, play, money, job, leisure, responsibility,* and *needs.* Cut the sheets to form puzzles and distribute the pieces. Ask students to find the other pieces to their puzzles. Have students show their word and pronounce it. Explain each word and use it in a sentence to reinforce the vocabulary.
2. *Picture Work/Play.* (Strand 2, *Skill:* Classifying Information)
    Ask students to cut out 3 work and 3 play pictures from magazines. Display them on a bulletin board. Some of the pictures may be categorized in both work and play—for example, a professional athlete or musician. The pictures can be mixed to play a game of categorizing. Divide the class into 2 groups and give each team and player an opportunity to select an activity from the box and label it correctly—play, work, or both. Contrast how each activity would be viewed by an older or younger sibling, parent, or even the students when they are grown. VARIATION: Have students put their names on the pictures of their favorite work and play activities and display on the bulletin board.
3. *Play or Work?* (Strand 2, *Skill:* Summarizing Information)
    Explain to students that a game will be played. Empty a box that contains 50 marbles, sticks, or blocks on the floor. The object of the game is for the class to pick up the objects and make sure that all are returned to the box. Repeat emptying the box of objects on the floor until students start complaining or noticeably become bored. When this happens, explain that you are going to empty the box of objects 1 more time and they now will work instead of play to pick up the objects. Discuss the differences between work and play.
4. *Work Responsibility.* (Strand 3, *Skill:* Social Responsibility)
    Make a list of responsibilities for the classroom, including: picking up books, arranging desks, emptying the pencil sharpener, distributing books, taking up assignments, and turning off lights when leaving room. Make a chart listing the activities and the responsible students. As the day progresses, mark the chart when tasks are completed and reward the workers or class with extra time to play or do something they find enjoyable. Discuss why they should be responsible for class chores.
5. *Work/Play at Home.* (Strand 2, *Skill:* Interpreting Information)
    Ask students to become detectives in finding work and play activities as they go home and return the next day. They should ask their parents to describe the work they do. Discuss and record observations on the chalkboard. Emphasize the environments in which the activities occur and have students identify the jobs that would be drudgery and the ones that would almost be play and why. Discuss opportunities in the work for experiencing self-fulfillment and satisfaction.

6. RESPECT FOR OTHERS

DETECTION Students may have difficulty mastering key concepts if they:

- Do not listen to suggestions from their peer group
- Are taking things from other students against their will
- Are exerting their point of view most of the time
- Make prejudgments about people
- Cannot empathize with others
- Appear to have low self-concepts

Description. Various ethnic and cultural groups are gaining more access to a variety of jobs and opportunities in most regions of the United States. Women and blacks, especially, have gained more opportunities in a male, white dominated business world in recent years. Because society is made up of a variety of ethnic and cultural groups, it is important to realize an equality and tolerance for all people. Prejudgmental feelings and ideas about other groups that are different from one's own group interfere with constructive communication and interaction. The fundamental democratic principles are exemplified through offering equal opportunities and rights to all people.

Causation. Respect is a two-way concept. Those who are constantly berated as well as those who don't respect themselves have difficulty respecting others. How students perceive other groups or individuals different from themselves will reflect the information or experience they have had. Students who have had limited opportunities to interact with blacks, Asians, native Americans, and other groups, will form opinions based on hearsay. Prejudiced viewpoints may be formed through family and community values and experiences. Textbooks, television, and movies have in the past perpetuated stereotypical views about women, blacks, native Americans, Eskimos, and other cultural groups.

Implications. Contact with individuals who are culturally different will help students develop their own information base for making decisions. As information increases about various groups, students soon discover more likenesses than differences. The increased respect that students demonstrate for other ethnic and cultural groups enables greater participation and understanding in the world community. (Note that this concept is also related to Self and Self-Concept, presented in Topics 1 and 3.) As students begin to feel better about themselves and their unique differences, they can feel better about others' differences.

CORRECTION   Modify strategies for topical and learning needs.

1. *Vocabulary.* (Strand 1, *Skill:* Vocabulary)
     Write these words on the chalkboard: *share, respect,* and *care.* Ask students to illustrate one of the vocabulary words by drawing a picture. Ask students to explain their drawings to the class. Culminate the lesson by making a list of situations, ideas, or expressions illustrating respect for others, such as: Can I help you? Excuse me. Thank you.
2. *More Alike.* (Strand 2, *Skill:* Interpreting Information)
     Explain to students that you are going to make a list of things that are similar and different about class members. Make 2 headings on the chalkboard and invite students to contribute ideas. Ask the questions: How are we alike? and How are we different? Students' comments concerning their differences may include things about their clothes, height, weight, hair, voices, sex, or fingerprints. Comments concerning similarities may include many of the same comments. Students should be asked to summarize what they have observed.
3. *Stereotypes.* (Strand 2, *Skill:* Analyzing Information)
     Have students roleplay to illustrate situations that show disrespect for others. Select different students to react to the following situations: 1) Girls are supposed to stay home and clean house; 2) Most blacks are on welfare; 3) native Americans just want to make trouble; 4) Old people can't do anything; and, 5) A woman would not make a good president. Bring the lesson to the conclusion that none of these statements is true. CAUTION: Teachers should be aware of the sensitivities of class members.
4. *Welcome to Class.* (Strand 2, *Skill:* Classifying Information)
     Ask students to pretend that a student their own age from another country or even another planet will soon visit their classroom. Make a list of questions that the students would like to ask and some of the information that could be passed on to the visitor. Extension: Have students write a group letter, asking some of their questions and explaining their country.
5. *Taste Buds.* (Strand 2, *Skill:* Evaluating Information)
     Bring in different foods from a variety of cultures for students to taste. Before tasting each food, ask students if they think they would like it or if they have ever eaten it before. Ask students to taste the foods and give their opinions. (Accept that some may refuse the foods.) Encourage students to form and explain their own opinions.
6. *Being Different.* (Strand 2, *Skill:* Summarizing Information)
     Select a student volunteer and leave the room with him or her. Make large red dots on his or her forehead and cheeks with watercolors. Return to the room and ask your volunteer to return shortly after. Students will probably laugh or stare at your volunteer. After a brief discussion, explain to students that many prejudices are formed because of outward appearances or physical handicaps.

7. PERSONAL HISTORY

DETECTION Students may have difficulty mastering key concepts if they:

- Are unable to recall events chronologically
- Cannot communicate about past events
- Do not recognize repeated behaviors as customs or traditions
- Have no concept of past, present, and future
- Have difficulty in seeing their role in history
- Do not understand growth and change

Description. History is the chronological record of significant events usually identified and explained with their causes. Family customs and traditions often shape people's personal histories and contribute to their sense of who they are and hope to become. All cultures have traditions and customs that govern behavior, yet these change and evolve over time, continually shaping individual identities and contributing to present and future personal goals. Everyone's personal history continues to expand with the passing of time. An individual cannot remember everything nor is everything that happens important. History is easier to remember when recorded through diaries or photographs.

Causation. Students who have moved often or live away from their extended or immediate families may not have had opportunities to share in family histories or to develop strong family traditions. Students who have not had stable and continuing environments at home or at school may not have developed the sense of time that other students their ages possess. Grandparents and older relatives give students perspective on age and share their stories about other times. Students without this resource may not have this sense of and appreciation for time. Students may need some stimulus, such as a photograph, to remember some of their history. All families do not keep a record of their history, however.

Implications. Having a personal history is important to individuals in establishing self-expectations and personal goals based upon what they have already accomplished—"Knowing where one has come from gives direction to where one is going." Significant events that make up one's history are remembered easily if related to other significant occurrences in our society. For example, most adults remember what they were doing when John F. Kennedy and Martin Luther King, Jr., were assassinated. Significant common experiences enable people to share a part of the total human experience and even make history. The knowledge that customs and traditions define to a large extent who we are helps students understand how they fit into groups they have chosen or perhaps inherited and to accept and live more comfortably within those groups.

CORRECTION Modify strategies for topical and learning needs.

1. *History or Tradition?* (Strand 1, *Skill:* Vocabulary)
Write the word *history* on the chalkboard. Discuss and define the word, explaining that history consists of important past events that have been recorded. Write examples and nonexamples of historical events on PostIts. Have each student draw one, decide if it is an example of history, and, upon class consensus that it is, come to the board and stick it under the word *history.*

2. *Personal Timeline.* (Strand 1, *Skill:* Classifying Information)
Ask students to draw (or provide a drawing for them) a timeline with a year designated for each year of their lives. They should then label those significant events that have occurred at given points in their lives. If students have photographs of significant events, they could bring those to share also. CAUTION: Be sensitive to adopted students and those who can't fill in details of their backgrounds.

3. *Family Tree.* (Strand 2, *Skill:* Analyzing Information)
Provide students with blank drawings of a family tree (or provide a simple genealogical form) for them to fill in; they should include the members of their immediate family and as many of their past relatives as their parents can supply. Provide space beside each family member's name to enter occupations and where he or she lived. Look for patterns of similarities and differences.

4. *Traditional Tales.* (Strand 2, *Skill:* Summarizing Information)
Ask students to tell whether they believe and/or practice any of the popular superstitions that have been passed down through the years: walking under a ladder, stepping on a sidewalk's crack, having a black cat cross the path, breaking a mirror. Discuss how these tales influence behavior today.

5. *Family Fun.* (Strand 2, *Skill:* Classifying Information)
List commonly celebrated holidays in columns on the chalkboard (or on handouts). Ask students to tell what their families do, and eat on these holidays. Compare the responses and discuss.

6. *Changing Times.* (Strand 2, *Skill:* Interpreting Information)
Ask students to identify some changes that have occurred in their lives and why they think those changes occurred. Have students bring in photographs of themselves at different ages and compare them to the present.

7. *Mapping Relatives.* (Strand 1, *Skill:* Maps, Globes, Graphics)
Ask students to find out where their relatives live. Post a large map of the United States or the world and have students place pins where relatives live.

8. *When I Was Little.* (Strand 2, *Skill:* Summarizing Information)
Assign students to tell or write a story about when they were "little" (younger). Share stories in class.

8. SOCIAL PARTICIPATION

DETECTION Students may have difficulty mastering key concepts if they:

- Are not aware of their inappropriate behavior
- Have difficulty interacting socially with other students
- Are not aware of the effects of their behavior on others
- Have difficulty demonstrating appropriate social behavior
- Have inconsistencies in their social behavior

Description. Students learn social skills just as they do academic skills. Listening, following directions, learning to work in groups, and demonstrating accepted behaviors when going to the movies, using the library, or playing baseball are just as important skills as learning social studies academic content. Learning to work in groups is one of the most important social skills. School and society are organized around various groups to accomplish simple and complex tasks. Students learn that cooperation is essential for large groups of people to interact and function together. As students get older, more complex social skills are required in peer, family, and work relations. The resolution of conflict through discussion or mediated intervention rather than aggressive action is essential for effective social interaction. Give and take and sharing of responsibilities helps individuals become accepted members of groups. Since a person's self-worth is to some degree determined by perceptions of others, effective social participation skills will contribute to a healthy self-concept.

Causation. Special students may exhibit inappropriate behavior that has been learned through inappropriate models. Certain disorders, such as aggressive or withdrawn behavior, may be associated with special learners. Students may be immature or lack opportunities to interact with their peers to learn social behavior. Special learners may not have had the specific intervention to learn appropriate behavior. These learners may simply not know what is acceptable behavior in various social situations.

Implications. Students must develop appropriate social behavior as well as learn academic skills and knowledge in school. Inappropriate social behavior in the classroom can interfere with academic learning, and students must learn that certain social behaviors are necessary for people to function cooperatively in various groups in our society. It is important that students learn to ask questions and make comments in school environments to be successful learners. Spending time developing appropriate social behaviors rather than reacting to discipline or conflict situations in the classroom is more productive for teacher and students. If students do not learn acceptable social behavior at a young age, it is possible that this behavior could escalate into antisocial behavior at an older age.

CORRECTION Modify strategies for topical and learning needs.

1. *Social Greetings.* (Strand 3, *Skill:* Personal Skills)

   Introduce students to the fundamentals of greeting people through a short roleplaying activity. Explain the importance of shaking hands for both boys and girls. Demonstrate the proper way of doing this before having the class practice shaking hands and asking, "How are you today?" Have students practice answering the question by talking about school, home, or other activities.

2. *Find the Treasure.* (Strand 3, *Skill:* Group Interaction)

   Form student groups of 5. Explain that a treasure hunt will begin and each group member will have a specific direction. Members of the group must cooperate and listen to each other to follow the directions to find the treasure. The teacher must hide an object (treasure) in the schoolroom or playground and develop sequential directions based on landmarks or measurements.

3. *Tell about Me.* (Strand 3, *Skill:* Personal Skills)

   Explain the importance of students introducing themselves and others in a social situation. Have students practice talking about themselves by telling their age, grade, hobbies, and favorite television show. Have students practice introducing themselves and listening to others. Arrange for outside people to come by the classroom to give students the opportunity to practice.

4. *I'm Sorry.* (Strand 3, *Skill:* Social Participation)

   Organize a roleplay by explaining that sometimes you hurt someone's feelings and an apology is in order (e.g., you accidentally spilled water on a person's schoolwork). Ask students to list on the chalkboard situations that would require an apology: bumping into someone; talking when someone else is talking; using someone's book by mistake; forgetting to return something you borrowed. Give the students opportunities to act out the situations and say, "I'm really sorry" or "I did not mean to hurt your feelings." This activity can be extended for students to learn to say "thank you" in specific situations.

5. *Asking Questions.* (Strand 3, *Skill:* Social Participation)

   Explain that students must sometimes ask questions to complete schoolwork successfully. When these questions are being asked, others should listen carefully, too. Give the students a simple task, such as drawing a rectangle and a triangle. Give students a hint, but emphasize that they must ask questions to complete the drawings.

6. *Making Decisions.* (Strand 3, *Skill:* Social Participation)

   Provide students with problems to solve through group consensus. For example: What should a student do when the assignment is not clear? After students learn to generate alternative approaches in their groups, give other situations for them to resolve: staying out of fights; teasing others; embarrassment; confronting fear or failure. Give students time to discuss alternatives before presenting them to the class.

9. SOCIAL INTERACTION

DETECTION Students may have difficulty mastering key concepts if they:

- Are not aware of overly aggressive behavior
- Have difficulty exhibiting appropriate social behavior
- Are overly withdrawn, shy, and self-conscious
- Use language that is socially unacceptable
- Have difficulty carrying out tasks within a group

Description. Behaviors that are not acceptable in our society become more pronounced and have more serious ramifications as students grow older. If these inappropriate behaviors are not corrected, serious intervention may result in later life. In addition, these behaviors often interfere with students' personal safety and social interactions with other people. Peer pressure and the search for identity through dress, music, and conversation are social means for belonging; students who deviate from the norm are quickly rejected by their peer group. Thus, it is important for students to learn how to engage in a conversation and participate as a cooperative member in group activities. The social and political processes in our society require individuals to negotiate and compromise in order to participate. The resolution of conflict requires individuals to talk it out rather than fight it out. Through effective social interaction, students learn behaviors that will help them become successful in their adult lives and to participate fully in our democratic society.

Causation. Special students may exhibit inappropriate social behavior due to developmental problems, immaturity, inadequate role models, peer pressure, or societal influences. Adolescents may have had difficulty at an early age with social interactions and reacted by withdrawing or being overly aggressive. If it is not controlled, this behavior will intensify over time and lead to destructive consequences.

Implications. The classroom provides an excellent environment for students to learn appropriate social behavior through carefully structured activities. Learning conditions can be established for students to experiment with appropriate social behavior in a safe environment. Students have opportunities in classrooms to learn to influence others as well as to compromise on various issues. If inappropriate social interaction is exhibited by students, then the academic learning will surely suffer, too. The sensitive and patient teacher can help students learn social skills that will help them accept social responsibilities associated with citizenship in a democratic society.

CORRECTION Modify strategies for topical and learning needs.

1. *Picture Us.* (Strand 3, *Skill:* Group Interaction)

    Ask students to bring pictures from magazines that illustrate social situations. Attach each picture to a large chart and give each student an opportunty to explain the social situation. Emphasize the proper behavior and rules that people must follow in order to live cooperatively.

2. *Rule Making.* (Strand 2, *Skill:* Decision-Making Skills)

    Discuss the importance of having rules in a society that enable people to cooperate and live together. Use a soccer or baseball game as an example of how people agree on certain rules to play by. Make a list of the rules around school for students to discuss and give reasons for the rules. Extend the activity by asking students to discuss what happens when people break rules in ballgames, school, or society.

3. *Dealing with Anger.* (Strand 3, *Skill:* Personal Skills)

    Explain that people do not have to use violence when confronted with conflict that makes them angry. Discuss with students situations that have made them angry. Reactions may have been to throw something, hit someone, or use insulting language. Using short roleplay activities, practice talking with the individual to clear up the misunderstanding. Students could also practice apologizing to each other.

4. *Complaining.* (Strand 3, *Skill:* Social Participation)

    Relate to students a personal example of purchasing clothes or some other merchandise and having to return it to the store. Solicit a list of similar examples from students and roleplay the situations. Emphasize the importance of being friendly with a thorough explanation as to why the merchandise is being returned.

5. *Group Puzzle.* (Strand 3, *Skill:* Group Interaction)

    Make a 5-piece puzzle from a large magazine picture by cutting it into irregular shapes. Give the shapes to the groups of 5 students and explain that the puzzle can be solved only through placing each piece on the floor in the proper place. Group members cannot talk or use gestures during the activity. Discuss with students the importance of cooperation during the activity.

6. *Spotlighting Strengths.* (Strand 3, *Skill:* Personal Skills)

    Have each student make a large personal shield, containing his or her picture and other personal information, such as favorite food, music, pets, and places. Provide an opportunity for each student to be spotlighted for compliments. The featured student will stand while the rest of the class gives a few compliments for the teacher to write on the personal shield.

7. *Group Production.* (Strand 3, *Skill:* Group Participation)

    Divide students in groups of 5 for a competitive activity among groups. Explain that each group will have to make as many 2" x 2" red squares in 3 minutes from 10 sheets of paper as possible. Give the students time to plan what each person in the group will do. After determining the most productive group, discuss with students the cooperation within the groups.

CHAPTER 5

HOME, FAMILY, AND SCHOOL

10. SHELTER

DETECTION Students may have difficulty mastering key concepts if they:

- Do not recognize differences in the types of shelters
- Take their shelter for granted
- Are not aware of factors affecting the types of shelters
- Do not recognize the importance of shelters for survival
- Have difficulty in noting functions of spaces in shelters

Description. Man must have some type of shelter for protection from the weather and for privacy to rest and survive. Factors that affect the types of shelters include the climate, available materials, and specific dangers in the environment. Early man used caves as shelters or built structures from what was readily available. The Eskimos can build an igloo from the packed snow in about one hour, which was necessary because they moved from place to place to hunt. In New Guinea, shelters are constructed on stilts to avoid the water beneath. In Mexico, mud and water are mixed to form adobe bricks to make shelters. Modern shelters include single-family houses, apartment and other multiunit complexes, and mobile homes. Usually, a modern shelter includes spaces designated as the kitchen, bathroom, living room, and bedroom. The style of a home depends upon individual tastes, climate, available materials, and the amount of money available for building. People have been very creative in constructing shelters to survive in various environments. The new challenges will be shelters to function in space and under the oceans.

Causation. Students are most familiar with homes in their immediate environments and may conclude that all people have similar shelters. Those with few travel opportunities, even in their own communities, will have a narrow concept of shelter. Limited exposure to history and other cultures also accounts for little information about shelters.

Implications. Understanding the basic purposes and the wide variety of shelters for meeting those purposes, students will begin to see many possibilities for future shelters. The relationship of economics as well as the availability of materials will help students make thoughtful decisions about constructing, buying, or renting homes or improving their own homes. Most importantly, students will develop ideas about other cultures and a deeper appreciation for the way they have creatively adapted to their environments.

CORRECTION Modify strategies for topical and learning needs.

1. *Shelter Words.* (Strand 1, *Skill:* Vocabulary)

    Introduce the word *shelter* and discuss how it meets our basic need for protection. Explain that people have adapted their shelters to the weather (hot, cold, wet, and dry) by using different materials. Ask students to collect or draw pictures of the following words: *shelter, house, apartment,* and *mobile home.* Review the pictures to insure that students understand the words. Have each child pronounce the words and select the type of shelter that they live in.

2. *Floorplan.* (Strand 1, *Skill:* Arranging Information)

    Provide a sheet of graph or blocked paper for students to complete a drawing of their shelter. Remind students to place at least 1 object in each room to note its main purpose. Some examples may be listed on the chalkboard (bed, bathtub, refrigerator, dining table, and fireplace). When students have completed their drawings, display them for discussion about the various types of floorplans and how they meet basic needs.

3. *Shelter Design.* (Strand 2, *Skill:* Analyzing Information)

    Describe the following environments and discuss with students the type of shelter needed to survive the elements and other dangers in each: a) rainforest that floods; b) desert that is hot in the daytime and cold at night; c) North Pole region where it snows most of the time. Assign the alternatives to the students and challenge them to design a shelter for their specific environment.

4. *Other Homes.* (Strand 2, *Skill:* Analyzing Information)

    Have students collect pictures from magazines to show shelters in other cultures. Discuss the pictures and explore the reasons why certain materials were used in these environments. The pictures can be compared and contrasted for differences in style from students' homes and critiqued for their value in their own culture.

5. *Home Survey.* (Strand 2, *Skill:* Analyzing Information)

    Ask students to survey their community to note the various kinds of roofs on homes. Drawings or photographs could be used to collect this information. Conduct a discussion to emphasize that different roof slopes are better suited to certain weather conditions (e.g., a steep roof enables water and snow to fall off easier). Also, the style of the roof adds to the appearance of the home.

6. *Space Homes.* (Strand 2, *Skill:* Synthesizing Information)

    Pretend that the class will be taken into space (or under the sea) for their lessons next year. Homes have to be designed for people to live in. The problems of providing shelter to protect against the lack of oxygen, gravity, food, and so on must be incorporated into the design. Also, the shelter has to support a family of 4 in a small space, since the materials will have to be brought from the earth. Discussion is necessary for students to understand the problems that will occur in developing good ideas.

11. FAMILY TYPES AND ROLES

DETECTION Students may have difficulty mastering key concepts if they:

- Are unable to understand the concept of family
- Do not recognize that families can be alike and different
- Have not had stable family environments
- Do not realize that family roles can vary
- Have had limited contacts with families in other cultures

Description. The family is society's most basic unit and the oldest of its human institutions. Every family is different in size, where and how they live, and how they distribute the work responsibilities. Other differences are determined by biological and environmental circumstances. Basically, a *family* is a group of people who function as a unit to love, share companionship, and sustain and take care of one another as needed. The functions of a family include provision of shelter, clothes, food, love, and the sharing of work responsibilities. As a social unit, the family establishes informal and sometimes formal rules that govern behavior and allow them to live in harmony. This small social unit makes up a part of the total environment in which people live, work, and have rules that govern behavior and allow people to function efficiently and effectively together. In recent years, the concept of family has undergone many changes. Mothers' and fathers' roles have changed significantly along with the economic and technological changes in many societies. World population concerns and longer life expectancies have also contributed to changes in the family. Divorce in families is very common and creates the need for all family members to learn to adapt to many changes.

Causation. Students who have not had stable family environments may not understand the significance of this unit or its contribution to modern-day survival. Children who have been abused need many positive examples to eliminate unfortunate views of the family. Also, stereotypical expectations of family role models have been perpetuated through popular reading material and television, while economic and sex-role changes in modern society have occurred quite rapidly.

Implications. In order to adapt and survive in society, students must depend upon the family unit to love them and provide care as they grow and become responsible members of society. At that point, they in turn must assume a different role as parents caring for their young and also for their parents and other needy family members. It is the family that provides protection and early training of the young. Through a mutual sharing of responsibilities, families are able to function as cooperative units. Helping young students understand that there are many different family configurations and that roles can shift and change will aid them in accepting and adjusting to the demands and changes in their lives.

CORRECTION Modify strategies for topical and learning needs.

1. *Who Is This?* (Strand 1, *Skill:* Vocabulary)
    Write on the chalkboard all the different words that describe family kinship relations: *cousin, aunt, uncle, great uncle, niece, nephew, father-in-law,* and so on. Make a crossword puzzle with these words and award a prize for the first person to find all of them.
2. *Are We Different?* (Strand 2, *Skill:* Interpreting Information)
    Ask students to bring a photograph or draw a picture of their family. Have each student introduce his or her family to the class and post pictures on the bulletin board. When finished, ask students to make a chart to describe the differences in families in terms of size, ages, who lives at home, works, goes to school, and the like.
3. *Going to Grandma's House.* (Strand 1, *Skill:* Maps)
    Have students draw maps of the route from their house to a relative's house (such as Grandma or someone they often visit). Ask students to orally describe where this relative lives and explain their map to the class. VARIATION: Use building blocks of different colors and shapes on a large table top to show routes.
4. *That's My Job!* (Strand 2, *Skill:* Classifying Information)
    Have students list jobs/responsibilities in their homes down the side of a page. Across the top of the page, they should list in columns each family member's name. Place a check in the grid square under the family member's name who's most responsible for the identified tasks. Compare the findings.
5. *Kinship.* (Strand 2, *Skill:* Synthesizing Information)
    Ask students to make a mobile showing their kinship to 5 people. Have students explain and display it in the classroom.
6. *What's a Family?* (Strand 2, *Skill:* Interpreting Information)
    Roleplay the following scenario: A spaceship has just landed on earth and two beings from outer space step out and encounter a family of 4, having a picnic in the park. The beings want to know what is happening here and who these people are. Have family members try to explain *family*, their relationships within that family, and why they are together in the park.
7. *Family Fun.* (Strand 2, *Skill:* Social Participation)
    Each student should list 4 things his or her family does for fun and what activity each member of the family considers his or her favorite thing.
8. *Name That Kid.* (Strand 2, *Skill:* Interpreting Information)
    Have students find out their complete names, who named them, and how that name was chosen. Consult a book of names and their meanings and share with the class.
9. *Animals' Families.* (Strand 1, *Skill:* Finding Information)
    Research what other animals live in families, for how long, and what their relationships and responsibilities are. VARIATION: Assign a specific animal to each class member.

12. CUSTOMS AND TRADITIONS

DETECTION Students may have difficulty mastering key concepts if they:

- Cannot identify any customs or traditions in their lives
- Have difficulties participating in common customs
- Have not developed an awareness of other people's customs
- Exhibit a negative attitude toward customs and traditions
- Cannot understand the purpose of customs in our culture
- Have not had stable family environments

Description. Customs are habitual patterns of behavior. When passed from one generation to another without benefit of being written down, they become traditions. Customs are reflected in behaviors by people: their eating habits, clothing, religion, and music. Many immigrants came to the United States and stayed together in order to continue their old customs while learning and accepting the new customs in America. Customs are not biologically determined but handed down from one generation to the next;and they are often practiced without question. Through custom, certain practices are expected of children, women, and men in all cultures. In a tribe in Africa, women are expected to grow the crops as well as care for the children, whereas the men are the hunters and warriors. In the United States, women are not used in military combat, but in Israel they stand alongside men to fight battles. In the U.S.S.R. and other cultures, it is customary for men to kiss each other's cheeks, whereas in the United States, this would not be acceptable practice. Generally, it is socially more acceptable to conform to customs than to ignore or create new ones.

Causation. Since cultures are generally passed on to the next generation through participation in society, many students may not be aware of the behaviors and practices they are learning. Young children are not given much choice as to whether or not to participate in certain customs of their parents—such as religion. Thus, the family is critical in the learning of customs. Students can develop a limited view of the world by becoming aware only of their own customs and not those of other people in their or other countries. Limited experiences can thus result in prejudices against other people and their customs.

Implications. Students may have trouble adjusting to society if they are not fully aware of the ramifications for not participating in certain customs. The United States practices a high degree of tolerance and even protects individuals who choose not to participate in certain practices (i.e., standing up for the Pledge of Allegiance). Tremendous social pressure is sometimes exerted on individuals who deviate from the norms of the customs and traditions in any culture. Students will gain a deeper understanding of people in other cultures through learning their customs. They will also grow in socially acceptable ways through participation in their own culture's customs and traditions.

CORRECTION Modify strategies for topical and learning needs.

1. *Birthday Parties.* (Strand 2, *Skill:* Analyzing Information)

   Discuss the activities that usually occur on people's birthdays, such as receiving and giving presents, having parties, and the like. Have students compare their typical family birthday celebration and then contrast these customs with those of 3 other cultures, such as China, Mexico, and the U.S.S.R.

2. *Eating Manners.* (Strand 2, *Skill:* Analyzing Information)

   Ask the class to list some of the eating practices in their homes and then compare them with those of another culture, such as Japan or China, where chopsticks are used, or Ethiopia, where much is eaten with the hands.

3. *What If . . . ?* (Strand 2, *Skill:* Synthesizing Information)

   List some of the classroom and school practices for students to discuss: going to school in the daytime; eating breakfast, lunch, and dinner; giving babies first, middle and last names; observing holidays such as Christmas and Hanukkah; parades. Evaluate the function of these customs/traditions, their purposes, and how they could be improved. Ask students to imagine, "What if you had to go to school at night? Discuss how these changes would affect their lives.

4. *Parades* (Strand 2, *Skill:* Summarizing Information)

   Use Valentine's Day, Independence Day, and Halloween as examples of customs and traditions practiced in our society. Valentine's Day is observed through exchanging cards, candy, and gifts; July 4th, Independence Day, is observed through parades and fireworks exhibitions. Lead discussion enabling students to conclude that customs and traditions are characterized through specific activities. Ask students to describe their family's activities on these days and make a list of some activities they would like to do, perhaps borrowing activities traditionally reserved for other occasions. Discuss why some activities are appropriate for some occasions but not for others and that certain groups have values that prohibit them from participating. CAUTION: Teachers must be sensitive to people's values in doing this.

5. *Pinata.* (Strand 3, *Skill:* Group Interaction)

   Other countries have traditions and customs that are different and very important to their cultures. For example, children in Mexico often break a pinata before Easter and Christmas. Using a large paper sack and papier-maché (strips of paper and glue), challenge students to make a pinata that resembles some animal, fill it with candy, fruit, and toys, and take turns trying to break it with a broom handle.

6. *Challenge to a Duel.* (Strand 1, *Skill:* Analyzing Information)

   The duel was once used to settle disputes over property, money, insults, and other differences among men. Through early times until the 1800s, the duel was a custom accepted in many societies. Ask students to compare and contrast how disputes are settled today, perhaps in the classroom or on the playground. Roleplay a modern version of the duel.

13. NEEDS AND WANTS

DETECTION Students may have difficulty mastering key concepts if they:

- Come from over- or underprivileged environments
- Are not able to differentiate between needs and wants
- Do not understand the importance of basic needs
- Do not understand the relationship of needs and wants
- Are not aware of the economics of needs and wants
- Have difficulty making good choices

Description. The basic needs of food, water, air and shelter are necessary for survival. Primitive humans were almost totally occupied with providing for these basic needs for themselves and their families. In modern societies, these basic needs are often taken for granted and people are not overly concerned about providing for them. More attention is given today to the things people would like to have—their wants, those things not needed for survival. Economics determines the degree to which people can provide for their needs and wants. Thus, the quality of satisfaction of needs and wants is an additional option. For example, a new car can be purchased for $7,000 or $20,000 or a person can buy a house that costs $50,000 or $150,000. Individuals must make choices with respect to the goods and services they want. Quality of life can be attributed to some degree to the various goods and services that make things easier and more efficient. For example, we could survive without a dishwasher or a microwave oven in the kitchen, but more time would have to be spent, a commodity many people want more of. New technology and developments have enabled us to spend more time satisfying wants as compared to needs. In the final analysis, many people want more than they can afford.

Causation.   Parents often provide for their children's needs and wants without explanation and to the degree that they are financially able. Children from affluent backgrounds as well as underprivileged ones certainly will have different perceptions of the number and quality of goods and services available to them. Students may not have had opportunities to think about why they want something or to control money and make decisions about spending it.

Implications. Whatever their economic background, students need to understand the economics of providing for their wants and needs. Most importantly, they need to learn to make their decisions based on some purpose or values. Students need more information and contact with other cultures to become aware that many people have difficulties in providing for their basic needs. Resources and services are limited in many cultures, irrespective of the apparent supply in the United States. Students will learn from experiences that they have to make the best choices among the many things they want, but explanations and simulations serve to create an important awareness.

CORRECTION Modify strategies for topical and learning needs

1. *Economic Words.* (Strand 1, *Skill:* Vocabulary)

	Place the following words on flashcards: *want, need, choice, money, air, food, shelter,* and *clothing.* Place pictures of the words on one side of the card to help students understand them. Pronounce the words and use them in sentences or give examples illustrating the ideas.

2. *Survival.* (Strand 2, *Skill:* Evaluating Information)

	Ask students to rank their basic needs for survival. Tell them to imagine they have been in a plane crash in the jungle and have to survive. They should discuss what they will need, rank their needs, and justify their lists. Their answers should be 1) air, 2) water, 3) food, and 4) shelter.

3. *Needs and Wants.* (Strand 2, *Skill:* Classifying Information)

	Make a list of items for students to label as needs (N) and wants (W). This list should include the following: clothes (N), a pet (W), a sled (W), air (N), a home (N), a radio (W), a soccer ball (W), and a new album (W). Have students suggest other things for labeling. Post the list and add to it. Discuss occasions when a need becomes a want and vice versa.

4. *Tough Choices.* (Strand 2, *Skill:* Decision Making)

	Give students a list of word pairs to choose from, such as: 1) hamburger or hot dog; 2) movie or ball game; 3) book or new ball; 4) watch television or finish homework; 5) play with your friends or go visiting relatives with parents. Ask students to give reasons for their choices.

5. *Shopping Spree.* (Strand 2, *Skill:* Decision Making)

	Give students $20.00 in play money or credit to spend for anything they may want or need. Use catalogs for students to make their selections. Monitor the students concepts of value, ask them to label their choices as a need or want, and then list what they had to give up for their choices.

6. *Trading.* (Strand 3, *Skill:* Social Participation)

	Distribute pictures of products obtained from magazines or newspapers to students. Explain that they will play a trading game and exchange products. Discuss with students their values in making choices for their trading decisions and whether these are wants or needs. Discuss their feelings about the things they attempted to trade for: Why did they want the things they chose? How did they feel when they didn't get them?

7. *All in a Day.* (Strand 5, *Skill:* Synthesizing Information)

	Give students circles divided to represent a 24-hour day. Tell them to divide their time into units for an ideal day. Draw pictures of objects in the appropriate timeframe. Start the activity by noting time for sleeping and going to school. Suggest that they include time for eating, playing, watching television, playing with friends, reading a book, and cleaning their room. When completed, display their 24-hour days and discuss their choices. Emphasize the ones that cost money or are basically free and how wisely they used their time. Other discussion should be centered around budgeting time and planning ahead.

14. RULES

DETECTION Students may have difficulty mastering key concepts if they:

- Disregard rules in the classroom
- Have difficulty playing games with their peer group
- Do not understand the purpose of rules
- Have difficulty making rules
- Are constantly trying to change rules

Description. Whenever people get together to hold a meeting or to play a game, rules are necessary to eliminate confusion, to encourage cooperation, and to foster harmonious and/or orderly social interaction. If rules do not exist, they must be created before others may participate. Observing the rules then becomes every participant's social responsibility and the consequences for not doing so can range from being ostracized from the group to being incarcerated as a criminal. Our lives would be very confusing if we did not have rules for the many complex social and economic situations in society. For example, we are accustomed to waiting in lines to buy tickets, to mail a package, and to pay for things in department stores. The rule is very simple: "You must wait your turn!" Almost every facet of living contains rules. Rules can become so necessary in our society that they are converted into laws. If rules have to be modified, they can be changed or updated. Differences over rules occur when there is no clear interpretation and no consistent enforcement. A basic tenet of democracy is the right to participate in making the rules.

Causation. Students may lack experiences in particular situations to have time to learn the appropriate rules. Depending on their ages and maturity, students may be used to getting their own way or always letting someone else make the rules. Students who are very self-centered or lack self-discipline may have difficulties in following rules established for group interactions. If students have been exposed to unfair treatment or the arbitrary interpretation of rules, they will certainly be skeptical. The importance of winning at any cost may have been instilled in students at early ages.

Implications. Students need to be exposed to rules and the social consequences for not following them through experiential activities. Many rules are abstract and need further explanation for understanding. The classroom and playground settings are ideal environments for students to help make and enforce rules. Students will be more successful in working with others if they learn and follow the rules. If rules are not followed, students must be aware of the consequences. It is important for students to have learning opportunities to modify or suggest rules for new situations. Students should be taught to ask questions and to clarify rules when confronted with new situations.

CORRECTION Modify strategies for topical and learning needs.

1. *Classroom Rules.* (Strand 2, *Skill:* Synthesizing Information)

    Have students suggest a list of classroom and playground rules. Rules about being quiet, doing one's own work, leaving the room, and being on time should be written for students to discuss their purpose and why they are needed. Ask students to suggest the consequences for infractions, post these, and stick to them.

2. *Community Rules.* (Strand 2, *Skill:* Analyzing Information)

    Ask students to draw pictures illustrating rules in their homes or in the community. For example, students may have rules about which television shows to watch, snacks between meals, bedtime, and so on. In the community, there are rules for crossing streets, keeping pets on a leash, or walking on people's lawns. Use these pictures to discuss the reasons for the rules and critique their utility.

3. *Fair Game.* (Strand 3, *Skill:* Group Interaction)

    Explain to the class that a new game will be played. Divide the class into 4 teams. Each team will have a turn guessing the number between 1 and 100 written on a card. The first team to guess the correct answer gets a point. After playing the game for awhile, change the rules without telling the class (e.g., if the girls miss on their first try, give them another try). Changing the rules should get some complaints from the rest of the class. Continue until you have made the point and discuss with the class how they felt about the game when the rules were changed.

4. *Finders Keepers.* (Strand 2, *Skill:* Decision Making)

    Pose the following situation: Susan found a pencil on the schoolground. What are the rules about finding a pencil? What should Susan do with this pencil? After discussion, pose a situation about finding money. Students should help each other determine the rules for these situations.

5. *New Game.* (Strand 3, *Skill:* Social Participation)

    Divide the class into 2 teams and place each team in a straight line. Give each team a ball and ask them to pass the ball to the person behind them. After a few tries, ask students to suggest rules for this game. For example, should the ball be passed between the legs to the person behind? How does the ball get from the back to the front of the line? Write and demonstrate the rules as students make them. Also, while playing the game, create new situations that will demand additional rules.

6. *Lost Ball.* (Strand 2, *Skill:* Decision Making)

    Pose this situation and ask students to determine a solution: If you borrow a new soccer ball from a friend and you lose it, what are the rules that are generally followed? Would the situation be different if your soccer ball were lost by someone else? A short roleplay would help the students analyze both sides of the situation. The roleplay could be expanded to include how parents fit into this situation and lead to the necessity for home and community rules in general.

15. GROUPS

DETECTION Students may have difficulty mastering key concepts if they:

- Cannot identify the groups to which they belong
- Do not understand the need to belong to groups
- Cannot identify the different purposes of groups
- Have difficulty becoming a cooperative member of a group
- Do not understand the roles of leaders and followers
- Have difficulty following social rules expected in groups

Detection. In a complex society, individuals have opportunities to belong to many groups related to their work and social lives. Groups develop unique personalities and identities just as individuals do. The dynamics of a group are reflected in the behaviors and interactions of its members. Individuals develop identities and assume a sense of efficacy through belonging to different groups. A group requires leadership and different roles for its members in order to function as a cohesive unit. Rules and generally accepted social behavior govern the participation of all members of a group. Formal groups develop very sophisticated organizational and procedural policies to conduct their business. Individuals must learn to accept leadership responsibilities as well as to follow in different group situations. Politics evolve through individuals trying to persuade others to follow their courses of action. The decision-making process involves the mixture of personal power of its members combined with real data and rational thinking.

Causation. How to work in groups is learned through experiences. Students learn to function in the family group through participation. When both parents work, group experiences may be increased or limited. Students may also have limited experiences with other groups due to being an only child, living in an isolated environment, or having protective parents. Play is one of the most powerful ways students learn to negotiate group rules. Students need to experience leadership to understand how it works. Students who are withdrawn, overly aggressive, or lack social skills may have experienced early rejection from groups and as a result may not have learned how to interact. It is also possible that students have belonged to groups whose agendas and values conflict (e.g., neighborhoods, age cohorts, teams, family, etc.) and they have been unable to resolve these conflicts satisfactorily.

Implications. Students must learn effective participation skills to function in groups. Individual identity is closely associated with belonging to various groups, and without positive experiences, students may develop feelings of powerlessness and alienation. It would be extremely difficult to function in our society without belonging to a few groups. Personal happiness and achievement can certainly be attributed to successful participation as a leader or follower in many group situations.

CORRECTION Modify strategies for topical and learning needs.

1. *Object Groups.* (Strand 2, *Skill:* Classifying Information)
   Use objects to develop the concept of groups. Give students a number of objects (marbles, different-size sticks, household items, etc.) and have students group them. After grouping the objects, ask students to label the various groups, discuss the similarities and differences, and what happens to an individual object when it does not conform to criteria.

2. *People Groups.* (Strand 2, *Skill:* Classifying Information)
   Explain that people can belong to more than 1 group. Introduce the activity by grouping students according to their height. Challenge students to form new groups (based on hair color, sex, clothes, interests); then discuss the similarities and differences of the groups.

3. *Reasonable Groups.* (Strand 2, *Skill:* Interpreting Information)
   Make a chart listing various groups on the left side (family, school, club, team). On the right, ask students to identify the reasons they belong to the various groups. Emphasize the reasons and purposes for belonging to a group and that people can belong to more than 1 group.

4. *Birdfeeder.* (Strand 3, *Skill:* Social Participation)
   Groups of 3–4 students are given the task of making a birdfeeder (or other group project such as a house from blocks). While the students are working, emphasize the importance of cooperation in the group. Also, discuss the different roles of individuals in the group and the formal and informal rules that govern each person's behavior and participation in the group. EXTEN-SION: Observe birds that feed and group them according to types.

5. *Follow the Movement.* (Strand 3, *Skill:* Social Participation)
   Form a circle so students can see each other. Explain that leaders have specific responsibilities in the group. Designate a leader to start a simple motion, such as swaying the arms back and forth or bending the knees. The rest of the class follows the action. Another leader is selected and a new movement is started. Discuss the importance of being a leader in a group and what happens to the group if everyone doesn't participate with the proper motion.

6. *Group Uniforms.* (Strand 2, *Skill:* Analyzing Information)
   Show pictures of groups dressed with similar uniforms or costumes, such as the military, police, prisoners, astronauts, dancers, or football players. Ask students to explain why they dress in similar clothes. Discuss the idea of discipline, cooperation, and communication in groups.

7. *Gestures and Flags.* (Strand 2, *Skill:* Synthesizing Information)
   Many groups dress alike and develop symbols or gestures designed especially for the members. Challenge groups of 3–4 students to develop a flag and a gesture (i.e., a handshake). Display the flags and ask students to explain their designs and demonstrate the gestures.

16. FRIENDS

DETECTION   Students may have difficulty mastering key concepts if they:

- Have difficulty making and keeping friends
- Lack social skills for developing friendships
- Have had few friends in the past
- Have had limited opportunities to make friends
- Do not recognize the value of friendships

Description. We are social animals enjoying groups and developing relationships. People need each other. The family provides the first and often primary satisfaction of this need. As people grow older, however, this need expands to include others around them and friendships are established. Friends learn from each other, share things, and help each other. Some friendships last only for a short time, while others may last for a lifetime. Friendships change as people move away, interests change, or they meet others with whom they have more in common. Friends are people who like each other, like to be together and talk with each other, and share truths they would not tell to all persons. Work is easier when others help and play more fun when someone shares the experience. Friends learn new things together and from each other. Friendships are established in neighborhoods, at school, and at other functions where people come together. They are based on things that people have in common: they live in the same area, go to the same school or church, belong to the same teams, and so on.

Causation. Students who have not had opportunities for making friends in contexts outside the home prior to entering school will often find it difficult to establish friendships. This is especially true when the other students have known each other and been together for several years. Others who have perhaps been only children or have been indulged may not have the social skills for sharing, interacting in groups, and cooperating with others, making opportunities for developing friends difficult. Special students often appear to have difficulty making and keeping friends due to a seeming lack of social skills.

Implications. It is through having and being a friend that we learn cooperation, social skills, and how to ask and receive advice for making decisions. Without friendships beyond the family, students cannot learn to develop independence for surviving in later years and to work together with others in society. School is a safe environment for students to develop skills for friendship as well as new friends. Most importantly, students must learn how to give and take from others around them.

CORRECTION Modify strategies for topical and learning needs.

1. *Friendship Circles.* (Strand 2, *Skill:* Analyzing Information)
    Ask students to draw a small circle in the middle of a page and to place their name there. Around this circle, they should draw another circle and place the names of their closest friends. On the next outer edge, they should draw another circle with names of friends that are not quite as close but still friends. On the next circle, write the names of persons who they would like to have as friends. Ask students what they learned about themselves and their friendship patterns.
2. *Guess Who?* (Strand 2, *Skill:* Interpreting Information)
    Have each student describe a friend, how they met him or her, and why they like him or her. Ask each student not to reveal the name and have other classmates guess who each student is describing.
3. *Tell Me . . .* (Strand 3, *Skill:* Personal Skills)
    Ask students to draw a grid with 4 columns across labeled: Self, Mother/ Father, Best Friend, Stranger. Have students list the following down the left side of the page: what I last cried about, a scary dream, something I am good at, something I am bad at, something taken that wasn't mine, what my favorite meal is, discontent with some part of my body. Ask students to make a checkmark in the column under each person they would feel most free in talking to about the above things.
4. *An Ideal Friend.* (Strand 3, *Skill:* Personal Skills)
    Have students describe a perfect friend. What would he or she look like (physical characteristics)? How would he or she act? What would he or she do? What special skills, talents, and interests would he or she have? What would be some of his or her favorite things?
5. *Special Delivery.* (Strand 3, *Skill:* Personal Skills)
    Have students imagine that the postman delivered a magic box to them and in the box could be 3 things for 1 (or more) of their friends. What would they want to be in the box for their friend (tangible or intangible)?
6. *Who's at the Door?* (Strand 2, *Skill:* Analyzing Information)
    Have students make a list of names of those people who have come to their houses to play or visit in the last year. Have them make a second list of those people they have visited or played with at their homes in the last year. Have them make a third list of 3 people they would invite to their houses next Saturday to play. Compare the names in the lists.
7. *Thank-You Note.* (Strand 2, *Skill:* Summarizing Information)
    Have students write thank-you notes to friends to thank them for 2 things they have done to make their lives happier or more pleasant.
8. *Friendly Advice.* (Strand 3, *Skill:* Personal Skills)
    Have students write letters to a new student in school, giving him or her some friendly advice about how to make new friends at school.

17. LEARNING

DETECTION Students may have difficulty mastering key concepts if they:

- Have not developed good skills for learning and study
- Are reluctant to try new ideas or activities
- Do not understand the need for practice
- Have difficulties seeing the purpose of learning
- Do not respond to motivational factors

Description. *Learning* is defined as the process by which behaviors (actions and emotions) are changed. Most things are learned through experiences in the environment that produce certain responses in consequence of particular stimuli. When students do not respond appropriately in social and teaching environments, the targeted learning cannot be mastered. It then becomes more important to concentrate teaching on the behaviors that interfere until they can be modified to allow for learning more academic tasks. Scientists are still studying the learning process; however, it is generally accepted that learning is stimulated through anticipation of some reward, or in some cases avoidance of punishment, and through imitation and practice. For students who experience difficulty in learning, it is recommended to structure the learning by first breaking it down into behavioral steps, modeling the appropriate behavior for students, having students practice the learning, receiving performance feedback, and finally transferring the learning to other real-life situations.

Causation. A small percentage of students have learning disabilities that interfere with normal processes of taking in or sending information. Others have not experienced good teaching practices and consequently have not had experiences that have allowed them to incorporate an adequate and independent learning style. Some home environments may be void of reading and learning materials or values conducive to learning. Students who have experienced constant failure and frustration in learning tasks both at home and at school are not likely to be motivated to learn and will even have overlearned those behaviors that continue to interfere.

Implications. Students need to experience success in the classroom under the guidance of an understanding and skillful teacher. It is important for students to have instructional materials that can be successfully completed. The motivation level will increase when students experience success and begin receiving praise and encouragement from teachers. It is important for students to realize that all people want to learn and must keep learning throughout their lives to stay current with a changing world. The incorporation of this value into students' world views will also aid in the development of their personal happiness and satisfying relationships with others.

CORRECTION Modify strategies for topical and learning needs.

1. *Stoplight.* (Strand 2, *Skill:* Classifying Information)

   Use the stoplight at an intersection to introduce the idea of learning. Ask students to make a stoplight on a sheet of paper with red, yellow, and green lights. Discuss the meanings of the colors to drivers or pedestrians.
2. *Learning Map.* (Strand 2, *Skill:* Synthesizing Information)

   Make a large timeline on the chalkboard, ranging from birth through 10 years old. Ask students to place significant learning events on the timeline: for example, when they learned to walk, talk, run, ride a tricycle, throw a ball, feed themselves, read, write, draw, ride a skateboard, and cross the street. Discuss the events in relation to other things they need to learn in life.
3. *Dog Tricks.* (Strand 2, *Skill:* Decision Making)

   Pose the problem of teaching a dog a trick, such as to sit down or to fetch a ball. Ask students to suggest ways of teaching this dog to do the tricks. Indicate that some type of reward is necessary to get the dog to perform. The reward could be food or a pat on the head. Compare and contrast the way dogs learn to the way humans learn.
4. *Foreign Language.* (Strand 2, *Skills:* Interpreting Information)

   Explain that people have to learn new languages or ways of doing things if they move to another country. Invite someone in to roleplay a teacher giving directions to students in another language. Afterwards, ask your visitor to teach the students a few simple words of another language. Discuss with students how they felt not being able to understand.
5. *Knot Tie.* (Strand 2, *Skill:* Interpreting Information)

   Ask half of the class to tie a shoe or a simple square knot. Then ask them to teach one of their classmates to tie the same knot. Discuss with them the ways that they taught their classmates through showing, practicing, correcting, and asking questions.
6. *Future Learning.* (Strand 2, *Skill:* Synthesizing Information)

   Discuss why many things cannot be explained fully and more learning is necessary for more understanding. The cure for cancer and other diseases are examples of problems posing new challenges for humankind. Ask students to draw pictures of things they would like to learn to do in the future: drive a car, build a house, operate a computer, pilot a spacecraft, or sew a dress.
7. *Puzzle Challenge.* (Strand 3, *Skill:* Social Participation)

   Take a large picture from a magazine and mount it on poster board. Cut the picture in 6–8 pieces forming a puzzle. Give each student a piece and challenge him or her to figure out the puzzle. Encourage the students to cooperate to get their puzzle pieces to fit together. Discuss with students how they felt putting the puzzle together. Explain that many things can be understood if people take their time and they talk and work with others.

REFLECTIONS

1. DETECTION and CORRECTION strategies have been presented in this section for special students who are learning about themselves in their immediate surroundings. Discuss the relationship between self-concept and the home, family, and school environments of students. Show how the home and family support the school's and student's learning environment. What are the ramifications of certain values taught in school being in conflict with home values?

2. There has been a proliferation of writing about the development of a positive self-concept and its importance in the learning process. Review some recent research concerning the development of positive self-concepts in the classroom. What are the backgrounds of the authors and their experiences in the classroom? Select some of these ideas to implement with students and evaluate their effectiveness.

3. Modern homes and families have undergone many significant changes in only a few years. Identify some of these major changes and discuss with others to verify your perceptions of their importance (e.g., technology, divorce, work specialization, entertainment, sex roles, etc.). Make some conclusions and some specific suggestions about what should be taught to students to help them cope with these changes.

4. This section stressed the relationship between having a positive self-concept and the learning process. Discuss this relationship with several teachers. Share personal experiences about learning difficulties or failures/ successes that were experienced in school. Do these experiences provide any insights for working with special students?

5. Researchers have argued about the impact of television on the development of home, school, and family values. View current television family shows and analyze the family structures, roles, and values depicted. Compare these situations to your own family background and to those of students in a selected classroom. What impact, if any, do you feel these programs have on young students?

6. There can be significant gaps in the planning of instruction and the actual lesson. Select a strategy in this chapter to teach to a small group of your peers. Videotape the teaching session and critique with respect to an actual implementation with younger students. Then try out the lesson with a student group. Compare the actual teaching situation with the microteaching session.

7. Students display behaviors toward home, family, and school through their classroom interactions, out-of-class activities, and speech and writing. Look over the DETECTION behaviors that are listed in the section before each topic. Observe the teaching of social studies in an elementary classroom for a period of time and note which of the behaviors seem most prevalent in this group. Make specific suggestions for adjustments in instruction that would be appropriate to these behaviors.

8. Adjustments in instruction often must be made because of an individual's particular learning problem. Select one or more of the activities in this section and perform the task from the vantage point of a student with a specified handicap. Write a summary paragraph of your observations and thoughts while performing the tasks. Make some conclusions about teaching this activity after having performed it yourself.

9. Teachers must recognize and analyze their own values and establish some harmony between their own and the school's to be effective in teaching and discussing values with others. Discuss your personal values about home, family, and school with other teachers. What are the alternatives when the teacher's values are in conflict with the teaching situation?

10. A number of suggestions for teaching about self-concept, home, family, and school relationships are presented in social studies texts. Compare and contrast discussions in these sources with the information and activities in this chapter.

Center, D. B. (1989). *Curriculum and teaching strategies for students with behavior disorders.* Englewood Cliffs, NJ: Prentice-Hall.

Evans, R. J. (1984). *Fostering peer acceptance of handicapped students.* Washington, DC: National Institute of Education. (ERIC Document Reproduction Service No. ED 262 498)

Herlihy, J. G., & Herlihy, M. T. (Eds.). (1980). *Mainstreaming in the social studies.* Washington, DC: National Council for the Social Studies. (ERIC Document Reproduction Service No. ED 186 346)

Long, J. D., & Williams, R. L. (1982). *SOS for teachers.* Princeton, NJ: Princeton Book.

Maxim, G. W. (1987). *Social studies and the elementary school child* . (3rd ed.). Columbus, OH: Charles E. Merrill

Ryan, F. L. (1980). *The social studies sourcebook: Ideas for teaching in the elementary and middle school.* Boston: Allyn and Bacon.

Samuels, S. C. (1977). *Enhancing self-concept in early childhood.* New York: Human Sciences Press.

Selakovich, D. (1970). *Social studies for the disadvantaged.* New York: Holt, Rinehart and Winston.

Simon, S. B., Howe, L. W., & Kirschenbaum, H. (1972). *Values clarification.* New York: Hart.

PART III

EXPANDING
COMMUNITIES

The continued use of the expanding community approach in this section enables teachers to use these activities in conjunction with the regular social studies curriculum or textbook. This approach is based on the premise that elementary students progress through developmental stages of social awareness. The social stages most often experienced by students begin with life at home and gradually expand to their neighborhood, community, state, country, and world. It is expected that, as students learn concepts in these expanding social environments, they can begin to apply them to other social studies learning.

The DETECTION sections in Chapters 6, 7, and 8 provide informal questions to pursue with students in selecting appropriate learning experiences in the dimensions of community, state, and country. The activities are designed to provide a range of very concrete experiences with historical and geographic concepts that correlate with the detection behaviors.

The Causation section provides teachers with further understanding about why special learners may have difficulties with the topics. A major contributing factor to lack of knowledge in these expanded environments is students' lack of experience and opportunities to travel. In addition, social studies is not often given priority in the early elementary grades, especially to special learners who may be struggling with basic reading and language tasks. Thus, students may not have had learning opportunities to develop these skills.

A variety of activities is available to meet a range of special learning needs related to the community, state, and country. Concrete learning experiences, such as Hat Play in Community Workers (Topic 23) and Cultural Dinner in Cultural Diversity (Topic 43), would be appropriate for limited-ability students. More abstract learning experiences would include New Shopping Malls in Shopping Centers (Topic 20) and Becoming a Citizen in Citizenship (Topic 39). Choose a Solution in Citizenship (Topic 39) and Auction in Free Enterprise System (Topic 44) are examples of many activities that involve an entire class, with special students taking cooperative learning roles. As much as possible, teachers should give students opportunities to select their own levels of involvement from several alternatives. Students usually select those activities that interest them as well as those that are within their degrees of difficulty.

The initial chapters of Part III should be interesting and relevant to special learners, due to the concreteness of the activities and the likelihood that all have had some background in local neighborhoods and shopping centers. Without some basis and experience to draw from, students may have difficulty, however, and it is especially crucial for teachers to be cognizant of students' previous learning. Special learners must become comfortable first with their immediate social situation and peer group before progressing into more abstract learning. Thus, if the special students have not developed some of the skills and knowledge presented in Part II, the material in this section may be very difficult and frustrating. The learner must understand a few concepts before being able to compare and contrast ideas and attach new learning to previous learning with the more difficult concepts in social studies.

Part IV continues to expand the concept of community into a wider and more world-view perspective. As in all sections, it is important to choose and modify each strategy to meet the specific learning needs of individual students.

CHAPTER 6

LIVING IN THE COMMUNITY

18. URBAN AND RURAL NEIGHBORHOODS

DETECTION Students may have difficulty mastering key concepts if they:

- Have not traveled in urban and/or rural neighborhoods
- Have difficulties making and expressing observations
- Do not recognize differences in neighborhoods
- Have difficulties describing neighborhood characteristics
- Do not understand the purpose for an address

Description. A neighborhood is made up of people living close together and is a part of a larger community group. Neighborhoods are described by explaining the geography, something about the people, and the various types of buildings located there. Urban neighborhoods have more buildings in closer proximity than rural or farm neighborhoods. A suburban neighborhood is usually characterized by an emphasis on the number of new houses in areas outside the center of an urban area. Generally, the people living in a specific neighborhood have similar income levels, as reflected in the rent or mortgage payments. A great deal of pride is often demonstrated in neighborhoods by keeping the streets and buildings clean. Immigrants and other groups sometimes live together in neighborhoods to continue to practice some of their customs and traditions. Other neighborhoods have festivals or social events to bring people together. Things are constantly changing in neighborhoods, with people moving in and out and buildings undergoing facelifts.

Causation. Many students do not have opportunities to travel to see various types of neighborhoods. Even students living in large urban environments may not have perceptions of the different neighborhoods within the city. Exposure to the ways other cultures organize into neighborhoods is sometimes limited to television and vicarious perceptions.

Implications. There are many alternative ways that people can live together in neighborhoods. Concepts of the way people live will be limited when students have only their own neighborhoods to learn about. Students can use their own neighborhoods to compare and contrast with other neighborhoods. More understanding about people in other cultures will evolve through increased exposure to the way other neighborhoods are organized.

CORRECTION Modify strategies for topical and learning needs.

1. *Home Address.* (Strand 1, *Skill:* Arranging Information)

    Write the school address on the chalkboard and explain the meaning of each line. Have each student address an envelope to another classmate at his or her home. Help the students write short letters describing the neighborhoods in which they live. Take the students on a fieldtrip to a neighborhood mailbox or post office to mail the letters. Ask students to bring their letters to school when they receive them at home.

2. *School Neighborhood Map.* (Strand 1, *Skill:* Map Making)

    Take students on a fieldtrip to observe the neighborhood around the school. Point out major landmarks, businesses, housing, streets, and open land for the students to observe and label. Upon returning to class, introduce students to map-making symbols (boxes for buildings, lines for streets, dotted spaces for open land, and other symbols for specific landmarks). Have each student make a map of the school neighborhood.

3. *Neighboring Sounds.* (Strand 2, *Skill:* Classifying Information)

    Open the windows and ask students to listen to all the sounds in the neighborhood. Match the sounds with the activities in the neighborhood.

4. *Neighborhood Signs.* (Strand 1, *Skill:* Comprehension)

    Ask students to observe and draw pictures of the street signs in the neighborhood. Post the pictures and ask students to explain the purpose of each sign. EXTENSION: Make these signs for students to observe and follow in the classroom.

5. *Neighborhood Services.* (Strand 2, *Skill:* Analyzing Information)

    Provide a list of activities that may or may not be available in certain neighborhoods (mail a letter, buy clothes, get a haircut, buy gas, catch a bus, get help for a fire, play football, observe wild animals, fish, hunt, climb trees, etc.). Ask students to label each activity "yes" or "no" as it pertains to their neighborhoods.

6. *Other Neighborhoods.* (Strand 2, *Skill:* Analyzing Information)

    Ask students to collect or find pictures in reference books of neighborhoods in other cultures. Use the question: How are the neighborhoods alike and different? Emphasize housing, business, geography, activities, and landmarks.

7. *New Shopping Mall.* (Strand 2, *Skill:* Evaluating Information)

    Pose the following situation to your class: What would happen to your neighborhood if a large shopping center were built on the vacant land? Discuss the impact on the neighborhood, emphasizing traffic, safety, convenience, and the like. EXTENSION: Obtain the future planning documents for the area and share with students.

8. *Urban/Rural Living.* (Strand 2, *Skill:* Analyzing Information)

    Make 2 headings on the chalkboard: Urban and Rural. Ask students to list things that are alike and different for these neighborhoods. Emphasize buildings, activities, and land forms. Go through the list again and label "yes" or "no" if these things are found in their neighborhoods.

19. NEIGHBORS

DETECTION Students may have difficulty mastering key concepts if they:

- Have difficulties naming some of their neighbors
- Do not understand the meaning of *neighbors*
- Are not able to describe their neighbors
- Exhibit prejudices toward different cultural groups
- Do not have cooperative attitudes toward their neighbors

Description. A neighbor is a person who lives near you. Neighbors can be various ages and have different backgrounds. Just because people live near each other does not necessarily mean they will be good neighbors. Neighbors have their peculiarities and can even be extremely eccentric. Most neighbors value their privacy, as demonstrated by the fences around their homes. It is not unusual for people not to know their neighbors very well. In modern society, neighbors are not as dependent on one another as in earlier times. A disaster such as a tornado or flood will bring neighbors closer together to help one another. Neighbors can help each other in many ways. In the pioneer days, neighbors used to have a barn raising; they would all help build a barn for one of the neighbors. Survival depended on neighbors cooperating and helping each other. In present-day society, neighborhood watches help to deter crime and make the area safer for everyone. Older neighbors need help during extreme weather conditions to insure that they are all right. Good neighbors respect each other, trying not to disturb or infringe on each others' rights.

Causation. Students may not know very much about their neighbors, especially if they live in heavily populated and mobile areas or have moved a lot themselves. Many parents teach their children not to be overly friendly with neighbors in order to protect them. Students may have had bad experiences with neighbors, especially if they have broken a window or infringed on the rights of another person. Also, students may have prejudices toward other cultural groups or people that are different.

Implications. Students need to understand the give-and-take relationship of having and being neighbors. In order to have a good neighbor, you have to be a good neighbor, too. Students need to learn that neighbors can be friendly and helpful but that they must not infringe on others' privacy. Neighbors sometimes have conflicts that must be resolved. To continue a good relationship, a neighbor's land and property must be respected and everyone must work together to make the neighborhood a better place to live. Diversity of cultural groups in any one neighborhood is becoming more prevalent, requiring a more open attitude toward people, irrespective of their background or the way they make a living.

CORRECTION Modify strategies for topical and learning needs.

1. *Name Your Neighbor.* (Strand 2, *Skill:* Classifying Information)

    Explain to students that neighbors are people who live close to you. Ask students to name some of their neighbors on a chart on the chalkboard. Have students complete the chart information by indicating if the neighbors have children, are elderly, or live alone and the type of work they do.

2. *Good Deeds.* (Strand 2, *Skill:* Synthesizing Information)

    Explain to students that neighbors usually share things and do good deeds for each other. For example, a neighbor may pick up your mail or feed a pet when you are out of town. Give students an opportunity to discuss some of the good deeds that neighbors can do for each other.

3. *Good Neighbors.* (Strand 2, *Skill:* Decision Making)

    Roleplay to explore the idea of being a good neighbor. Ask different students to respond to the following questions: 1) Would you loan your soccer ball to a neighbor? 2) Would you invite your neighbor to stay all night with you? 3) Would you pick up your neighbors' mail while they are out of town? 4) Would you ask your neighbors to turn their music down? 5) Would you invite your neighbor over for hamburgers? Conclude the lesson by summarizing characteristics of good neighbors.

4. *Country Neighbors.* (Strand 2, *Skill:* Synthesizing Information)

    Explain to students that countries such as the United States have neighbors, Mexico and Canada. Show the countries on a map. Country neighbors have conflict just as people have conflict. What are some areas of conflict that could develop between countries (boundaries, travel, immigration, pollution, and products)? How do countries and people settle their conflicts?

5. *Fences for Neighbors.* (Strand 2, *Skill:* Group Interaction)

    Make a fence using the classroom chairs and set up a roleplay to explain why neighbors build fences. Fences are more often found in cities, where people have small lots. Before initiating the roleplay, ask students to develop reasons why people build fences (privacy and security). Invite students to act out the situations.

6. *Student Neighbors.* (Strand 2, *Skill:* Evaluating Information)

    Explain to the class that students sitting next to each other are neighbors. Ask the class to contribute ideas that describe good and bad student neighbors.

7. *Disaster Aid.* (Strand 2, *Skill:* Interpreting Information)

    Explain to students that, during the pioneer days, neighbors used to help each other build barns in barn raisings. In modern times, we usually don't help people build, but we do help in times of critical need. Ask students to identify times of critical need, such as a blizzard, tornado, flood, fire, or crime. Students can finish the activity by drawing neighborly activities that might occur during a disaster.

20. SHOPPING CENTERS

DETECTION Students may have difficulty mastering key concepts if they:

- Have difficulty understanding the medium for exchanging goods in society
- Do not understand that shopping centers have evolved from an ancient concept of a marketplace
- Do not know the functions of a shopping center
- Do not understand the need for shopping centers
- Have difficulty recognizing the relationship between shopping centers and the community

Description. In all parts of the world, as early as ancient times, traders leased space in marketplaces to exchange goods. In the United States, the modern-day shopping center is relatively new; most were built in suburban areas because of lack of space and inconvenience in downtown shopping areas. A shopping center is a group of stores, businesses, and restaurants built around an open area often referred to as a mall. The stores are managed as a unit; however, they are occupied, managed, and operated individually. The primary advantage of this arrangement is convenience to the consumer. All types of desired goods and services can be located in one central place and the area can be heated and air-conditioned for the patrons' comfort. Services offered in many centers include banking, hotels, medical and dental clinics, theaters, and restaurants. Special events are also often part of the activity that occurs in a shopping center, including art exhibits, concerts, and fashion shows. Merchants typically pay rent for their space to a single firm or owner of the center. The owner has the responsibility of locating the area in a convenient place, providing and maintaining attractive facilities and parking, and making sure that stores and shoppers are protected from crime.

Causation. Students may have had little experience with shopping centers if they have not lived in areas where they are available and/or convenient. Students' experiences may have also been limited to only a few examples of shopping centers. Some parents have limited their children's chances to explore these environments because of the inconvenience of shopping with small or handicapped children.

Implications. Shopping centers are growing in numbers yearly and have significant impacts on local economies. Students should understand how people's basic needs for goods and services combines with their ingenuity to produce better, more convenient, and modern ways of providing for these needs.

CORRECTION Modify strategies for topical and learning needs.

1. *Design a Center.* (Strand 2, *Skill:* Synthesizing Information)
   Have students bring boxes of different shapes and sizes and build a shopping center. Label the stores and make a list of products a consumer might find in them.
2. *What's in a Name?* (Strand 2, *Skill:* Interpreting Information)
   Prepare a list of the stores that might be found in a shopping center. Ask students to identify what these stores sell. If the product is not apparent in the name of the store, ask students to predict what the store sells and why they think so. Have students make up names of stores.
3. *Shopping Around.* (Strand 2, *Skill:* Classifying Information)
   Ask students to make a list of all the products their families have purchased in the last month. For each product, decide if it is available in a local shopping center or if it would need to be purchased from a separate store in a different area of town.
4. *Mapping It Out.* (Strand 1, *Skill:* Maps)
   Make a list of all the shopping areas in town. Locate each on a map and place a marker to label it. Have students determine which shopping area is most convenient to where they live.
5. *Tell Me Why.* (Strand 1, *Skill:* Community Resources)
   Have students devise a questionnaire to find out who shops at the shopping centers. Questions should focus on how often respondents shop at the shopping centers, their opinions of the goods and services offered there, why they like to shop at shopping centers, their favorite store in the mall, and so on. Ask students to share their information and to make conclusions from their findings.
6. *Advertising It.* (Strand 2, *Skill:* Classifying Information)
   List all the products and services advertised in the newspaper on any one day. Ask students to identify whether or not these goods and services could be purchased at the local shopping center.
7. *Go Shopping.* (Strand 2, *Skill:* Decision Making)
   Take a fieldtrip to a local shopping area. Give each student a determined amount of money to spend hypothetically on an outfit of clothing, including shoes, pants, blouse/shirt, and other accessories. Have students keep notes on where they found each item they would have bought and how much they would have spent on it. Compare the economic experiences each student has. VARIATION: Give each student an assigned item to find (e.g., a shirt/blouse, shoes, belt). Ask students to list each store that offers an item of this type and compare the highest price they found for this item and the lowest price they found.
8. *No Shopping.* (Strand 2, *Skill:* Summarizing Information)
   Have students make a list of all the things they can see and do in a shopping center besides shopping. Compare lists and discuss the variety of activities.

21. CONSUMPTION AND PRODUCTION

DETECTION Students may have difficulty mastering key concepts if they:

- Cannot identify things consumed in the community
- Cannot identify things produced in the community
- Do not understand differences in production and consumption
- Cannot relate money to consumption/production process

Description. People and businesses specialize in certain aspects of the consumption and production process in order to fulfill the needs of a free-market economy. Consumption is using goods and services, whereas production is making and delivering goods and services for the consumer. A business can produce just about anything in a free-market society, as long as someone wants the product or service and is willing to pay for it. During the pioneer days, a family had to be self-sufficient in providing for their consumption through their own production. For example, food was provided through farming and hunting rather than purchasing it at the local store. In modern-day society, food is produced on large farms and shipped to supermarkets for sale and eventual consumption. People are dependent on each other to provide the goods and services that are needed and desired in modern society. The farmer is very dependent on the tractor producer who makes the equipment to cultivate the large fields to produce food for distribution and consumption. The exchange of products and services is facilitated through a monetary system. Every good and service has a monetary value determined by the competitive market. If a product is very scarce, then the demand drives its price higher.

Causation. The consumption and production process may not have been an overt part of students' backgrounds. Most students have not had the responsibility of participating actively in the production process but certainly have consumed a number of goods and services in their daily lives. The production process is usually controlled by the adults in modern society; students will be more familiar with the consumer role. Also, the economic power of most students is controlled by adult economic resources.

Implications. Students need to understand the consumption and production process and that they are actually a part of the overall economic system. In order for people to participate in a free market, they must provide products or services to obtain money to exchange for other products or services. The most skilled services or valued products demand the higher prices in modern society. Communities, states, and countries are interdependent with one another in producing goods and services. Our quality of life depends upon exchanging goods and services produced by other communities throughout the world.

CORRECTION Modify strategies for topical and learning needs.

1. *Goods and Services.* (Strand 2, *Skill:* Classifying Information)
   Distinguish between *goods* and *services.* Make index cards with examples of either goods or services performed by people listed on them (e.g., pencils, groceries, gasoline, clothes, repairmen, salespeople, waiters, police officers). Distribute 1 card to each student and have him or her place it in 1 of 2 boxes marked goods and services.
2. *Popcorn Trail.* (Strand 2, *Skill:* Synthesizing Information)
   Bring popcorn to class for a snack for students to consume. Challenge students to reconstruct the way popcorn was obtained and eventually brought to class. The consumption/production process will include a farmer growing the popcorn, purchase by a distributor, delivery to a supermarket, purchased by a consumer, and then popping it for consumption. Other items could be traced, such as the pencils or books that students use. Students could roleplay the various parts to further develop the process.
3. *Clothes Label.* (Strand 2, *Skill:* Summarizing Information)
   Ask students to look at the labels in their shirts and shoes to see where the items were made. Make a list of the places and locate them on a map or globe. Discuss with the students why so many of their clothes are made outside of the United States.
4. *Fast Food.* (Strand 2, *Skill:* Synthesizing Information)
   The interdependence of communities and people providing goods and services is important in a specialized environment. Mark on a timeline showing minutes the length of time it takes a person to eat in a fast-food restaurant (i.e., 10 min.) or a regular restaurant (i.e., 20 min.), or to prepare and eat the food at home (i.e., 60 min.). Use other examples, such as buying vs. making a dress or shirt, and mark the information on a timeline. Discuss with students how this helps people specialize and become more interdependent with others.
5. *Primitive Life.* (Strand 2, *Skill:* Analyzing Information)
   Explain to students that an imaginary trip will take them back in history to live with a primitive family. Primitive people were both producers and consumers of almost everything. For example, the family had to secure a place to stay, make their clothes, hunt for food, and build and care for the fires. Relate these activities to a 24-hour day and ask students to draw pictures to indicate the amount of time necessary for these tasks. Compare this schedule to daily life today.
6. *New Business.* (Strand 2, *Skill:* Social Interaction)
   Discuss with students goods and services difficult to obtain in their community or neighborhood. Divide students into small groups and have them propose a new business for their community by drawing a picture or describing the business. Ask other students to react to the pictures or suggestions by indicating whether or not the community would accept a new store, factory, or business.

22. GOVERNMENT

DETECTION Students may have difficulty mastering key concepts if they:

- Cannot identify jobs associated with government
- Are not aware of how laws are made or enforced
- Do not understand the overall purpose of government
- Have difficulties understanding levels of government
- Do not understand the process for government participation

Description. Government is a vital part of every community, state, and nation. Its processes enable group members to live in harmony with each other. Laws are developed that usually affect the lives of the total group by requiring or forbidding certain behaviors. Most people obey the laws willingly in society, with a small percentage trying to exist outside the laws. Enforcement of the laws is the responsibility of local and state police. People charged with breaking the law are entitled to be heard in court, working through the judicial system. The United States has a democratic form of government, which is ruled by the people in the society. People in a democracy have opportunities to vote for political leaders who become representatives to develop laws. Separate governments exist in the United States; certain responsibilities are vested at the federal, state, or local levels. Government can take many forms; leaders can be presidents, prime ministers, kings or queens, or dictators. All of these different types of governments exist and work to establish a process for making and enforcing decisions that affect the group.

Causation. Even though students are very much a part of and are affected by various governments, they may not be aware of the overall process due to their lack of overt participation in an adult-controlled activity. The nature of government and many of its processes requires students to understand abstract concepts that may be beyond their developmental levels. Students may come from families who feel powerlessness in relation to government.

Implications. The classroom is an ideal environment for students to learn about government through active participation in some of the fundamental democratic processes, such as electing leaders and participating in rule making. Students must learn the skills and requirements for participating in the democratic process, whether by becoming a leader or casting an informed vote. Even in a democracy, fierce competition exists for government financial resources. In addition, learning about governments helps students to understand people living in different countries.

CORRECTION Modify strategies for topical and learning needs.

1. *World Leaders.* (Strand 1, *Skill:* Maps)

   Have students collect pictures from newspapers and magazines of different countries' leaders. Place the pictures on a bulletin board with a string connecting the leader with the country.

2. *Letter to Congress.* (Strand 2, *Skill:* Summarizing Information)

   Write a class letter to one of the United States senators or representatives, requesting information about some aspect of government or outlining a specific problem in the community.

3. *Class Election.* (Strand 3, *Skill:* Social Participation)

   Stage a political election, with students belonging to political parties called the Plats and Tiggs. Each party should outline goals that they support. Explain that a class president, vice president, and secretary will be elected. Help students to select candidates for each of the offices from both parties. Organize a ballot listing all the nominees and their offices for the rest of the class to vote for in private elections

4. *Government Leaders.* (Strand 3, *Skill:* Social Participation)

   Identify the mayor of the city, governor of the state, and president of the United States. Explain to students that all these individuals are political leaders. Discuss with students the role of each of these individuals and the relative powers at their respective levels.

5. *Whose Law Is This?* (Strand 2, *Skill:* Evaluating Information)

   Many of our laws are differentiated based upon whether they are local, state, or federal. Explain this to students and use several examples to illustrate the point (e.g., federal laws or state laws are enforced at the local level, but local laws are not enforced at the federal level). List laws, such as the speed limit, that students know about and decide what levels govern their enforcement.

6. *My Way/Our Way.* (Strand 2, *Skill:* Summarizing Information)

   Organize a roleplay for students to experience the differences between democratic and dictatorial forms of government. The teacher will play the different roles of leaders. Decisions will be made by a dictatorship first as to lining up to leave the room, seating arrangements, playground activities, and so on. Some of the decisions need to be blatantly arbitrary to make the point about the power of dictators. Then switch roles and use some democratic processes for making the decisions in the above situations. The teacher could let students vote on certain things, with the majority ruling. Discuss the basic differences between the two forms of government.

7. *Community Problems.* (Strand 2, *Skill:* Decision Making)

   List on the chalkboard some of the problems in the community that local politicians and people are facing, such as zoning or major community projects. Ask students to express opinions and give reasons. The class could invite the mayor or councilmembers to discuss the problems.

23. COMMUNITY WORKERS

DETECTION Students may have difficulty mastering key concepts if they:

- Cannot identify community helpers or workers
- Cannot describe the functions of community workers
- Cannot identify the relationship between needs and community workers
- Do not perceive the need for shared responsibility
- Do not understand the economics of community services and workers
- Have difficulty understanding the concept of specialization

Description. Although communities vary in characteristics, they all carry on the same basic activities: protection, trade and industry, transportation, communication, education, recreation, government, religion, and the arts. Within each of these areas, people work to maintain and meet the responsibilities for a quality life environment. Jobs related to the provision of the goods and services needed in a community range from the professional level to labor and are more complex as the size of the community grows. As communities have become larger and more complex, workers have specialized their work to save time and to provide higher levels of service and quality. Population growth requires additional resources and workers in the community to support the supply of goods and services. Thus, it becomes more necessary for people to depend upon each other and to share responsibilities for accomplishing the common activities of a community.

Causation. Students who lack experience in complex organizations or have not been observant of their environment are likely to be unaware of the many jobs and responsibilities required in the efficient operation of a community. In most homes and communities, the common activities and jobs are provided so efficiently that many students will have taken these for granted, not realizing the degree of cooperation and interrelatedness required. Students may have had limited contact with community workers.

Implications. By studying the various dimensions of work and workers in the community, students will build an awareness of career opportunities and can plan their futures around the opportunities for contributing to and participating in the continued growth and improvement of a community. Students also learn about using important community resources, especially for reporting emergencies of all types. It is important for students to learn the value of all types of work in providing for the complex needs of an expanding community. Through increased cooperation among workers, stronger communities can be built and essential needs can be better met.

CORRECTION Modify strategies for topical and learning needs.

1. *Work List.* (Strand 2, *Skill:* Classifying Information)

    List the following community activities on the chalkboard: protection, trade and industry, transportation, communication, education, recreation, government, religion, and arts. Ask students to name all the jobs or workers they can and classify them under the appropriate headings.

2. *Help Me.* (Strand 2, *Skill:* Decision Making)

    Print the following situations on strips of paper and have each student draw 1 and decide who he or she should call for help: a) house fire, b) broken arm, c) broken water pipe, d) garbage, e) robbery, f) recreation, g) learning to read, h) car repair, and i) power failure.

3. *Whose Job?* (Strand 2, *Skill:* Interpreting Information)

    Draw symbols or find pictures in magazines that represent various occupations. Ask students to identify and explain how the symbol relates to the work. Examples: stethoscope (doctor), books and pens (teacher), plumber's helper (plumber), bag of groceries (grocer), clerical collar or other religious symbol (religion), hammer and nails (carpenter), wrench (mechanic), water hose or ax (firefighter). VARIATION: Collect several types of "tool boxes" and ask students to list 5 tools they might expect to find in each worker's box: doctor's bag, teacher's bag, carpenter's apron, plumber's tool box, tailor or seamstress's sewing box, homemaker's utility drawer, mechanic's tool box.

4. *Hat Play.* (Strand 3, *Skill:* Social Participation)

    Collect or make several kinds of hats that are associated with various jobs. Ask students to select a hat and roleplay this person in a job-related situation. For example: a nurse's cap and a nurse about to give a patient a shot; a police officer's hat and a police officer giving a speeding motorist a ticket; a hard hat and an engineer building a large office building.

5. *What Would Happen?* (Strand 2, *Skill:* Analyzing Information)

    Ask students to discuss how things would be different or what would happen if: a) teachers did not come to work (a strike was called); b) firefighters were not trained and ready; c) all the mechanics in the community left town; d) the secretaries refused to work; e) the sanitation department closed down.

6. *Spokes of the Wheel.* (Strand 2, *Skill:* Analyzing Information)

    Draw a wheel on the chalkboard and place the name of the school in the middle (hub). Draw spokes from the middle and ask students to think of all the jobs necessary for running a school; label each spoke with a job (e.g., principals, teachers, clerical help, PTA, maintenance, books and supplies, food, safety, money, etc.).

7. *When I Grow Up.* (Strand 2, *Skill:* Synthesizing Information)

    Ask students to draw a picture of what they might like to do for a career when they grow up. List the tasks they think they will perform in this job and 5 things about themselves that they think will be helpful to them in doing this job well.

24. TRANSPORTATION

DETECTION Students may have difficulty mastering key concepts if they:

- Do not know the functions of transportation systems
- Have had limited travel experiences
- Are not careful observers of the world around them
- Do not perceive the interrelationships of transporting people and goods and services

Description. Transportation brings communities the goods and services they need and takes people where they need and want to go. Common transportation forms include automobiles, trains, trucks, airplanes, ships, and even pipelines that carry oil and gas across our country. Without these forms, a community would not have food, mail, and energy resources. Modern transportation has given society access to other communities, making the world more interdependent. The three main types of transportation are land, water, and air; each of these has advantages and disadvantages. The kind of transportation selected for moving goods depends to a great extent upon the costs involved. Usually, the slower the moving, the lower the cost. Goods must be transported cheaply in order for consumers to afford them. However, some products must be moved more quickly and must take the higher-priced forms of travel. Other factors that must be considered in choosing forms of transportation include weight of goods shipped, distance shipped, and even comfort and safety. In primitive times, people tamed animals for carrying their goods and eventually invented the wheel to make it easier to move heavier burdens. Organized systems of roads and expanded water travel helped to bring people in remote areas and goods closer together, forming larger and more complex communities.

Causation. Opportunities to observe more primitive means of transportation may have been limited for students in modern and urban communities. Goods and services are so readily available in our society, primarily because of our excellent transportation systems, that students often do not realize the intricacies for providing them. Transportation hubs are usually located in isolated sections of cities, away from neighborhoods, thus making them inaccessible and unfamiliar to students.

Implications. Without transportation, modern society would not exist. It would be necessary for us to spend much of our time growing our food and a lot more of our personal energy providing for our basic needs. In order to maintain and improve the level of support provided through the transportation system, people must contribute by paying taxes, enforcing laws, and keeping the environment safe for the future. Students today will have essential roles in these systems in the future.

CORRECTION Modify strategies for topical and learning needs.

1. *Toy Parade.* (Strand 2, *Skill:* Classifying Information)

    Ask students to bring toys from home that are part of the transportation system. Display the cars, airplanes, trucks, trains, and ships on a table and discuss the kinds of goods and services delivered by these vehicles.

2. *Beasts of Burden.* (Strand 2, *Skill:* Interpreting Information)

    Ask students to name all the animals they can that have been used for transporting materials. This form of transportation is still used today in many parts of the world. Discuss where and why animals are still being used. For each animal discussed, ask students to list in separate columns the disadvantages in using this beast and the advantages. Animals will include horses, mules, llamas, oxen, elephants, camels, pigeons, dogs, and humans. Aspects to discuss for each animal include climate and weather, distance and geography, fuel, safety, and impact on the environment.

3. *Mapping It Out.* (Strand 1, *Skill:* Maps)

    Find (or draw) a grid map of the community and locate its centers of transportation. Label these locations with symbols: a picture of an airplane for the airport, a bus for the bus depot, train, subway, and so on.

4. *Collage.* (Strand 2, *Skill:* Synthesizing Information)

    Make a collage of pictures from magazines of every form of transportation that can be found.

5. *See It, Feel It.* (Strand 1, *Skill:* Community Resources)

    Ask a truck driver to bring his truck to school and let the students see it both inside and out. Have the driver tell the class about his experiences moving goods across the country. VARIATION: Take a fieldtrip to a truck stop and have the manager speak to the class.

6. *Wheels, Wheels.* (Strand 1, *Skill:* Synthesizing Information)

    Give students a picture of a wheel with spokes dividing it into several units. Ask students to draw pictures of forms of transportation that have wheels in the divided areas of the big wheel. Post the drawings on the bulletin board.

7. *Plan a Trip.* (Strand 2, *Skill:* Synthesizing Information)

    Ask each student to plan a trip. Give them the following guidelines to research, make decisions about, and share with the class: location, number of miles to be traveled, means of transportation, time trip will take, and round-trip transportation.

8. *Cars, Trains, Planes.* (Strand 2, *Skill:* Analyzing Information)

    List the 3 most common types of people transportation on the chalkboard. Under each type, list the advantages and disadvantages associated with it.

9. *Primitive Days.* (Strand 2, *Skill:* Group Interaction)

    Select a group of students and assign roles of family and other persons found in the primitive community. Have students roleplay how they would travel to hunt a mammoth, carry their tools and supplies, and bring back meat for family members who could not go along.

25. COMMUNICATION

DETECTION Students may have difficulty mastering key concepts if they:

- Cannot identify various ways of communicating
- Do not know the major events and people who contributed to the development of communication
- Do not recognize alternative systems for communication
- Have limited forms of communication themselves

Description. *Communication* means sharing information, both sending and receiving, and is a basic human activity. If we had no communication, our entire way of life would cease to exist in its present form. The human voice and bodily gestures are important means of communication as are other methods, such as letters, telephones, books, magazines, newspapers, signs, radio and television, and motion pictures. Communication and transportation are so closely linked that it would be impossible to have one without the other. Before a letter can be delivered, for example, it must first be transported to its destinations. All forms of transportation depend upon some type of communication for goods and services to reach their destination. A lot of our communication depends upon face-to-face gestures and signals that can be carried on even without words. Pictures and symbols have always been significant communication devices between people because they are possible without a common language. After language was developed, it became easier for man to share information with others. Where many languages are spoken, this may slow the communication process somewhat. The growth of communication was rapid in history and many important events and people contributed to its development. Television, computers, and satellites have brought dramatic advances in recent times. As a consequence of these advances, alternative forms of communication have been invented to aid the blind, deaf, and speechless in participating fully in society.

Causation. Limited experiential learning often contributes to language deficits and underdeveloped communication skills. Early identification, resources, and programs for young children are often not available in some communities. Family environments are sometimes limited in range and level of communication among members. Certain physical anomalies contribute significantly to students' abilities to communicate in common ways.

Implications. We are surrounded by communication. It is necessary to insure health, safety, economic well-being, and personal happiness. Students need to realize how crucial to survival communication is and to know that there are alternative means for communicating, should the common means not be available. Communications systems have made our world smaller by bringing people together and offer hope for maintaining peace and harmony in the future.

CORRECTION Modify strategies for topical and learning needs.

1. *What Was That?* (Strand 2, *Skill:* Summarizing Information)

    Tape record a sentence or series of sentences that tell a short story. Whisper the information to 1 student and have that student whisper it to another student until all have heard it. Ask the last student to say what he or she heard. Compare what was heard to the tape recording. Discuss the implications.

2. *Braille.* (Strand 1, *Skill:* Arranging Information)

    Bring examples of Braille to class and have students experiment with reading it. Discuss how this form of communication is used. EXTENSION: Learn how to write in Braille and write a short paragraph.

3. *Sign Language.* (Strand 2, *Skill:* Interpreting Information)

    Learn the American Sign Language alphabet, practice it, and use it in class for an entire day. Discuss with the class their feelings about not being able to communicate orally.

4. *Biographical Profiles.* (Strand 1, *Skill:* Finding Information)

    Assign students the names of people who have made significant contributions to the development of communication (Alexander Bell, Thomas Edison, Benjamen Franklin, Samuel Morse, etc.) and have them give short oral presentations.

5. *Picture This.* (Strand 2, *Skill:* Synthesizing Information)

    Ask students to make a booklet of pictographs or symbols used in their communities. Examples: no parking, bus stop, railroad crossing, no smoking.

6. *Timely Events.* (Strand 2, *Skill:* Synthesizing Information)

    Make a timeline of the history and development of communications.

7. *Hand Signals.* (Strand 2, *Skill:* Interpreting Information)

    Ask students to interpret several hand signals and then to think of several on their own for their classmates to interpret (e.g., hello, good-bye, OK, that way, be quiet, anger, prayer, etc.).

8. *Dot, Dash, Dot.* (Strand 2, *Skill:* Interpreting Information)

    Learn Morse code and practice sending messages to others.

9. *Rebus Writing.* (Strand 2, *Skill:* Synthesizing Information)

    Have students write a letter to a friend. Ask the students to rewrite the letter using as many pictures as possible to substitute for the words.

10. *Hieroglyphic Fun.* (Strand 2, *Skill:* Interpreting Information)

    Explain how early people used hieroglyphics to tell stories. Ask students to draw stories and give to someone else to interpret. Discuss the limitations of this form of communication.

11. *Computers All Around.* (Strand 1, *Skill:* Technical Skills)

    Ask students to observe in their environments for a full day to determine how many times and in what ways that lives are touched by computer technology. Examples will include clocks, radios, television, mail, banking, grocery checkouts, cash registers, and the like. Make a list of these and discuss the implications of computer technology for their lives.

26. GEOGRAPHY

DETECTION Students may have difficulty mastering key concepts if they:

- Do not know or understand cardinal directions
- Cannot identify geographical features of their community
- Do not understand how geography contributes to and influences life in a community
- Have not compared geographical features of other communities to their own

Description.   *Geography* is the study of the relationships between the earth and its people. Geographers study where people, plants, and animals live and where geographic features, such as rivers, lakes, mountains, and cities, are found. The interrelationships of these features and their impact on people and the environment are the primary concerns of this field of study. The major tools of geographers include maps and more recent advances in computer technology that allow for scientific interpretations of information. The geography of a community influences many aspects of lives of the people who live there. Often people choose to live in an area primarily because of certain advantageous features of its geography. For example, farmers want to own land where crops can be cultivated in good soil conditions, favorable climate, and with adequate water supplies. Other people find work in areas where there are coal deposits or large forests of trees, while some choose living areas for climate and health reasons. The growth of cities often depends on rivers, and the quality of water from these rivers depends on the cities' use of them. Climate and weather conditions influence what people do from day to day. Extremely hot or cold temperatures limit what food can be grown, influence how shelters are built, and determine the kinds of industry that can be established. The growth of populations in communities is greatly influenced by geographical features of the area.

Causation.   Limited geographical knowledge usually is a consequence of few firsthand experiences with a variety of geographical features. Students who have traveled little, have not explored nature's different features, and have not had opportunities to compare and contrast their communities with others may not realize the differences that exist among areas due to geographic features. Much of our knowledge about other places is learned from reading, motion pictures, and television. Students with limited backgrounds or only media exposure to other places will have limited understandings.

Implications. Students need basic information about world patterns of population, occupations, climate, land forms, and natural resources to fit events into their proper geographic settings and to make intellectual decisions about changes in the environment that they depend on and can influence.

CORRECTION Modify strategies for topical and learning needs.

1. *Geo-Pictures.* (Strand 1, *Skill:* Interpreting Graphics)

    Ask students to go on a photographic expedition of the community, taking pictures of all features that are examples of distinguishing geographic features (lakes, hills, trees, highways, etc.).

2. *Community Survey.* (Strand 1, *Skill:* Finding Information)

    Prepare a community survey to be completed by each student with help from parents and other community members. Questions for the survey: What are your community's major natural resources? Describe the present transportation and communications systems that exist. What ethnic, social, and cultural groups live in the community? What are the major occupations of the working people? Describe the lay of the land in the community.

3. *Community Sell.* (Strand 2, *Skill:* Synthesizing Information)

    Write an advertisement for the community in which you live that points out its favorable features and would convince someone to move to the area.

4. *Map It Out.* (Strand 1, *Skill:* Maps)

    Draw a large map of the local community on butcher paper, including all the landmarks and notable features, such as rivers, streams, lakes, and parks. Have students print their names and addresses on the map in the areas in which they live.

5. *Global World.* (Strand 1, *Skill:* Maps)

    Make a world globe by blowing up balloons and covering them with papier-maché. Draw the land and sea surfaces, and paint and label them. Locate your own continent, country, state, and community on the globe and put markers there.

6. *House Adaptation.* (Strand 2, *Skill:* Synthesizing Information)

    After studying how climate affects housing in various parts of the world, ask students to draw 4 different types of houses and to label the features of each that reflect geographical conditions.

7. *State Maps.* (Strand 1, *Skill:* Maps)

    Gather as many different state maps as possible and study the geographical features that can be determined from each. Make a list of those features that are most apparent for your home state. Compare and contrast neighboring states. Make a chart of these features and display it on the bulletin board.

8. *Room Directions.* (Strand 1, *Skill:* Maps)

    Label each wall of the classroom with the appropriate direction. Teach directions by having students orient themselves to these points when they are in other parts of the school building. Eventually, move outside the building and check for understanding.

9. *Geographical Jobs.* (Strand 2, *Skill:* Interpreting Information)

    List all the major geographical features of your community. Decide which jobs in the community are directly related to these features and make a bulletin board showing them.

CHAPTER 7 /
LIVING IN THE STATE AND REGION

27. HOME STATE

DETECTION Students may have difficulty mastering key concepts if they:

- Cannot locate their home state on a United States map
- Have difficulty identifying major political leaders
- Cannot describe major home state historical events
- Have difficulty describing major home state attractions
- Cannot identify state writers, inventors, or heroes

Description. The 50 states in the United States have a number of similarities and differences. States grouped in the same geographical region, such as the West or South, tend to have more in common than some of the other states. States engage in friendly competition to attract industry and to improve the quality of life for people. People are highly influenced by the values and traditions that evolve in their region and state. Language differences or dialects are noticeably different in various regions. Populations vary, depending on the location of states near major transportation facilities. Historical events help students to understand the uniqueness of each state's contribution to the United States' democratic way of life. It is essential for states to cooperate to keep the air and water clean, to build bridges linking major population areas, and to improve the quality of life in larger areas.

Causation. Students with limited contact or information can develop stereotyped views of people living in other states. Although an efficient transportation and communication system is established in the United States, time and money are necessary to use these systems. Many students lack travel experiences to form their own opinions and thus rely on textbook or vicarious information for learning. The study of students' home states is often limited in many curriculum guides and results in inadequate timeframes to teach significant concepts.

Implications. Students can better understand themselves through the study of the people and environmental factors that have affected their lives. Communication and even personal habits are sometimes determined by birthplaces or states. Students can learn a lot about themselves and others by comparing and contrasting their home states with other states. In daily conversation, it is often evident that people are curious about life, weather, personalities, and folklore of various states. Students will also increase their opportunities in our society by learning about the resources and options in all the states.

CORRECTION Modify strategies for topical and learning needs.

1. *State Headlines.* (Strand 2, *Skill:* Classifying Information)

    Place an outline of the home state and all the surrounding states on a bulletin board. Ask students to watch the newspapers (local, state, and national) and collect stories about these states. Place the stories on the states making the news. Provide time to discuss the headlines and important events related to each story.

2. *State Location.* (Strand 1, *Skill:* Map)

    Place the name of the home state and all the states in the region on cards. Provide students with an opportunity to select a card at random and find the state on the United States map. Place the card back in the box and repeat the activity for other students.

3. *Population Growth.* (Strand 1, *Skill:* Arranging Information)

    Ask students to locate the population of the state for various time periods (1600, 1700, 1800, 1900, 1988, and projected 2000). Provide an outline of a graph for students to plot the population growth during these time periods.

4. *Historical Events.* (Strand 1, *Skill:* Arranging Information)

    Provide or ask students to find information identifying significant events in their home state's history. Make a timeline and mark these events in the appropriate place.

5. *Early State History.* (Strand 1, *Skill:* Comprehension)

    Read students a short selection about the early history of the state. Ask students to draw and display pictures based on the selection.

6. *State Tour.* (Strand 3, *Skill:* Group Interaction)

    Explain to students that people from another state will be making an imaginary visit to their state. Working in groups of 2, plan a tour to visit 5 of the most important places in the state. Encourage students to use resources and ask other people in the community to identify the places. Provide an opportunity for students to share their tour schedules and routes on a map.

7. *State Trivia.* (Strand 2. *Skill:* Summarizing Information)

    Play a State Trivia game, with students making up some of the questions about their state. Include the major political leaders, population, state bird, flower and song, historical events, and so on. Divide the class into teams; each team gets 2 points for a correct answer.

8. *Flag Day.* (Strand 1, *Skill:* Arranging Information)

    Obtain a state flag (or picture) and explain the meaning of the various parts. Ask students to draw pictures of the state flag and display them in the classroom.

9. *State Problems.* (Strand 2, *Skill:* Synthesizing Information)

    Invite a state politician to discuss some of the state's major problems in the areas of crime, education, transportation, and the like. Make a list of these discussion problems and solutions and invite students to express their opinions. Culminate the activity by writing a class letter about 1 of the problems to the local newspaper.

28. STATE AND REGIONAL GEOGRAPHY

DETECTION Students may have difficulty mastering key concepts if they:

- Do not know the concepts associated with geographical terms
- Cannot describe how the state and region's geographical features contribute to living conditions
- Cannot describe the likenesses or differences of areas and how they contribute to people's lives
- Do not understand the relationship between population distribution and geographical features of a state and region

Description. Geographers are engaged in the study of people through investigations of how and where they live, how many others live nearby, how the climate affects living conditions, and how other physical and cultural conditions contribute to and influence life in a particular area. By gathering data about certain places, geographers make conclusions about why people choose to live in particular areas and make predictions about future changes that might significantly affect life patterns in an area. Major similarities and differences among various locations also provide a basis to divide areas into regions. Groupings of states with similar features are called regions. Regions in the United States include the Northeast, the mid-Atlantic, the South, the West, the Midwest, the Northwest, and the Southwest. Categories of states are formed on the basis of physical features, common agricultural crops, the shape of the land, and other common features. Population growth and distribution are important for understanding how the land is being used and why people choose to live in certain areas. The tools geographers use for this study include maps, charts, photographs, graphs, and census data.

Causation. Lack of familiarity with scientific modes of inquiry may limit students' abilities to apply and use information to solve problems and make decisions. The opportunities for application of critical thinking skills may have been limited for students who have had difficulty with basic skills.

Implications. The geographical study of states and regions allows students an opportunity to apply knowledge, techniques, and skills used by geographers to make conclusions and informed decisions about existing living conditions in various areas. The study of likenesses and differences among regions helps students understand how these conditions affect people's lives. Using the appropriate geographical tools for studying states and regions will assist students in becoming independent in collecting and analyzing data for other purposes.

CORRECTION Modify strategies for topical and learning needs.

1. *Geography Language.* (Strand 1, *Skill:* Acquiring Information)
    Teach the following terms: *coast, delta, island, lake, mountain, peninsula, plain, plateau, river, valley, continent, gulf, ocean,* and *sea.* Ask students to draw or paint these concepts. Make a search-a-word puzzle of the words using computer software (Elementary Language Arts, available through the Minnesota Educational Computing Consortium, Lauderdale, MN).
2. *State Pride.* (Strand 2, *Skill:* Summarizing Information)
    Develop a collage of drawings or write an essay on the state's major features about which its citizens have the greatest pride. Ideas to consider: national and state parks, mountains, lakes, historical sites, sports, colleges, or state flower, tree, or bird.
3. *Region Roundup.* (Strand 2, *Skill:* Synthesizing Information)
    Provide an unlabeled United States map and ask students to locate and label their home state on it. Identify all states that border the state and determine if all are classified in the same region. Ask students to read about each of these states and make a summary chart of how each is different or like the home state.
4. *Who Lives Here?* (Strand 2, *Skill:* Arranging Information)
    Have students find information to complete the following outline:
    I.   Home State
       A. Native Americans who lived here
       B. First European settlers
       C. Why settlers came
       D. Major crops and industries
       E. Population
       F. Capitol city
    II. Bordering States
    Conduct a class discussion of students' findings and require students to speak from their outlines.
5. *Earliest People.* (Strand 2, *Skill:* Interpreting Information)
    Present an informative lecture or ask students to research the earliest people who settled the state and region. Ask students to roleplay a scene where the early European settlers discuss with the native Americans who inhabited the area (perhaps at a tribal council) who should own the land and how it should be used.
6. *State Relief Map.* (Strand 1, *Skill:* Maps)
    Make a large relief map of the state with a mixture of salt and flour. Note all significant geographical features and paint it with appropriate colors.
7. *Sea Level.* (Strand 2, *Skill:* Interpreting Information)
    Ask students to measure their height from the base of their bodies (feet). Explain that the earth's hills and mountains are measured from base to top, where the base is sea level and the measurement is referred to as elevation. Determine the elevation of the state and its highest peaks.

29. NATURAL RESOURCES

DETECTION Students may have difficulty mastering key concepts if they:

- Have difficulty identifying natural resources
- Cannot understand the importance of natural resources to the economic system
- Have difficulty understanding how natural resources are converted to useful items in our society
- Do not understand the importance of conserving natural resources

Description. All states have natural resources that include to some degree minerals, varied soil types, water and air resources, and animal life. Air and water resources have become increasingly more important in modern times, due to pollution and contamination. Not all states have clean and abundant resources. Usually, states have to depend on other states or countries to supply many of the natural resources needed to maintain the quality of life and to support industry. For example, many states do not have oil and must bring it in from other states and countries. States usually capitalize on their natural resources, as reflected by the way people make a living. During the 1600s through 1800s, animals were important natural resources for the early settlers' food as well as for basic bartering and trading. A state may have excellent land to grow crops, but have to look to other states for steel products. People have been creative in discovering and utilizing natural resources for various purposes. Modern equipment and technology provide the means to make the best and most efficient use of natural resources. Unfortunately, some produce negative side effects. An attitude now prevails that natural resources are limited and must be used with care to preserve a high quality of life for future generations.

Causation. Natural resources may seem abundant to students who have not had opportunities to discuss the issues of scarcity and pollution. Students have to be sensitized to their environments and the natural resources that are sometimes taken for granted (i.e., good drinking water). The abuse of natural resources is not easily demonstrated or observed, since a long period of time is usually necessary for the evidence to become apparent. Students may have difficulties understanding the long-term effects of air or water pollution.

Implications. An attitude toward conserving and utilizing natural resources has to be developed before students can help preservation efforts. Students may themselves discover new and different ways to utilize natural resources by understanding some of their potential. Students' lives are clearly impacted by the natural resources in their states and region.

CORRECTION Modify strategies for topical and learning needs.

1. *Natural Resource Terms.* (Strand 1, *Skill:* Vocabulary)

    Place the following words on the chalkboard for students to use in sentences and pronounce: *gold, silver, oil, coal, copper, iron ore,* and *uranium.* Emphasize that a limited supply of these natural resources exists in various states. Challenge students to find out if any of these minerals are found in their state.

2. *Natural Resource Map.* (Strand 1, *Skill:* Maps)

    Have students make a map of their state to illustrate some of the natural resources, including soils, minerals, water, forests, and animal life. Students can focus on a particular natural resource area and display their maps for the rest of the class.

3. *Resource Conservation.* (Strand 2, *Skill:* Decision Making)

    Explain to students that there is a shortage of wildlife in the state and certain controls have to be determined to prevent overkill. You have to decide what controls are necessary to protect the species. What are some of the controls that you would pass to protect the deer population?

4. *In and Out Resources.* (Strand 2, *Skill:* Analyzing Information)

    Make a list of resources and ask the class to determine whether each is brought in or shipped out of the state.

5. *Pure Air.* (Strand 2, *Skill:* Interpreting Information)

    Monitor the local pollution counts for air and keep a chart of this index along with the local weather conditions. At the end of the week, ask students to determine the significance of the data.

6. *Water Sample.* (Strand 2, *Skill:* Summarizing Information)

    Bring samples of water from local areas, such as lakes, wells, ponds, and rivers, for students to compare with the water they drink. Ask students to compare the samples through sight and smell and discuss possible ways that water can be contaminated or polluted in their state. Students could research state and federal laws related to water pollution.

7. *Resource Exchange.* (Strand 3, *Skill:* Group Interaction)

    Distribute at random 3 cards to each student, describing specific natural resources found in the state. Include soils, minerals, animals, and water on the cards. Explain to students that they are going to exchange resources to obtain all 3 cards of the same type. In other words, students will trade cards until they have obtained 3 water cards or 3 gold cards.

8. *Historical Note.* (Strand 2, *Skill:* Summarizing Information)

    In the pioneer days, wild animals were one on the chief natural resources that settlers hunted and trapped for food and trading. Also, forests had to be cleared to raise crops. Ask students to determine what animals and other products were used in their state. Students can draw pictures to explain and compare the way of life in pioneer days vs. modern times.

30. CLIMATE AND WEATHER

DETECTION Students may have difficulty mastering key concepts if they:

- Cannot define *climate*
- Cannot describe the climate of their local environment
- Do not know how climate and temperature affect life conditions in their state and region
- Do not know what conditions determine climate

Description. *Climate* refers to weather patterns over a period of time. Temperature and precipitation are 2 of the most important factors in describing climatic conditions of an area. Other factors include latitude, elevation, seasonal changes, and location near oceans or mountains. The earth's movement around the sun determines the amount of sunlight an area receives; this in turn determines the seasons of a year. Latitude, or distance north or south of the equator, also determines how hot or cold the climate of an area will be. Climate is also affected by elevation above sea level. Thus, the higher the area, the cooler it will be. Rain and other forms of precipitation are also important aspects of climate. Oceans and other large bodies of water can also affect the climatic conditions of an area, as the winds and currents interact to carry warm and cold air in certain patterns.

Causation. Concrete experiences with weather patterns over a long period of time are sometimes difficult to provide. Consequently, students may have missed opportunities to learn about weather and climate. Many times these concepts are assigned to the science area for study and may not have been emphasized because other concepts were deemed more important. Students sometimes realize that weather and climate cannot be controlled and thus do not feel motivated to learn about them.

Implications. The climate of an area has a significant affect on the people who live there. It may determine the kind of clothes they wear, the crops they grow, their economic concerns, and the houses they live in. Wind, rain, and ocean waves actually change the surface of the earth over a long period of time. More sudden weather conditions, such as hurricanes and tornadoes, can cause great amounts of damage to life and property. Students should realize that climate and the development of cultures are interwoven. People must be able to grow food and sustain life in supportive environments. People have adapted in many creative ways to climate and other aspects of nature in order to survive and provide for future generations.

CORRECTION Modify strategies for topical and learning needs.

1. *House Hunt.* (Strand 2, *Skill:* Analyzing Information)

    Ask students to look around their homes and local communities for examples of adaptations to various weather conditions. Examples will include air conditioners, heaters, car shelters, and storm cellars.

2. *TV Weatherforecaster.* (Strand 2, *Skill:* Interpreting Information)

    Ask students to take turns watching or listening to the weather on TV or the radio and reporting each morning to the class the forecast for the day's weather. Ask someone to record predictions at the first of the day and note the accuracy at the end of the day. At the end of a week, compute the accuracy of the forecaster's predictions. Write to local TV weather forecasters for summaries of how they compute accuracy ratings.

3. *What's Your Season?* (Strand 2, *Skill:* Classifying Information)

    After discussing the seasons of the year and their characteristics, share some of the *Color Me Beautiful* literature that claims that people can be classified as "seasons" by their hair, eye, and skin color. Analyze each student and determine his or her season.

4. *Dressing Up.* (Strand 2, *Skill:* Synthesizing Information)

    Give each student a cut-out of a doll figure. Ask them to cut out of magazines or draw and color clothes for the doll for each season of the year.

5. *Farmer for a Day.* (Strand 1, *Skill:* Using the Library)

    Tell students that they are going to be farmers in their area of the country and assign them a particular crop to try and grow. Students should research their crop and decide whether they can grow it in their local area. Ask students to report on their conclusions, telling why they could or could not grow the crops.

6. *Climate Map.* (Strand 1, *Skill:* Maps and Graphs)

    Collect weather maps from the local or national newspaper over a period of time. Ask students to make bar graphs of the high and low temperatures for their state over a 7-day period. VARIATION: Compare their home state with another state of the students' choice and make bar graphs showing comparisons.

7. *State Comparisons.* (Strand 2, *Skill:* Interpreting Information)

    Ask students to choose a state and compare its elevation from sea level with that of their state. Compare average temperatures over a week's time and other similar data and make conclusions from the data.

8. *Gauge It.* (Strand 2, *Skill:* Summarizing Information)

    Make a weather chart for the bulletin board and post each day's weather. Devise a rain gauge that can be placed in easy access of the classroom and have students include measured precipitation in their daily notes on the chart. At the end of the month, summarize the information and determine averages for the numbers of rainy, sunny, and cloudy days and the amount of precipitation per month.

31. URBAN AND RURAL ENVIRONMENTS

DETECTION Students may have difficulty mastering key concepts if they:

• Cannot differentiate between urban and rural environments
• Cannot describe characteristics of urban and rural environments
• Have developed concepts based on misinformation about life in urban and rural environments
• Cannot locate urban and rural environments on a map
• Cannot identify problems associated with living in urban or rural environments

Description. All of the 50 states have urban and rural environments, but due to population and geographic size, the characteristics of these urban and rural environments vary. Some of the northeastern states are more urban and the midwestern and southern states are more rural. New York is the largest urban area in the United States. Most of the large urban centers have evolved near sea or river ports. Others have developed due to transportation points throughout the United States. Urban environments are more complex due to the increased variety of business and service activity available. Governmental services are larger due to the number of people served in large urban areas. Large shopping centers enable people to purchase their goods and products in one location. More opportunities for cultural activities in the arts are available in urban environments. Business is conducted in large office buildings or in manufacturing and distribution centers. Urban environments have unique problems with crime and other environmental concerns including air and water. Rural environments are very dependent on the farming industry. People living in rural environments have to travel to urban areas to sell their products and to obtain goods and products not readily available. Today many people choose to move to rural environments to live and commute to urban centers to work. Rural environments usually have less air and water pollution and are for some a more desirable place to live.

Causation. Students develop an understanding of their environments based on their experiences. The environments in which students live make a great impression on concepts and ideas about urban or rural living. Students often lack opportunities to experience and learn about the different ways people adapt to urban and rural environments in their states.

Implications. Students can use their immediate urban or rural environment to learn concepts about other environments. Although some similarities exist among urban or rural living, differences are apparent in the way people adapt to the land and resources. Quality of life depends upon people making intelligent choices about living and working together.

CORRECTION Modify strategies for topical and learning needs.

1. *Big City.* (Strand 2, *Skill:* Analyzing Information)

    Identify the major urban environments in your state and develop a graph illustrating their populations. Compare these to the populations of New York, Chicago, and Los Angeles. Project the populations in these urban environments for the next 10-year period.

2. *Crowded Cities.* (Strand 2, *Skill:* Synthesizing Information)

    Place a string around 1 corner of the room to illustrate an urban area. The rest of the room will be the rural environment. Make a set of cards for students to draw to move to their living areas (3 urban to 1 rural ratio). Explain that students will draw cards to determine where they live. Ask students to move to their areas when they draw their cards. The urban environment will obviously be crowded with plenty of room for the rural people to establish their home place. Discuss with students the problems that could evolve in crowded urban or sparsely populated rural areas.

3. *Map City.* (Strand 1, *Skill:* Maps)

    Locate on a state map the major urban centers in your state and region. Indicate how these cities are connected by interstate, rail, and air transportation systems.

4. *Day on the Farm.* (Strand 1, *Skill:* Comprehension)

    Arrange a fieldtrip to a rural area for students to observe the way people live there. A visit on a farm will enable them to understand life in a rural environment. Upon returning from the fieldtrip, have students write about what they observed and learned while on the trip.

5. *Urban Living.* (Strand 2, *Skill:* Summarizing Information)

    Tape large sheets of paper together for students to map their urban or rural environments and draw significant geographic features and major roadways. Ask students to place major rail, interstate, or airport transportation facilities on their maps.

6. *Country Store.* (Strand 2, *Skill:* Synthesizing Information)

    Explain to students that the class is going to open up a country store that has limited shelfspace and room for only the essential items. Give students an opportunity to suggest things for the store and give reasons for their choices.

7. *Picture Living.* (Strand 2, *Skill:* Interpreting Information)

    Ask students to collect pictures from magazines and categorize on the bulletin board under urban and rural living in my state. Give students an opportunity to explain their picture.

8. *Amenities.* (Strand 2, *Skill:* Interpreting Information)

    Give students the following list and ask them to categorize items for an urban or rural environment: art gallery, shopping center, airport, lake, forest, field, apartment house, horses, market, tractor, truck, hunter, police officer, firefighter, university, and hospital. Give students an opportunity to justify their answers. Some of the ideas could be found in both urban and rural environments.

32. INDUSTRIAL DEVELOPMENT

DETECTION Students may have difficulty mastering key concepts if they:

- Cannot describe the functions of industry
- Do not know what raw materials are needed by local industry and how they are provided
- Cannot categorize local industry and products as types of industry

Description. Many years ago, people made everything they needed and wanted by themselves. As we progressed in time, skill, and knowledge, the making of the necessities of life became more complex. Today, we describe the activities that provide us with the things we need and want as *industry.* Modern industry has evolved through the discovery of new techniques, tools, power sources, and new and creative applications of raw materials. Industry has been encouraged by a free-enterprise economic system that supports the creation of new ideas. Natural resources, labor, capital, and management are the primary ingredients in all industrial activity. The first factories and industries were established close to rivers and sources of raw materials needed to produce and transport the products. People work, or labor, to turn raw materials into products. Capital goods are those things needed in production and include raw materials, machines, tools, factories, and transportation systems. The bringing together of resources, labor, and capital to produce products and services is carried out by management, or those people who make the decisions and act responsibly for the owners of the company. Useful classifications of industry include the following: 1) agriculture, forestry, and fisheries; 2) communication; 3) transportation; 4) construction; 5) finance, insurance, and real estate; 6) government; 7) manufacturing; 8) mining; 9) public utilities; 10) wholesale and retail trade; and 11) business and personal services. Presently, economies are moving from being industrialized to becoming information and service oriented.

Causation. Students may not have had opportunities to classify the work of their parents and the people in their communities into industrial categories. Due to their level of abstraction, these concepts may be difficult for some learners. The teaching and understanding of the interrelationships of ideas is problematic when there are few examples in a local community.

Implications. Industry provides jobs and affects the quality of life for workers. It is helpful for students to understand their roles as producers and consumers in the industrial nation in order for them to be better participants in the economic system. They must realize that industry is constantly changing and that their work opportunities will depend upon their level of skill and participation.

CORRECTION Modify strategies for topical and learning needs.

1. *My Job.* (Strand 2, *Skill:* Classifying Information)
   List major categories of industry on chalkboard. Have students write down or discuss their parents' jobs. Discuss which industrial categories the jobs fit in.
2. *Industry in Our Community.* (Strand 1, *Skill:* Community Resources)
   Identify all major industries in the local area and state. Decide what raw materials are needed for production and discuss the relationship between the location of the factory and the raw materials.
3. *Industrial Visit.* (Strand 1, *Skill:* Community Resources)
   Organize a fieldtrip to a local factory and observe the manufacturing process. Find out what raw materials are used, who uses the products, how much labor is required, where products are shipped, and how much they cost. VARIATION: Ask a member of management of one of the local industries to visit the classroom and discuss the industry.
4. *Where Is It From?* (Strand 2, *Skill:* Interpreting Information)
   Ask students to examine labels in their clothing and other items to find where they were manufactured. Discuss which items were made locally and which may have been made in faraway places. Discuss why they were made where they were and how students received these products.
5. *Our Factory.* (Strand 2, *Skill:* Synthesizing Information)
   Create a simulation of a factory with an assembly line producing some product (e.g., paper cars). Decide who will manage the company, assemble each part, what raw products will be needed and how they will be provided, and how products will be sold and distributed.
6. *Environmental Impact.* (Strand 2, *Skill:* Analyzing Information)
   Discuss the impact of industry on the natural environment. Many of the raw materials needed in the manufacture of products are not replenishable. What are the implications? Some industries produce byproducts and create wastes that can be harmful to human health. Provide some examples and discuss the implications.
7. *Labor Skills.* (Strand 2, *Skill:* Interpreting Information)
   Choose a local industry and find out how many people it employs, what the average wages are for workers, what the qualifications are for the various jobs, what employee risks are required, and what benefits are provided.
8. *Foreign Industry.* (Strand 2, *Skill:* Analyzing Information)
   Research what foreign industry has come into our country and discuss why and how it is able to produce goods and services that compete with our country. Ask students to collect information about foreign industry from the newspaper or magazines.
9. *Why Here?* (Strand 2, *Skill:* Interpreting Information)
   Write an advertisement for your local area that would convince potential industries to locate their businesses there.

33. AGRICULTURE

DETECTION   Students may have difficulty mastering key concepts if they:

>   • Cannot identify crops that are grown in their local area
>   • Do not know where their food products come from
>   • Do not know how the local economy and agriculture are related
>   • Are not aware that there is hunger in the world

Description. From earliest time, people have learned how to grow products that feed, clothe, and shelter them. The process of plowing the soil, sowing seed, and harvesting crops is repeated in every part of the world today. The crops farmers grow depend upon the soil conditions, climate, and water supply in their areas. Some farms raise only small amounts of crops and animals, while others operate as extremely large and well-paying businesses. Farmers sell the crops and animals they grow, providing essential products to others in the world who need them. As the world's population increases, the need for food increases, also. Grain is the world's most basic food and 3 crops—rice, wheat, and corn—are the most common of these grains. The farmers in the United States often produce a surplus of crops and sell their products to other countries who cannot grow these crops in sufficient amounts to feed the people. Likewise, crops that cannot be grown in the United States can be imported, thus establishing more global interdependence between countries. In addition to having enough food to eat, people must also choose the proper variety and balance of foods in order to be healthy. In all countries, there are people who not only do not get enough to eat but also do not have the proper diets to be well-nourished, resulting in malnutrition.

Causation. Because farming is now so highly technical and each stage is so specialized, students may not have had opportunities to observe the process involved in getting food to grocery stores. In the United States, many programs work to feed people who are hungry, which students may not realize. The provision of food is one of the most basic of human activities. Without economic support for farmers and farm programs, our country would not be able to maintain its high level of health. This would, in turn, affect all aspects of life in our country. Keeping the air, water, and soil free from contaminants so that crops and animals can grow is essential to our survival, also. Fostering cooperation among states and other countries is also essential to provide the choice of foods needed to maintain well-balanced diets and general good health of people.

CORRECTION Modify strategies for topical and learning needs.

1. *Where Is this Food From?* (Strand 2, *Skill:* Interpretation)

   Ask each student to bring in some item of food. Analyze packaging information to decide where the food was processed. Research the crops that are involved and decide where each might have been produced.

2. *Calorie Counting.* (Strand 2, *Skill:* Analyzing Information)

   Using a calorie chart, compare the number of calories each food contains and classify each food into high, medium, and low groups. Discuss the implications of eating too many calories and too few calories.

3. *Food Groups.* (Strand 2, *Skill:* Classifying Information)

   Make a list on the chalkboard of all the foods that students can name. Have students divide a sheet of paper into 4 columns and label them Milk Group, Meat Group, Vegetable and Fruit Group, Bread and Cereal Group. Classify each food listed by category. VARIATION: After studying basic food groups, make a deck of 52 cards in sets of 4 (3 cards with foods listed and 1 card with the group listed). From 2–4 students can play a type of rummy game; 7 cards are dealt to each player who can lay down and discard cards when he or she has the group card and 3 examples of the group in their hand. The first player to lay down all cards wins the round and points are awarded.

4. *Fieldtrip.* (Strand 1, *Skill:* Community Resources)

   Arrange for a fieldtrip to a local grocery store and ask the grocery manager(s) to discuss where the foods come from. Allow students to watch produce being loaded and unloaded.

5. *Food All Around.* (Strand 1, *Skill:* Community Resources)

   Write to the local and state farm agencies, asking for literature about your state's farming activities. Identify major crops grown in the state and ask students to prepare a bulletin board showing those products grown locally.

6. *Hunger Programs.* (Strand 1, *Skill:* Community Resources)

   Survey the local community to find out what food programs and services are available for the unemployed and elderly. Visit some of these places or have representatives come to class to discuss their programs and services.

7. *Grow Some Grains.* (Strand 2, *Skill:* Interpreting Information)

   Plant some rice, wheat, and corn on the schoolground. Research the appropriate time of the year for planting, how much water and fertilizer is required, soil and growing conditions needed and so forth. Observe and make notations about crops. Discuss conclusions after completion of the project.

8. *Let's Eat.* (Strand 2, *Skill:* Interpreting Information)

   Plan lunch for the entire school for a week. Make sure all meals are well-balanced nutritionally and if possible secure permission to prepare these meals through the school cafeteria. Have the cafeteria director discuss with the class the decisions that must be made about the planned menus.

34. MAPS AND GLOBES

DETECTION Students may have difficulty mastering key concepts if they:

- Do not recognize that maps and globes are representations of the state, region, country, and world around them
- Cannot understand and use the legend on a map or globe
- Cannot use the latitude and longitude coordinates on a map or globe
- Cannot distinguish between land and water forms
- Cannot locate their state or country on a map or globe

Description. A significant part of history and political geography can be traced on maps and globes over a period of time by the changes in boundary lines. Many of these boundary lines represent natural land or water features that separate states and countries. Maps and globes are a combination of colors, symbols, and words representing part or all of the geographic environment. Various symbols that are presented on a legend are the keys to understanding the purpose of the map or globe. A globe, a very small model of the earth, illustrates less detail than a state map or a city map. The globe is used to illustrate earth movements that cause daylight and darkness as well as the various seasons. Maps are projections of selected segments of the globe. Maps are used to depict more detail about specific areas such as states. State maps usually present enough detail to illustrate the geography explaining why cities developed in certain locations as well as the reasons for other human activity.

Causation. Many classrooms are not properly equipped with maps and globes to enable teachers to use them for instructional purposes. Recent research has suggested that many teachers lack geography skills and consequently do not devote much instructional time to them. Also, because of the symbolic nature of maps and globes, students who are functioning cognitively at very concrete levels are likely to have difficulty with these concepts.

Implications. State and world problems can be placed in context by using a map to identify the specific locations of these occurrences. Events in the global community impact on the daily lives of all people; students have a better understanding of global concepts today as compared to earlier times due to advances in communication and transportation systems. Many of these concepts could be developed in more detail through the use of maps and globes. Effective use of maps enables students to interpret their environments and to understand how people make a living and depend on others. Maps are essential for people who travel and depend on transportation systems to exchange goods and services. Maps and globes should be used at every learning opportunity to illustrate the nature of this tool in understanding people's adaptation to the earth.

CORRECTION Modify strategies for topical and learning needs.

1. *Around We Go.* (Strand 2, *Skill:* Summarizing Information)
   Set up an experiment in the classroom to illustrate the rotation of the earth around the sun, causing day and night as well as the seasons. A flashlight can be used to represent the sun and a globe to represent the earth. Help students to locate their state and surrounding states and mark them with masking tape. The flashlight (the sun) remains stationary while a student (the earth) walks around it to illustrate the day and night changes. Complete the experiment by showing how the globe tilts on its axis to cause the seasons.

2. *Around the World.* (Strand 3, *Skill:* Social Participation)
   Form groups of 3–4 and ask students to plan a trip by car, air, or boat around the world. They should begin and end the trip in their home state. Students can indicate their mode of transportation between cities.

3. *Legend Puzzle.* (Strand 1, *Skill:* Maps and Globes)
   Using a state or United States map, introduce the map legend by explaining the symbols and illustrating examples. Ask students to locate cities, mountains, rivers, railroads, and state boundaries by using the legend. The idea can be expanded to using a globe to locate continents and oceans.

4. *Location Game.* (Strand 1, *Skill:* Maps and Globes)
   Make up a game for students by using latitude and longitude lines to locate major cities in the state. Students would be given the latitude and longitude readings to locate the cities or other geographic features in the state.

5. *Travel Game.* (Strand 1, *Skill:* Maps and Globes)
   Provide students with a state map and distance problems to figure out between cities. Students will compute the distance between 2 cities using the scale on the map. Strips of paper or rulers could be used as measuring instruments.

6. *Personal Map.* (Strand 1, *Skill:* Maps and Globes)
   Provide an outline of the state and have students make a legend using colors to illustrate the rivers, mountains (elevation), valleys, and other geographic features. Students can place their city as well as the surrounding states on their map. Display the pictures in the room and discuss the different legends illustrating the same concepts.

7. *Historical Maps.* (Strand 2, *Skill:* Analyzing Information)
   Locate maps from eras in the state's history and compare to an updated map. Ask students to note the similarities and differences in the maps. Students could make a map illustrating the future.

8. *Mobile Society.* (Strand 2, *Skill:* Summarizing Information)
   On a United States map, have students locate cities and states that they have lived in; connect these cities with their present homes by string. Extend the activity by providing students with an opportunity to extend other strings to where they may live or would like to live in the future.

35. LIFE IN THE COLONIAL UNITED STATES

DETECTION Students may have difficulty mastering key concepts if they:

- Cannot describe some of the reasons for the early settlements in the United States
- Have difficulty describing the life of the colonist
- Cannot relate the early settlements to timeframes
- Cannot describe the conflict that evolved among native Americans, the British, and the colonial settlers

Description. Europeans came to America in the 1600s for religious and economic reasons. They were offered free or cheap land in America, with the promise to develop the property. Along with land ownership, settlers had the right to vote. Houses and furnishings were built from the plentiful supply of wood. Most of the colonists were English, but others included Germans, Scotch, Irish, French, Dutch, and Swedes. The early colonists faced great hardships and dangers establishing a living in the new land. They had to provide for food by hunting and farming in an unfamiliar environment. In the early period, the colonists lived in harmony with the native Americans; they learned to grow corn in the Plymouth Settlement. Only later did they experience conflict when more and more land was required for the increasing number of settlers. The colonists were very successful in raising livestock, growing crops, and cutting lumber to exchange for manufactured goods from other countries. Each colony had a governor and legislature that was under the control of the British government. The colonists were very independent from British control, due to distance and basic conflicts in philosophy of government. The conflict finally resulted in the Revolutionary War of 1775, which ended the colonial period.

Causation. Many students will find it difficult to understand the basic life of colonists because it is so removed from their present lives. For example, modern kitchen equipment with ranges and microwave ovens is quite an advancement from cooking over an open flame. Students who have experienced camping or rural living will have some experiences similar to colonial life.

Implications. Students will certainly appreciate the skills of the early Europeans to adapt and survive new obstacles. The fight for the democratic ideals that regulate our everyday lives were conceived and preserved by the early colonists.

CORRECTION Modify strategies for topical and learning needs.

1. *Colonial Words.* (Strand 1, *Skill:* Vocabulary)
   Place the following words on the chalkboard or bulletin board for students to learn during the study of the colonial U.S.: *colonies, Jamestown, Plymouth, England, king, democracy, religious freedom, Sabbath, witchcraft,* and *native Americans.*

2. *Rule Breakers.* (Strand 2, *Skill:* Analyzing Information)
   Explain to students that the colonists often punished people that broke minor rules or laws through public whippings or disgrace. The ducking stool or the pillory were used for punishment by public display. Have students roleplay a situation where a person had been seen drunk in public and determine the punishment. Discuss the feelings of a person being on public display and its effectiveness in society.

3. *Village Life.* (Strand 3, *Skill:* Social Participation)
   Have students read about colonial village and native American life. Assign groups of 3 to design and build a replica of a colonial or Indian village (or draw and paint). Display the pictures and/or models and have students explain the purpose of the various buildings and the commons areas.

4. *Colonies.* (Strand 1, *Skill:* Maps)
   Give the students a map of the Eastern United States. Write the names of the colonies and early settlements on the board for students to place on their maps (Massachusetts, Connecticut, Rhode Island, New Hampshire, New York, New Jersey, Pennsylvania, Delaware, Virginia, Maryland, North Carolina, South Carolina, and Georgia).

5. *Tool Making.* (Strand 2, *Skill:* Summarizing Information)
   Take students on a fieldtrip to a museum to view tools and implements used in colonial times. Some of these tools may be available through students' parents or local resource people. Compare these tools to modern day electric or gas powered equipment. For example, ask students to compare cutting down a tree with an ax to using a power saw.

6. *Hard Beds.* (Strand 2, *Skill:* Synthesizing Information)
   Ask students to design a piece of furniture (stool, bed, table) as a colonial person. Emphasize the importance of using the materials that can be found in the local environment (wood and stone). If materials are available, students could actually make the furniture.

7. *Colonial Games.* (Strand 3, *Skill:* Social Participation)
   Many games that colonial children played are still popular today, such as hopscotch, leapfrog, and blindman's bluff. Discuss with students the similarities of these games. Make a list of all the games the students know and determine how many could be played by colonial children.

8. *Colonial Trade.* (Strand 2, *Skill:* Interpreting Information)
   The colonists used specific trade routes to exchange goods with Africa, England, and other European countries. Have students trace these routes on a world map, describe the products that were traded, and the use of these goods.

36. EVENTS THAT SHAPED THE UNITED STATES

DETECTION Students may have difficulty mastering key concepts if they:

- Cannot associate major events in U.S. history with certain time periods
- Cannot explain the impact of major events on other aspects of life
- Cannot describe the reasons causing some of the major events in U.S. history
- Cannot distinquish between major and minor events in U.S. history

Description. Some of the most significant events that shaped U.S. history include the following: The Continental Congress declared independence from England and formed the United States of America by adopting the Declaration of Independence (1776). The American people created the Constitution (1787), which formed the basis for our government. The Bill of Rights (1791) was added to guarantee more individual rights. The abolitionists opposed slavery that began during colonial times and finally resolved this issue during the Civil War (1861) with the Emancipation Proclamation (1863), which freed all slaves. World War I (1917–18) was fought against Germany to help the European Allies and to stop acts of aggression. The Depression (1930s) affected millions of Americans who lost their jobs, land, and money. Franklin D. Roosevelt's New Deal helped to pull the country out of the Depression. World War II (1941–45) was fought against Japan and was ended by dropping atomic bombs. After the war, the United States experienced an economic boom. Television became popular in the 1950s along with other major appliances that changed life-styles. Space exploration became a reality with a trip to the moon in the 1960s. The Civil Rights Movement of the 1960s involved both blacks and whites in demonstrations for equal rights and treatment. The Civil Rights Act (1964–68) outlawed discrimination based on race for jobs, voter registration, and housing. The Watergate scandal (1973–74) forced Richard Nixon to resign, the first time a U.S. President ever did so. In 1987, President Reagan and Premier Gorbachev of the U.S.S.R. reached agreement on arms control.

Causation. The study of history in many classrooms is a collection of names, places, and dates. Students need meaningful information to help them remember and to determine the significance of important events. Since students have no experience base for most of these events, it is difficult to motivate them to learn the information and understand its impact on modern times.

Implications. Many of these events affect the values of people in this country and throughout the world. Students can better understand developments in modern times by knowing about the events that influenced history. Also, students need to know the struggle that shaped our democratic way of life.

CORRECTION Modify strategies for topical and learning needs.

1. *Room for a Soldier.* (Strand 3, *Skill:* Social Participation)
    Obtain copies of the Declaration of Independence for students to study. Discuss with students some of the most important features, such as free trade, taxation, self-government, and the like. Organize a roleplay with some students portraying the colonists and others portraying the British. Role-play the requirement that the colonists must provide quarters and supplies for the British troops.

2. *"Fire!"* (Strand 2, *Skill:* Decision Making)
    Obtain a copy of the Constitution of the United States and discuss with students the Bill of Rights. Discuss the first amendment freedoms of religion, speech, and the press. Ask students if a person can shout "fire" in a crowded theatre. Can a newspaper print anything they want to about people?

3. *Patriotic Songs.* (Strand 2, *Skill:* Social Participation)
    Americans were very patriotic during World War I. Introduce students to the songs "Over There" and "You're a Grand Old Flag." Discuss the meaning of *patriotism.*

4. *Soup Line.* (Strand 2, *Skill:* Summarizing Information)
    Introduce the Depression of the 1930s by describing soup lines and unemployment. Have students collect contemporary newspaper and magazine articles about the homeless and compare this information to what is known about this problem in the 1930s. Discuss with students some of the solutions.

5. *Atomic Bombs.* (Strand 1, *Skill:* Community Resources)
    Explain to students that the U.S. dropped atomic bombs on Hiroshima and Nagasaki in 1945 to end World War II. Invite a guest speaker from Japan to describe the impact of this disaster. Obtain a book presenting a Japanese account of the bombing.

6. *Early TV.* (Strand 2, *Skill:* Interpreting Information)
    Obtain a 1950s television program and show it to the class. Compare the black-and-white program to favorite programs on television today. Discuss with students how television impacts leisure time.

7. *Home Buying.* (Strand 3, *Skill:* Social Participation)
    Explain to students that they will be given play money to purchase homes for their families. Explain that some will play roles of minority groups such as, blacks, native Americans, and Hispanics. On a large fictitious map, invite students to select where they want to live. Some, of course, will not be able to have their choice due to their race. Discuss the roleplaying.

8. *Space Travel.* (Strand 1, *Skill:* Arranging Information)
    Develop a chart with students to trace space developments from the first flight in the 1960s through achievements and disasters up to the 1980s.

37. PEOPLE WHO SHAPED THE UNITED STATES

DETECTION Students may have difficulty mastering key concepts if they:

- Cannot name individuals who have made significant contributions to the United States
- Have difficulties associating events with key individuals
- Cannot describe the leadership characteristics associated with key individuals
- Have difficulties relating key individuals to time periods

Description. Throughout history, certain individuals emerge to help solve problems or to make technological advances to improve the human condition. These individuals usually possess leadership characteristics that are utilized within the context of cultural events and circumstances. A certain amount of risk is necessary for individuals to emerge as leaders during these times. Christopher Columbus risked the unknown by sailing the seas and discovering America. Many presidents, by nature of their position and their individual characteristics and beliefs, accomplished historical deeds through their actions. Abraham Lincoln provided the leadership to free the slaves and pave the way for greater equality in the U.S. for all people. Great inventors, such as Benjamin Franklin and Eli Whitney, made contributions that still affect modern society. Martin Luther King Jr., provided the leadership for nonviolent demonstrations to focus attention on the unequal treatment of blacks in U.S. society. King and John F. Kennedy were victims of assassinations in a time of dramatic social change. Women have fought for equal rights throughout history and made advances in many areas of government, arts, and business. Sandra Day O'Connor became the first woman justice of the Supreme Court. Many individuals have made contributions in social movements, wars, the arts, education, business, sports, entertainment, and other areas to help formulate the basic tenets of democracy.

Causation. Lack of student interest in the significant individuals who have made contributions to U.S. society may in part account for their lack of information about these people. Many of these individuals are associated with the past, and students may be more focused on present leaders who capture their attention on television or in the press. Curriculum plans do not always provide students with opportunities to learn about the contributions of great leaders in various fields.

Implications. Students need to understand the qualities of leaders and the risk involved in contributing to a better society. Through studying these individuals, students will better understand their own capabilities as well as support good ideas to improve our society.

CORRECTION Modify strategies for topical and learning needs.

1. *Sail to New World.* (Strand 2, *Skill:* Synthesizing Information)

    Christopher Columbus (1492) discovered North America for the Spanish. Ask students to read about or listen to a description of the voyage. Form student groups of 3 and have them list the supplies needed for the journey to America; Have students draw pictures of their chosen ship—the Santa Maria, the Pinta, and the Nina—and place their list of supplies on it.

2. *Franklin's Life.* (Strand 3, *Skill:* Social Participation)

    Divide the class in groups to study the life of Benjamin Franklin. Each group will develop a short skit to illustrate the contributions Franklin made as an inventor, statesman, and writer. Encourage students to use props and illustrations in presenting their skits.

3. *President Wheels.* (Strand 2, *Skill:* Analyzing Information)

    Provide a list of presidents for the class to choose from and to learn 1 thing about each of their contributions to the U.S. Students can place the name of the president in the center of a wagon wheel and list the contributions on the spokes of the wheel. Display the wheels for discussion.

4. *Martin Luther King, Jr.,* (Strand 2, *Skill:* Evaluating Information)

    Martin Luther King, Jr., effectively used nonviolent methods to focus attention on the unequal treatment of blacks in America. He emphasized changing laws and policies through political means by registering voters. Design a form and have each student register to vote in all class elections and decisions. Play a record of one of King's famous speeches or write some of his famous quotes, such as "I have a dream . . ." Develop a leadership profile of King.

5. *Women Leaders.* (Strand 2, *Skill:* Summarizing Information)

    Explain to students that women have only recently had the opportunities to accept leadership roles. Sandra Day O'Connor, Geraldine Ferraro, Elizabeth Dole, and Jeanne Kirkpatrick are only a few of these leaders. Challenge students to find other women in history who have made significant contributions and prepare oral reports with visual aids. Students can draw or collect pictures from news sources.

6. *Inventors.* (Strand 2, *Skill:* Synthesizing Information)

    Provide a list of inventions: telegraph, telephone, steamboat, steam locomotive, cotton gin, automobile, electric light, phonograph, sewing machine, photography, safety pin, dynamite, and zipper. Ask students to tell a story about one of the inventions or one of their own ideas for an invention.

38. ELECTIONS AND VOTING

DETECTION Students may have difficulty mastering key concepts if they:

- Do not understand the election process
- Have negative attitudes toward voting
- Have difficulty in relating the election process to democratic ideals
- Do not understand the purpose of political parties
- Do not understand representation of elected officials

Description. Under the Constitution, the right to hold elections is guaranteed in the United States. Voters choose their political leaders and determine some of the major policies. A fundamental process in a representative democracy is that people will be governed by leaders of their own choosing. The Constitution requires that representatives be elected every 2 years, senators every 6 years, and a president every 4 years. Candidates align themselves with 1 of the 2 political parties, Democrats and Republicans, or remain Independents. Political parties adopt platforms that establish their major positions and policies. The best candidates within the political party are usually nominated before having an election to fill the office. Candidates appear in political advertisements and make speeches prior to the election. Candidates debate the issues to clarify their positions and to convince voters of their leadership ability. Political action groups contribute money to finance the high costs of elections. Election day is the first Tuesday after the first Monday in November for national and state elections. Amendments to the Constitution gave women (19th) and blacks (14th and 15th) the right to vote in elections. The twenty-sixth amendment lowered the voting age from 21 to 18. All states have some residency requirements and registration procedures for voters. Election officials monitor the polls to insure a fair election. Although all citizens have the right to vote in a democracy, many do not exercise this privilege.

Causation. Due to their age, students are not usually interested in the political process or the elections; since the impact is not readily observed in their everyday lives. They can also be influenced by a feeling of powerlessness due to ideas developed in their homes or communities.

Implications. Students must understand the election right as well as the responsibility for using their vote wisely. At an early age, students can understand the political process through active participation, even in real elections. Students can pass out literature and help at political rallies for the candidates of their choice. Through this process they can begin to develop a sense of efficacy for not only casting their vote but also for participating in the total process.

CORRECTION   Modify strategies for topical and learning needs.

1. *Slogans.* (Strand 2, *Skill:* Summarizing Information)

    During an election year, have students collect the various slogans and news articles of candidates. Place these slogans on the bulletin board for discussion. Discuss the meanings of these slogans with students. Have students make their own slogans that would appeal to the group.

2. *Political Qualities.* (Strand 2, *Skill:* Analyzing Information)

    Make a list of factors and experiences that help candidates obtain political office in modern society: communication, appearance on television, experience, and family and personal life. Compare these factors with those that were relevant during the time in which George Washington was elected.

3. *Class Election.* (Strand 3, *Skill:* Group Interaction)

    Explain to students that an election will be conducted in the room for class president and vice president. First, students have to determine their political party, such as Trots or Waks. Within the political party, they will decide the candidates for the class election and the party platform. Candidates will have an opportunity to campaign for a few days before the election. A debate could be arranged with the candidates. The election is then conducted, with the candidates' names listed on a secret ballot. The results are tallied by the poll officials and announced.

4. *News Conference.* (Strand 3, *Skill:* Social Participation)

    Organize a simulated news conference where students ask questions of the president of the United States or a candidate running for office. Ask students to write their questions ahead of time. Extend the activity if a real political official can visit the classroom. Videotape the session to make it more real.

5. *Right to Vote.* (Strand 2, *Skill:* Decision Making)

    Explain to students that, at one time, women and blacks could not vote in the United States. Amendments to the Constitution have insured these voting rights in modern society. Ask students to determine whether or not criminals should have the right to vote. Emphasize the reasons, pro and con. Explain later that certain classes of felons and some others are deprived of the right to vote by law.

6. *Can't Read.* (Strand 2, *Skill:* Decision Making)

    Explain that a voter must be a resident of a state, of a certain age, and registered to vote. Find the specific voting requirements in the state and discuss. Ask students to determine whether or not a person should be required to pass a literacy test to determine if they can read before being able to vote. Discuss why this is not legal today.

7. *Pollster.* (Strand 2, *Skill:* Summarizing Information)

    Television reports the results of polls to predict the outcome of elections. Make up a simple poll for students to conduct in their school about some issue. Emphasize the importance of remaining neutral while taking the poll. After conducting the poll, summarize and discuss the results.

39. CITIZENSHIP

DETECTION Students may have difficulty mastering key concepts if they:

- Cannot define the concept of *citizen*
- Do not know what the rights and responsibilities of citizenship are
- Do not know how to act responsibly and cooperate with others to solve problems rationally
- Do not know how to become a citizen of a country

Description. A *citizen* is someone who has full membership in a country, state, or city. Citizens have certain rights as a consequence of their citizenship, but they also have duties and responsibilities. Citizens' rights, such as the right to free speech, are provided in our country's Constitution. In return for these rights, citizens are expected to support the government with taxes, obey its laws, and defend it. The U.S. system of government is based on the premise that citizens are capable of making rational judgments and choosing reasonable actions and that people can do this in ways that are not coercive or destructive. Because it is not possible for all citizens to participate directly in the governance of a country or state, representatives are selected to vote on issues. Citizens have the responsibility of choosing these representatives and letting them know how they wish them to vote, thus sharing cooperatively in all the decision making. Under the fourteenth amendment to the Constitution, all people born or naturalized in the U.S. are citizens of the country and the state in which they live. People who were not born in this country but who wish to become citizens may do so by following certain procedures. It is also possible under certain circumstances for people to give up or lose their citizenship.

Causation. Citizenship is an abstract concept often taken for granted because it was awarded at birth to most students. Students who have not learned to cooperate with others and who do not have value systems consistent with the concept of rights and privileges bearing responsibilities and consequences may have difficulty understanding citizenship.

Implications. All groups work best when people share responsibilities. Also implied by these responsibilities is the opportunity to choose from alternatives. Making wise choices depends upon careful consideration of the options and the probable consequences. These choices can sometimes produce conflict. Conflict can be managed in constructive ways if people work together and share responsiblities through governance. It is important for everyone to share in the decision making by choosing responsible representatives who vote for alternatives that will ultimately affect all citizens.

CORRECTION Modify strategies for topical and learning needs.

1. *Crosswords.* (Strand 1, *Skill:* Vocabulary)

    Choose from the following words and make a crossword puzzle: *alien, Bill of Rights, Boys' State, Citizenship Day, civics, civil rights, community, democracy, deportation, freedom, Girls' State, government, human relations, immigration/emigration, nationality, naturalization, patriotism, pledge to the flag,* and *voting.*

2. *Whose Responsibility?* (Strand 3, *Skill:* Social and Political Participation)

    Relate the following situation: A beautiful park where people enjoy having picnics and playing ball has become so littered with smelly trash and broken glass that it is not safe any longer. Conduct a discussion about why this is a problem; who caused the problem; why people litter and cause damage; and how the problem can be solved. EXTENSION: Select a schoolwide citizenship project to work on, such as litter. Brainstorm ways students can help solve this problem. Ask a custodian to talk to the class about the problem of litter. Discuss several alternatives or suggestions from the class and try them out.

3. *Choose a Solution.* (Strand 2, *Skill:* Decision Making)

    Roleplay a courtroom scene of the following situation: Mrs. Simpson who is almost deaf, lives in an apartment house with her dog, who barks and lets her know when a stranger comes to the door. Several of the neighbors have complained and want the manager of the apartment to make her move. Choose characters to represent Mrs. Simpson, the judge, lawyers, the manager, neighbors who want her to move, others who don't mind the dog, and others with animals in the same apartments. Have the class vote on their decision and give reasons why they voted as they did.

4. *Vote My Way.* (Strand 3, *Skill:* Political Participation)

    Choose an issue that students can make a decision about such as, how the class can make money for a class project. Ask the class to elect representives who will make the decision for them. Decide what criteria should be used for choosing representatives: one person from each row; equal numbers of boys and girls; certain ages; only A students; most popular students, and so on. List the advantages and disadvantages of each criterion and then vote on the representatives.

5. *Citizen for a Day.* (Strand 3, *Skill:* Group Interaction)

    After discussing the characteristics of a good citizen, tell students that they will choose 1 person at the end of the day (or week) as an Outstanding Class Citizen. Ask students to nominate and support their candidate with examples of how that person has practiced good citizenship. Vote on the nominees and choose 1 at the end of each week.

6. *Becoming a Citizen.* (Strand 2, *Skill:* Summarizing Information)

    Research the requirements for becoming a citizen of the U.S. Read and interpret the "Oath of Allegiance" (see the *World Book Encyclopedia*). Discuss the implications.

40. LAWS AND SOCIETY

DETECTION Students may have difficulty mastering key concepts if they:

- Do not understand the purpose of laws and consequences of infractions
- Do not have respect for authority
- Do not know the reasons for following laws and rules
- Do not understand the social consequences of a criminal record or bad reputation
- Cannot explain the importance of sanctions for an orderly society

Description. Rules of conduct are necessary wherever people choose to live together. The rules the government enforces in our society are called *laws.* They are needed to settle disputes, run the government, and help people live together peacefully. There are two primary types of laws—criminal and civil—that govern most of our society's activities. Society is commanded to obey criminal laws and those who do not are fined, sent to jail, or even executed. Civil laws govern the business dealings people have with each other, including contracts, real estate, and personal injury. Cases in civil courts are called *lawsuits.* In a democracy, laws are made by the people through their acceptance of a Constitution and through the people they elect to represent them in the government. Judges also help to establish law by making rulings they consider to be fair and just and that represent the customs and wishes of the community, as each judge understands them. This is called *common law* and is an important source of rules in many countries. When people do not obey the law, they are forced to appear in court, where a jury or a judge will hear the related information and make a decision about the guilt or innocence of the accused. Appropriate action or punishment is then determined for those found guilty and they are sentenced to conform to this judgment.

Causation. Students who have lacked consistent discipline in their home lives are likely to have difficulty understanding why rules cannot be easily changed or consequences manipulated for their own personal satisfaction. Self-indulgence and lack of concern for others are also personal qualities that cause people to have problems being governed by rules. Misunderstanding of the reasons for rules sometimes make them appear arbitrary and illogical for some. Inconsistent application of school rules also contributes to poor citizenship.

Implications. All societies require that rules and laws be established and obeyed for the health, welfare, and safety of its people. This is an irrefutable requirement for all members and those who choose not to abide must either not belong or expect to suffer the sometimes harsh consequences.

CORRECTION Modify strategies for topical and learning needs.

1. *Name That Law.* (Strand 3, *Skill:* Personal Skills)

    Explain to students that laws regulate the conduct of people within a society. Ask students to identify laws dealing with driving, business, manufacturing, advertising, school, and property. Discuss the reasons these laws are good laws.

2. *Not My Coat.* (Strand 2, *Skill:* Decision Making)

    Explain the following situation to illustrate the ambiguity of the law. Joe borrowed a coat from Jeff. On the way home, Joe had an auto accident. The police officer on the scene noticed that some marijuana had fallen out of Joe's coat pocket. Although Joe explains that the marijuana is not his, the officer arrests Joe. If you were the judge listening to this case, what would you do?

3. *Penalty.* (Strand 2, *Skill:* Analyzing Information)

    Write the word *deterrence* on the chalkboard. Explain that it describes the philosophy that penalties for certain laws should be severe enough to prevent people from breaking them. For example, the penalty for committing a murder is more severe than that for stealing a car. Discuss with students other laws and their penalties. Do harsher penalties deter people from breaking the laws (i.e., driving while drinking)? Finally, ask students to determine penalties for stealing a bicycle, shoplifting, stealing a car, skipping school, and breaking a neighbor's window.

4. *Finder's Keepers.* (Strand 2, *Skill:* Interpreting Information)

    If a person leaves his/her purse or wallet on a chair and you find and keep it, have you committed a crime? Explain to students that the crime is called *larceny,* the theft of anything of value. Discuss other instances of larceny.

5. *Guns.* (Strand 3, *Skill:* Social Participation)

    Explain to the class that a teen-ager was shot and killed when he pointed a toy pistol at a police officer. Set up groups of 4 students and have them suggest new gun laws to present to the city council to prevent this. Extend the activity by asking students to decide whether or not to ban guns completely.

6. *Arrested Again.* (Strand 2, *Skill:* Summarizing Information)

    Explain to students that the police must do certain things when they arrest someone. List and discuss the following on the chalkboard: A) Do not struggle, be cooperative; B) give your name and address; C) ask to make a telephone call; D) do not say anything about the case unless your lawyer is present; and E) Miranda statement (a person must be informed of his or her right to remain silent and that anything said can be used against them in court).

7. *Consumer Laws.* (Strand 3, *Skill:* Group Interaction)

    Organize a roleplay in class where students are trying to return a radio. The store owner will not take the radio back unless the consumer has a sales receipt, the original box, and reason for returning the merchandise. After the roleplay, discuss with students precautions when buying new things.

41. GOVERNMENT

DETECTION Students may have difficulty mastering key concepts if they:

- Have difficulty explaining the concept of government
- Do not understand the role of government established through the Constitution
- Have difficulty explaining the different branches of government
- Cannot differentiate between different types of governments

Description. The Constitution describes the basis for government in the United States. Government has the right to make and enforce laws in society at the local, state, and national levels. Government provides for internal and external security as well as welfare services, education, and regulations on the economy. The three branches of the U.S. government include 1) the legislative, the law-making branch, which includes the House of Representatives and the Senate; 2) the executive branch, the management branch, which includes the president and his staff; and, 3) the judicial branch, the Supreme Court and all the courts. The Constitution established a balance of power to insure that any one of the branches does not have too much power. Each branch has given controls over the other branches. This system is referred to as *checks and balances.* The Supreme Court has the power to determine the constitutionality of laws. The president can veto any law that Congress makes, and Congress can override a veto with two-thirds majority. Since the United States is ruled by the people through their voting power, it is a democracy. Democratic principles are used in clubs, organizations, and meetings through exercising the voting process to decide issues and to make rules. Government has many bureaucratic layers to perform all the services expected in a modern society.

Causation. Students may not have experienced situations where they were given the opportunity to vote on questions. Families do not necessarily include their children in major decisions with an equal vote. Adults control the decision-making processes in government and students do not always have a lot of opportunities to learn to express their opinions through voting.

Implications. The classroom is a miniature cross-section of society where situations can be formulated for students to participate in democracy. It is important that students learn to vote and express their opinions and have reasons for their decisions. They can become functioning members of society through learning to participate with their voting privileges. The continuation of a democratic form of government depends upon full participation of all people.

CORRECTION Modify strategies for topical and learning needs.

1. *Government Vocabulary.* (Strand 1, *Skill:* Vocabulary)

    Introduce the following words: *Constitution, president, legislative, judicial, Senate, House of Representatives, Supreme Court, checks and balances, veto, democracy,* and *Bill of Rights.* Explain these words and give examples.

2. *Hands Up.* (Strand 2, *Skill:* Decision Making)

    Present a number of issues for students to vote on and tally the votes on the chalkboard. Issues could include wearing certain colors of clothing to school on certain days; certain games to play, such as soccer or kickball; ideas for story writing; or classroom rules. Explain to students that, in a democracy, it is all right for people to disagree on issues.

3. *Government Power.* (Strand 2, *Skill:* Analyzing Information)

    Ask students to make a chart, with the legislative, executive, and judicial branches at the top. List the powers of each under the appropriate heading. Introduce the idea of checks and balances for discussion.

4. *Great Seal.* (Strand 2, *Skill:* Summarizing Information)

    Ask students to examine a dollar bill to inspect the Great Seal of the United States. Emphasize the meaning of the eagle holding the olive branch and arrows. Discuss the meaning of the pyramid on the other side (see discussion in an encyclopedia or other sources). Conclude the activity by asking students to offer design changes to the Seal and explain their reasons.

5. *Letter to Congress.* (Strand 3, *Skill:* Group Interaction)

    Write a group letter to a senator or representative, expressing the class's concern over an environmental, domestic, or foreign policy issue. Students can vote on the issue and decide whether or not they want to sign the letter. Mail the letter and wait for the response.

6. *Democracy Pictures.*(Strand 2, *Skill:* Summarizing Information)

    Ask students to make a drawing or collect pictures to paste on a sheet to illustrate their idea of democracy. Post the pictures and give students an opportunity to explain them to the rest of the class.

7. *Bill Passing.* (Strand 3, *Skill:* Social Participation)

    Assign students roles of legislators who are trying to pass a bill for their state. These bills could include building a state prison; establishing a state park; or funding a new highway or weather station. Students will be given different bills to pass and attempt to get their bill through the simulated Congress. Explain that only 1 of the bills will get passed this session. Give students time to speak informally to each other before voting for the bills.

8. *Political Cartoons.* (Strand 2, *Skill:* Analyzing Information)

    Ask students to collect political cartoons about governmental issues. Discuss the meanings of these cartoons. Emphasize the importance of the press having the freedom to criticize government in a democracy.

42. U.S. GEOGRAPHY

DETECTION   Students may have difficulty mastering key concepts if they:

- Do not know what the study of geography encompasses or how it relates to their lives
- Cannot explain how the earth changes with the way people use it
- Cannot describe elements of the earth's space and resources
- Do not recognize geographical characteristics of various areas in the United States
- Do not know the relationship between space, resources, people, and ecological problems

Description. Geography is the study of space, resources, and people on the earth. Knowing where people live tells us how they live, and how people live determines how the earth is changed as they use it. Geographical space is the land and water forms that make up the area known as the United States. It also includes that space used for different functions, such as homes, shopping, airports, farms, highways, and playgrounds. The resources of the earth—land, water, and air—are used by people and without them we could not exist. Most of the resources of the earth are changed so much as we use them that it is difficult sometimes to realize that they came from the earth. Our resources can be classified into 2 categories—renewable, meaning we can replace them when they are used, and nonrenewable, which cannot be replaced. Air and water resources seemed so abundant in the past that we took them for granted for many years. Because the population of the earth has expanded so greatly and people have developed highly technical ways of living, our water and air pollution problems are increasing, creating situations that are dangerous to human health. The world's population covers all parts of the world and numbers several billion today.

Causation. Ecological concerns are generally considered to be adult problems and thus, students may have had little opportunity to consider them. Analysis and interpretation of the consequences of using the world's resources have not often been a high learning priority in schools. Therefore, students have had little opportunity for studying the balance of nature and the contribution of geography.

Implications. Knowing how geographers study the earth's space, resources, and people will help students understand the necessity for predicting future needs, basing decisions on reliable information, and making decisions that will ultimately affect their lives and many others'. Future careers and opportunities are determined by many of the geographical features of our land and students need to appreciate how these elements affect their lives.

CORRECTION Modify strategies for topical and learning needs.

1. *Physical Map.* (Strand 1, *Skill:* Maps)

   Give students an outline map of the United States. Ask them to identify major mountain ranges, rivers, lakes, and forests. Decide how much space each feature has proportionally and make a pie chart showing these proportions.

2. *Interstate Map.* (Strand 1, *Skill:* Maps)

   Give students a map of the United States showing the interstate highway systems. Ask them to determine all the patterns they can discern from this map and note them on the chalkboard. Examples: numbering system, more populated areas, loops around major cities, distribution areas, any determiners from geographical features of the land.

3. *Renewable Resources.* (Strand 1, *Skill:* Interpreting Information)

   Select several types of soil and plant a vegetable in each type. Keep all conditions the same and observe the plants. Discuss conclusions that can be drawn from the experiment.

4. *Nonrenewable Resources.* (Strand 2, *Skill:* Decision Making)

   After discussion of the consequences of using up the earth's nonrenewable resources, decide on a class project for recycling resources (collect aluminum cans, newspapers, etc.).

5. *Water Jug Pollution.* (Strand 2, *Skill:* Analyzing Information)

   Bring in several containers of drinking water and add different types of pollutants. Ask students to decide how they affect the water's drinking quality (e.g., oil, salt, wastes). Discuss the consequences for other animal life.

6. *Air Pollution.* (Strand 2, *Skill:* Analyzing Information)

   Demonstrate the effects of air pollution and discuss the consequences (e.g., smoke, gasoline fumes, hairspray).

7. *School Census.* (Strand 2, *Skill:* Summarizing Information)

   Discuss how the census helps in identifying present and future needs of people. Do a census of the entire school. Have students work in groups to decide what questions they will ask and how they will collect the information. Design the surveys and collect the information. Summarize the data, graph it, and make conclusions and predictions from the information.

8. *Follow that Coal.* (Strand 2, *Skill:* Analyzing Information)

   Trace the origination of coal through its mining, distribution, and transformation into other products. Draw sequences of events and discuss the implications of this nonrenewable resource being exhausted.

9. *Industry Location.* (Strand 2, *Skill:* Decision Making)

   Choose a large industry and have students pretend that they have the responsibility for choosing where to place it in the United States. Research the geographic needs of the industry and which regions in the country would be suitable. Have students present their decisions to the class, who will challenge their decisions based on the ecological impact of the industry on the area.

43. CULTURAL DIVERSITY

DETECTION Students may have difficulty mastering key concepts if they:

- Cannot identify different cultural groups living in the United States
- Demonstrate prejudice toward different cultural groups
- Do not understand the contributions of cultural groups
- Cannot distinquish the differences between cultural groups
- Have difficulty relating to the freedom struggles of various cultural groups

Description. Europeans from many countries helped establish the U.S. as the land of opportunity. Immigrants left hardship and persecution to become part of the "melting pot" society. Various cultural groups did not blend in as expected and retained many of the customs and traditions unique to their homelands. Different languages kept people from adjusting quickly in the United States. The "melting pot" idea has evolved, emphasizing the cultural and pluralistic nature of the United States. In the last decade, the largest immigrations have been non-European (i.e., Asian and Latin American). Many people come to this country as illegal aliens to accept low-paying work in hopes of receiving some of the benefits from the economy. Due to the large numbers of immigrants, Congress had to pass quota laws to limit the number that would be permitted to enter the country. Blacks, the largest minority group in the United States, came to this country as slaves and have been denied their full civil rights more than any other minority group. The Civil Rights Acts of 1964 and 1968 established strong penalties for racial discrimination. The cultural diversity of the United States remains one of the strengths for testing the tenets of democracy in providing equal opportunity for all people. Even though laws have been passed to end discrimination, prejudices still exist in the attitudes and practices of many Americans.

Causation. Students belonging to minority groups would certainly have firsthand knowledge in dealing with the prejudices of other people. But due to the separation of cultural groups into communities, many students do not have the experiences to interact with and to form their own opinions about other people.

Implications. Students need to learn that a person's skin color, language, or other attributes are not enough information to form prejudicial attitudes. Living and working in harmony with people from all cultural groups is essential in a pluralistic society, especially as the world becomes "smaller" and cultures tend to overlap in more numerous ways. Integration of people, their talents, and contributions can serve to create more beneficial and effective ways of solving human problems.

CORRECTION Modify strategies for topical and learning needs.

1. *Cultural Survey.* (Strand 2, *Skill:* Interpreting Information)
   Conduct a survey in the class to determine the different cultural groups present. Discuss with the students the things that are different and alike about the groups. Make a list of their ideas on the board.
2. *Prejudice Moments.* (Strand 2, *Skill:* Evaluating Information)
   Give each student a handout listing various cultural groups down the lefthand side of the page and characteristics of groups across the top. (Cultural groups: native Americans, Chinese, Jews, blacks, Germans, Italians, etc.; Characteristics: smart, lazy, good cooks, hard workers, good athletes, good businesspersons, etc.) A discussion should reveal that these characteristics would be appropriate for almost any of the groups.
3. *Back of the Bus.* (Strand 3, *Skill:* Social Participation)
   Set up a roleplay where students pretend that they are riding a bus. Some of the students will portray black students who have to give up their seats for whites. Discuss with students their feelings about this practice and explain that it is against the law in our society now. Extend the discussion to include native Americans having to give up their land to live on reservations.
4. *Business Survey.* (Strand 2, *Skill:* Analyzing Information)
   Ask students to survey their community to locate businesses owned and operated by different cultural groups. Make a list of their findings and discuss any patterns.
5. *Immigrants.* (Strand 3, *Skill:* Social Participation)
   Set up a roleplay about immigrating to the United States. Explain that preference was given to people who had relatives in the United States and had skills to enter the labor market. Criminals and people who were ill would not be permitted to enter. Ask students to give reasons why they should be permitted to enter the United States. Focus also on the limited ability to speak English.
6. *Cultural Dinner.* (Strand 2, *Skill:* Evaluating Information)
   Arrange for a snacktime involving foods from different cultural groups. Ask students to taste the foods and decide on their favorite choices. Afterwards explain the origins of the foods.
7. *Immigrant Home.* (Strand 2, *Skill:* Decision Making)
   Pose the following situation to students: You are an immigrant (emphasize immigrant or a specific cultural group) coming into the United States and have to choose a place to live and get a job. How would you choose? After students have made their choices, explain that immigrants usually live in the same communities as their cultural group.
8. *In the News.* (Strand 2, *Skill:* Analyzing Information)
   Have students collect newspaper articles and pictures of different cultural groups making the news. Post the pictures on the bulletin board and have students discuss any patterns with the material.

44. FREE-ENTERPRISE SYSTEM

DETECTION Students may have difficulty mastering key concepts if they:

- Do not understand the concept of supply and demand
- Cannot explain the difference between goods and services
- Have difficulty explaining the consumer's role in the economy
- Have difficulty understanding profit
- Do not understand the need for competition in a free-enterprise system

Description. The United States has a free-enterprise system operating with limited economic controls imposed by the government. People are free to make decisions about what goods or services to sell or buy. Consumers can also make decisions about how to earn their income within the limitations of the opportunities in the economy. Competition is one of the most central factors in developing an economy where people pursue their own interests. In a competitive economy, a person could offer a product or service that the consumer does not want or purchase and thus suffer a loss. A person can also produce a product that people want and are willing to purchase at a high price to generate a profit. The free-enterprise system emphasizes the freedom to start and operate a business. The United States government regulates the economy by controlling foreign trade and maintaining fair competition through regulations and laws. Other laws balance the interactions between unions and business through collective bargaining. The government has become more active in the economy in recent years through the space, welfare, and military programs and as an employer. Government intervention can sometimes interfere with the principles basic to free enterprise; however, government intervention also prevents tremendous fluctuations in the market to avoid depressions and stock market crashes.

Causation. Due to the abstract nature of studying the economy on on a large scale, students will have a difficult time understanding many of the concepts without concrete examples. The study of economics is also limited in schools and does not provide adequate background for learning. Students usually are participants primarily as consumers and have only experienced production of goods or provision of services on a limited scale.

Implications. Students need to understand the free-enterprise system operating in the United States and in other countries to enhance their future participation and ability to earn a livelihood. Education and training will provide the background for students to become full participants in the information and technological businesses dominating the marketplace.

CORRECTION Modify strategies for topical and learning needs.

1. *Job Hunting.* (Strand 2, *Skill:* Interpreting Information)
   Bring newspapers into the classroom and encourage students to job hunt. Have students print their job needs on a large sheet of paper, along with qualifications and pay. Explain that in our society a person can choose his or her work. Discuss with students other factors involved, such as having the qualifications and experience to obtain work in the first place.

2. *House Building.* (Strand 3, *Skill:* Social Participation)
   Divide the class into 3 groups, with each group having the same objective: to construct a house from paper products. Distribute the paper supplies to group 1, the tools (rulers and scissors) to group 2, and the dimensions of the house to group 3 (House: 18" x 24" with flat roof overhanging 1"; windows (1" x 2"; doors 2" x 3"). Students will have to cooperate to complete the house. Discuss the cooperation after the activity is completed to emphasize product quality.

3. *Advertisement.* (Strand 2, *Skill:* Evaluating Information)
   Explain to students that advertisements are designed to help the consumer make a decision to buy a certain product or service. Collect advertisements from magazines and help students analyze the messages. Emphasize the role of advertising in fostering competition. Extend the activity by having students design a new advertisement for a selected product and display it in the classroom.

4. *Make a Profit.* (Strand 2, *Skill:* Summarizing Information)
   Explain to students that a person has to make a profit in a business to pay rent, buy materials, and pay employees and themselves. Mr. Smith owns a bicycle shop and pays $500 a month rent and makes an average of $75 on each bicycle. He pays himself $400 a week and an employee $100 a week. Ask students to determine the number of bicycles Mr. Smith would have to sell in order to break even (40 bicycles) or to make a $500 profit (60 bicycles). Discuss with students what would happen to the shop if Mr. Smith did not make a profit. VARIATION: Use the computer program "Lemonade Stand" (MECC) to illustrate the concept.

5. *Auction.* (Strand 3, *Skill:* Social Participation)
   Give each student $10 in play money to purchase items in a class auction. Ask students to bring games and things to donate to the auction. Emphasize after the auction how people made choices and determined value of products by their offers to buy.

6. *Budget Making.* (Strand 2, *Skill:* Decision Making)
   Explain to students that people must live on the amount of income they make by having a budget. Ask students to make a budget for living in their community to provide for housing, food, car, and other things.

7. *Monopoly.* (Strand 2, *Skill:* Synthesizing Information)
   Use the game of Monopoly® to illustrate some of the principles of a free-enterprise system.

45. TECHNOLOGY

DETECTION Students may have difficulty mastering key concepts if they:

- Cannot describe examples of technological utilization in our society
- Have difficulty understanding the beneficial aspects of technology
- Have difficulty understanding the harmful side effects of technology
- Cannot compare and contrast the technological development of other countries with that of the United States

Description. Technology refers to the inventions and discoveries that improve the quality of life by making work easier and more productive. The simple tools of primitive times and the complex computers of today are examples of technology. Technology is advanced through people's intellectual power to make important discoveries in business, health, industry, communication, transportation, space, and other fields. Technological developments affect other aspects of people's lives. Television and VCRs have affected the entertainment industry. The invention of the airplane has certainly impacted travel and delivery services. Space travel enables us to utilize space for scientific experiments, travel, and other advancements. The invention of the atomic bomb changed the meaning of war in modern time. The United States is a world leader in inventing and putting technology to use. Along with the advancements in technology come harmful side effects that pose new and different problems for people to solve. For example, the increased number of automobiles has a side effect of air pollution. The problem was partially solved through installing systems on cars to remove some of the harmful gases from unleaded gasoline. Another example of technology developing at a rapid pace can be traced through the evolution of computers. Our advancements are limited only by our ingenutity in solving problems.

Causation. Students are surrounded by and utilize technology in everyday living and playing, as well as in education. The development of technology can be taken for granted if students do not have a sense of evolution or do not realize that there are always opportunities to improve on what already exists. This is the core of problem solving and it may not have been taught or encouraged as a process.

Implications. The development of new technologies requires new skills and continuous learning. Students must learn to use the new technologies as well as to envision and help make advancements to solve new or previously unsolved human problems. Assistive devices for the physically handicapped and advances in medical technology are quickly changing and improving life.

CORRECTION Modify strategies for topical and learning needs.

1. *Tool Technology.* (Strand 2, *Skill:* Summarizing Information)
   Bring a box full of tools and ask students to determine the specific function of each one. These should include simple tools, such as hammers, screw drivers, pliers, wrenches, nails, bolts, saws, and screws. Discuss the function of the tools by having students give demonstrations. Extend the activity by demonstrating a power screw driver or drill. Discuss the development of the technology of tools. Summarize the discussion by defining technology as human knowledge at work to make things easier and faster.
2. *Machine Technology.* (Strand 2, *Skill:* Interpreting Information)
   Have students collect pictures of machines that demonstrate the use of technology. Make a large bulletin board for students to display and explain their pictures.
3. *Tractor Farming.* (Strand 2, *Skill:* Analyzing Information)
   Show students a picture of a farmer plowing a field with horses or oxen and another farmer using a tractor. Ask students to determine the impact of the tractor on farming. Include cost, amount of profit, number of acres, and labor to plant and harvest crops.
4. *House Survey.* (Strand 2, *Skill:* Classifying Information)
   Give students a sheet of paper with 2 headings: Technology and Function. Ask students to survey their homes and list uses of technology. Review the surveys with an emphasis on function.
5. *Computer Use.* (Strand 2, *Skill:* Summarizing Information)
   Computers have impacted modern society, with uses ranging from data storage to guiding rockets into space. Have students draw pictures of computers being used in a variety of ways.
6. *Assembly Line.* (Strand 3, *Skill:* Social Participation)
   Assembly-line production is used to produce automobiles at a rapid rate. Set up an assembly line where students draw a car, with each person having a specific responsibility. For example, 1 person would draw the wheels with other students drawing the front, back, top, lights, antennas, and decorative strips on the sides. Students will need a planning session to decide on the type of car and the responsibilities of the group members. Discuss with students the advantages and disadvantages of an assembly line.
7. *Technological Problems.* (Strand 2, *Skill:* Decision Making)
   Technology has created a number of problems in society. Ask students to identify the problems that technology has created with the environment, safety, health, and other areas. Develop possible solutions for these problems with the class.
8. *Super-Fast Food.* (Strand 2, *Skill:* Evaluating Information)
   Pose a futuristic situation, explaining that within the next 10 years all food will be prepared in 1–3 minutes. Ask students to design a kitchen or a super-fast-food store to accommodate this situation. Post their drawings and give students an opportunity to explain them.

REFLECTIONS

1. The activities in this unit are centered around the students' immediate community as a resource for understanding the concept of community. Since students bring this frame of reference to the classroom, discuss how the neighborhood and community environment affects their motivation and learning of social studies concepts.

2. Due to limited markets, materials about individual states are scarce. Brainstorm a list of all possible sources of teaching materials that could be collected (e.g., chamber of commerces, travel agencies, and governmental agencies) for use in teaching about the history, economics, and government of the state. Request some of these materials and organize them for various learning needs of students.

3. There are implicit values in many of the activities in this section. Identify these values and discuss how they impact the way certain social studies concepts related to the United States are taught. Are these values consistent with your belief system? Develop a personal values chart to share with your class.

4. Every community has unique and distinguishing features that contribute to living in that environment. Discuss with others those places in the local area community that are possible fieldtrip sites. Generate a list of these places.

5. Review the DETECTION strategies in this section and design a pretest and posttest for the most important concepts related to the study of your community and state. For special students, interviews or demonstrations may be more appropriate than paper/pencil tests. Have your test examined by another teacher and a special education teacher.

6. The importance of students learning to read and develop study skills is reflected in curriculum materials and testing procedures. Look at each strategy in this chapter and suggest ways study skills can be developed and reinforced through the activities.

7. Structured speaking opportunities need to be integrated into the assessment of concepts students are learning. Plan two speaking activities to be incorporated into the concepts being emphasized in the study of communities.

8. Special learners often need very focused and carefully planned questions to guide their thinking and comprehension. Working with others, develop a set of questions to determine mastery of the content and ideas presented in this section. Match your findings with the strategies found in this section.

9. Supplementary visual and auditory materials are especially useful for special learners. Consult the school and community media resources to locate audio or video recordings describing life in other cultures or other parts of the United States. Develop a conceptual framework for comparing and contrasting communities. Research the frameworks used in various textbook series to study about community life.

10. Most social studies texts address the concept of communities. Compare and contrast discussions in these sources with the information and activities in this section.

Cornbleth, C. (1986). *An invitation to research in social education.* Washington, DC: National Council for the Social Studies.

Dobkin, W. S., Fischer, J., Ludwig, B., & Koblinger, R. (1985). *A handbook for the teaching of social studies.* Boston: Allyn and Bacon.

Edmunds, P. (1985). *Resource manual on disabilities: A count me in project.* Minneapolis, MN: Pacer Center.

Harmin, M., Kirschenbaum, H., & Simon, S. (1973). *Clarifying values through subject matter.* Minneapolis, MN: Winston Press.

Henley, M. (1985). *Teaching mildly retarded children in the regular classroom.* Bloomington, IN: Phi Delta Kappa Educational Foundation.

Jarolimek, J. (1977). *Social studies competencies and skills.* New York: Macmillan.

Michaelis, J. U. (1987). *Social studies for children.* Englewood Cliffs, NJ: Prentice-Hall.

Morgan, J. C., & Schreiber, J. E. (1969). *How to ask questions.* Washington, DC: National Council for the Social Studies.

Savage, T. V., & Armstrong, D. G. (1987) *Effective teaching in social studies.* New York: Macmillan.

Shaftel, F. R. (1967). *Role playing and social value.* Englewood Cliffs, NJ: Prentice-Hall.

Shaver, J. P., & Curtis, C. K. (1981). *Handicappism and equal opportunity: Teaching about the disabled in social studies.* Reston, VA: Foundation for Exceptional Children.

PART IV

TOWARD A
SMALLER WORLD

Part IV includes many of the current topics of concern in social studies education related to the world community. Issues such as protecting the environment, controlling population growth, monitoring technological advances, and solving world conflict are vital concerns with which today's students must contend. Harmony in this smaller world community hinges upon people working cooperatively to meet world challenges.

Special learners cannot be exempted from these concerns because of their achievement difficulties, but rather ways must be found to help them understand the issues and learn to cope with the changes and decisions. Social studies education has as its ultimate goal the preparation of all students to face today's challenges and to meet the unique conditions of the future.

Unlike earlier sections, most of the activities in Part IV are beyond the immediate experience of students and will require teachers to provide sufficient background, explanation, and experience to develop the concepts. This degree of removal from students' immediate lives will make this section more challenging for teachers and for students who are experiencing severe learning problems.

The DETECTION sections highlight behaviors that can be expected of students who are having difficulties with the concepts focused upon in this unit as well as many regular students who have not been exposed to these concepts. The more specificity teachers can glean regarding the detection of difficulties, the greater success in correcting the problems is likely to be.

Part IV begins with an overview of historical events that have shaped the present. While it is often argued that past events are perceived as irrelevant and even boring to today's students, it is nonetheless imperative to help students find the relationship of the past to the present, lest they ignore history and be doomed to repeat it. Limited contact with other people and places contributes to students' lack of ability to accept and live cooperatively with those different than themselves. These differences are focused on in World Cultures, Topic 47, for the purpose of identifying what is actually common among people. Four of the most immediate and influential countries in today's world are highlighted for study in this section to build upon students' awareness of the interrelationships and cooperation needed for continued survival and peace.

To be effective, corrective instruction must include ample learning opportunities that involve interactions of all types. Structure listening, viewing, speaking, reading, and writing activities and integrate them throughout the selection and adaptation of activities. Television, newspaper, and magazine articles will provide the most current information available, as textbooks will be dated for many of the topics in this unit. For general guidelines for selecting and adapting strategies to teach identified special learners, refer to the practices and corrective principles in Part I. As with any set of teaching ideas, select and modify the CORRECTION strategies to meet the learning needs of individual students.

CHAPTER 9 /
THE WORLD: THEN AND NOW

46. WORLD EVENTS THAT SHAPED THE PRESENT

DETECTION Students may have difficulty mastering key concepts if they:

- Cannot identify or describe significant world events
- Do not understand the relevance of certain world events to their personal lives
- Do not have a sense of the chronological order of history

Description. History was first recorded about 5,000 years ago. We know from this writing that farming was one of the most important steps in history, allowing people to settle in communities and develop structured civilizations. The first of these, the "cradles of civilization," were begun in four river valleys: the land between the Tigris and Euphrates Rivers in Southwest Asia, along the Nile River in Egypt, along the Indus River in Pakistan, and along the Yellow River in China. The Greeks developed one of the first advanced civilizations and contributed many of the principles of democracy. The Romans' culture developed more slowly but they conquered much land and created a vast empire. The Fall of Rome marked the beginning of the Middle Ages, a 1,000 year period that brought many ideas, inventions, and people together. Christianity grew during this time and became the most powerful political and social influence in Western Europe. On the American continents, highly developed Indian civilizations flourished until they were conquered by European explorers. A 300-year period of cultural awakening, known as the Renaissance, resulted in many of the world's masterpieces of art and literature and discoveries in science. Trading and exploration led to colonization of other countries. The Industrial Revolution brought new ways of doing business and a middle class of people developed. Conflicts such as World War I and World War II occurred, leading to the development of the atomic bomb. The Space Age brought exploration beyond the earth and led to inventions and medical discoveries that improved life.

Causation. Characteristically, young people do not have a strong sense of the past. They are present oriented and do not see relevance in events or places removed from them.

Implications. The focus of this study should be on the world as the home of many different people who work with the forces that shape their lives. The events selected for study should illustrate changes through time that develop a knowledge of and appreciation for the contributions of many cultures to the collective wisdom of the human race.

CORRECTION Modify strategies for topical and learning needs.

1. *What's the Connection?* (Strand 2, *Skill:* Analyzing Information)
    Give students 1 of the following terms and ask them to find a connection between their term and someone else's: *farming, cradles of civilization, Greeks, democracy, Romans, laws, romance languages, feudalism, Christianity, exploration, colonization, native American cultures, Industrial Revolution, World Wars I and II, atomic bomb, and Sputnik.* Have students explain to the class the connections they make.
2. *Around the World in a Week.* (Strand 2, *Skill:* Summarizing)
    Ask students to collect newspaper articles of events that occur in other countries for a week. Make a list of the major events on the chalkboard and discuss which are most likely to have impact on other countries and particularly on their lives and which events are probably only local.
3. *Relevance Research.* (Strand 1, *Skill:* Information Search)
    Assign students (individually or in cooperative groups) a major world event and have them read about it. Ask students to make a list of all the ways this event affected the future and their lives. Have students report orally and encourage the rest of the class to add to the lists after the reports.
4. *What If... ?* (Strand 2, *Skill:* Synthesizing Information)
    Choose several world events and reinterpret them in terms of what might have happened if things had been changed in some way. Example: What if Columbus had disappeared at sea instead of finding the Americas? What if *Sputnik* had exploded?
5. *Play It Again.* (Strand 2, *Skill:* Interpreting Information)
    Form students into groups and ask them to choose a historical event to roleplay as it might have occurred in ancient days and then to reinterpret the event as it might occur today. Encourage simple costumes and props and videotape the presentations.
6. *Art and History.* (Strand 2, *Skill:* Classifying Information)
    Assign groups of students different periods of world history to study (i.e., ancient times, Middle Ages, modern times). On a wall or side of the classroom, have each group develop a mural, display objects, draw, and/or create their interpretations of life at this time in history.
7. *Working It Out.* (Strand 1, *Skill:* Comprehension)
    Paint a simple jigsaw puzzle white and allow to dry. Begin at the upper-lefthand corner and write an event on this puzzle piece. On each connecting piece write about a person or event related to the first event and so on until the puzzle is completed.
8. *Read All about It.* (Strand 1, *Skill:* Comprehension)
    Select several books for young readers that discuss aspects of world history. Read various selections to the class and make the books available to them for independent reading and research. Examples: Van Loon, *The Story of Mankind* (Liveright, 1972); Quennell, *Everyday Life in Prehistoric Times* (Putnam, 1959); selections from Auel, *Clan of the Cave Bear* (Crown, 1983).

47. WORLD CULTURES

DETECTION Students may have difficulty mastering key concepts if they:

- Have had limited contact with other persons and places outside of the United States
- Have not studied how people have utilized and adapted themselves to particular geographical conditions
- Do not have experience in living cooperatively with persons who are different from themselves
- Do not realize that all people have the same basic needs
- Do not know that all cultures have some form of religion or guiding belief system

Description. The world is made up of a variety of cultures that reflect each group's way of doing things, their beliefs, customs, traditions, and traits. Although there are many differences among the world's cultures, people share common needs that unify them: food, security, friendship, and opportunities to have families. As people have learned new ways of doing things, these ideas have spread to other cultures and influenced their development. Changes have occurred more and more rapidly throughout the world as science and technology have increased. The invention of the airplane, television, radio, and motion pictures have had a significant influence on most of the cultures in the world. This rapid process of cultural exchange has led some people to predict that someday there will be a common world culture, with many of the differences among people disappearing. Examples of how this has already occurred to some extent are the spread of Westernized ways of dressing and the fact that different types of food and cooking once found only in certain areas and countries are becoming common in many places in the world today. Religion is also a common need of all people and occurs in some form as part of every culture. Religious teachings help people to accept the mysteries of the world and promote understanding and goodwill.

Causation. Students who have limited experiences with other countries and peoples often view those who are different as inferior. They do not readily accept them into their friendship circles because they do not trust them or see them as being like themselves.

Implications. Students must become competent to live in an emerging world community and the school can be a model and laboratory for teaching and practicing this concept. They must learn to think in terms of the dignity and worth of all humans and to appreciate the contributions of people from all parts of the world. The interdependence of all nations is becoming so complex that it ultimately will effect the way all people live and think.

CORRECTION Modify strategies for topical and learning needs.

1. *Cultural Inquiry.* (Strand 2, *Skill:* Summarizing Information)

    In order to understand any culture, information must be obtained about its government, religion, education, arts, economics, history, technology, and social organization. Ask students to draw large circles for each of the preceding concepts and collect information about a specific culture. The concepts could be modeled by the teacher to provide clarity. Also, the circles could be displayed for the class to review.

2. *Cultural Exchange.* (Strand 3, *Skill:* Group Interaction)

    Divide the class into 3 groups each representing a different culture. Give each group a specific nonverbal behavior that makes them different such as: wanting to touch while talking to you; always looking away while talking to you; covering your mouth while talking; and using 1-word sentences. Ask students to play the specific role of their culture in an attempt to get others to join it. After the experience, provide students with the opportunity to discuss the unusual behaviors of the different groups or cultures.

3. *Cultural Differences.*(Strand 2, *Skill:* Analyzing Information)

    Explain that all cultures are different and unusual when compared to the culture that one lives in. Ask students to collect different habits and practices of other cultures from the newspaper or television to explain to the class.

4. *Lost in a Strange Land.* (Strand 2, *Skill:* Decision Making)

    Explain to students that they are visiting another culture and cannot speak the native language. They are staying in a hotel and want to wander around the city. Divide students into groups and explain that they may get lost and would need to return to the hotel. Have groups discuss what they could do to communicate where they were staying. (Clue: Take a matchbook from their hotel with them.)

5. *Religion.* (Strand 3, *Skill:* Personal Skills)

    People in different cultures have religions that explain many of their cultural practices. Ask students to share stories of the religious practices in different countries. Compare some of these practices to their own.

6. *New Handshake.* (Strand 3, *Skill:* Social Participation)

    Challenge students to invent a new handshake for their class. During recess, ask students to teach the handshake to other people in the school. Discuss with students the idea that cultures have similar habits and practices.

7. *Cultural Costumes.* (Strand 2, *Skill:* Classifying Information)

    The way people dress establishes a cultural identity. Have students collect pictures of different costumes in various cultures and post on a bulletin board. Ask students to react to the following question: What would happen to a person's dress if he or she moved to another culture?

48. ANCIENT EGYPT

DETECTION Students may have difficulty mastering key concepts if they:

- Are not aware of the history of any other cultures
- Cannot compare ancient Egyptian culture with that of the United States
- Do not understand the advancements in civilization
- Cannot describe the ancient Egyptian culture
- Do not know the ancient Egyptian contributions to world history

Description. Ancient Egypt was characterized by pharaohs and kings dating back to 3,000 B.C. who built giant temples and pyramids. The pharaoh was worshiped as a god and had complete authority to enforce the devine commands. Ancient Egyptian history can be divided into 30 dynasties that dominate in the various kingdoms. Much of the history has been reconstructed because dry air and sand preserved many records and artifacts. The Egyptians developed an organized government, a 365-day year, and invented paper. Most of the major cities were built along the Nile River, the longest river in the world. The Nile River would flood every year, leaving behind rich black soil to farm. Egyptians also made their living in other ways by working in mines to obtain gold and copper. Other craftsmen worked in quarries to obtain the stone to construct the giant pyramids. The Egyptians developed a written record of their language, as indicated by the famous Rosetta stone. Archaeologists are still exploring pyramids to reconstruct history. Weapons, colored pottery, and wood and limestone carvings are just a few of the artifacts that reveal clues about this civilization.

Causation. Special students may have difficulty understanding ancient Egyptian history not only because of the vast time period but also because of the wide diversity of the many aspects of this rich heritage. Textbooks devote very little space to studying this culture and present only a brief overview of thousands of years of development and conflict during this time period. Many students may have stereotypical views about the pyramids and the various gods that the Egyptians worshiped. This, of course, is determined by their own religious teachings and beliefs. People that dress differently and practice unusual customs are often perceived stereotypically. Limited exposure and experience of students often perpetuate these perceptions.

Implications. Special students use their immediate culture to filter the customs and practices of other people. The study of Egypt will help students see the vast contributions that were made thousands of years ago to modern society. Students will better understand their own behaviors and beliefs through studying other cultures. Students are usually fascinated by the accomplishments of the Egyptians in their building of the giant pyramids and the elaborate stone and metal sculptures.

CORRECTION Modify strategies for topical and learning needs.

1. *Egyptian Vocabulary.* (Strand 1, *Skill:* Vocabulary)

    Place the following vocabulary on the chalkboard and have students pronounce the words and draw pictures or give examples: *Nile River, Rosetta stone, papyrus, pyramid, pharaoh,* and *mummy.*
2. *Egyptian Life.* (Strand 2, *Skill:* Evaluating Information)

    Give students a blank map of Egypt and the surrounding countries but showing the Nile River. Explain that Egypt has practically no rainfall. Group the students in 3s and have them locate cities on the map and determine how people made a living in Egypt.
3. *Mummies.* (Strand 2, *Skill:* Interpreting Information)

    Explain to students that the Egyptians decorated mummies with special colors and jewelry. Mummies were wrapped tightly in layer after layer of linen to preserve them. Explain to students that the Egyptians believed in life after death. Ask students to conjecture about how mummies have been preserved for thousands of years. EXTENSION: Have students write a short group story about a mummy that visited the United States.
4. *Pyramid Building.* (Strand 3, *Skill:* Group Interaction)

    Divide the class into groups of 3 and ask them to construct pyramids of clay blocks. After constructing the pyramids, the groups should make lists of things the Egyptians would probably place inside. Ask students to make lists of the things from their culture they would place inside today.
5. *Mask.* (Strand 2, *Skill:* Synthesizing Information)

    Give each student materials to make an Egyptian mask. Explain that the mask should have some evidence of the culture. Using reference books, have students find examples of Egyptian art to get ideas. Students should display their masks and explain the cultural relationships.
6. *Pharaoh's Power.* (Strand 3, *Skill:* Group Interaction)

    Explain that the pharaoh's power was absolute in most kingdoms in ancient Egypt. Give students the opportunity to pose problems to the pharaoh (another student) to make decisions. Some coaching may be necessary to get the pharaoh to make unpopular decisions. Compare and discuss the difference between the pharaoh's and president's power.
7. *Hieroglyphics.* (Strand 2, *Skill:* Interpreting Information)

    The Egyptians used hieroglyphics in their writing, in which pictures represented certain ideas and letters. Develop a system of hieroglyphics for the alphabet (each letter represented by a picture). Ask students to use the hieroglyphics to write a brief message for other students to interpret.
8. *Pyramid Power.* (Strand 2, *Skill:* Synthesizing Information)

    Challenge students to figure out a system for moving 500-pound blocks to the tops of pyramids in ancient times. Remind them that modern technology was not available.

49. OUR NEIGHBOR: CANADA

DETECTION Students may have difficulty mastering key concepts if they:

- Have not traveled outside the United States
- Do not know where Canada is located
- Cannot describe anything about Canada
- Do not know why it is important to have strong allies
- Cannot describe any cultural features of Canada

Description. Canada borders the United States on the north across the entire east-to-west boundary. Second only to the U.S.S.R., Canada is one of the largest countries in the world, covering the entire northern half of North America except for Alaska and Greenland. Only about one-tenth as many people live in Canada as in the United States, however, and most live very close to the southern border because of the extreme cold in the northern areas. North American Indians and Eskimos live in Canada and were its first inhabitants, but most of the people who live there today are from Europe, primarily of British and French descent. The name *Canada* comes from the Iroquois Indians' word *Kanata,* or *Kanada,* which means "group of huts." Canada has 2 official languages, English and French. Canada's form of government is known as a constitutional monarchy. It is a member of the Commonwealth of Nations and Queen Elizabeth, of Great Britain, is the monarch. Nonetheless, Canada is a self-governing, democratic nation. The federal government consists of 10 provinces and 2 territories. Its capital is Ottawa, located in the province of Ontario. Schools in Canada are taught in English or French, depending on where they are located. Most elementary schools have 8 grades and high schools have 4. Some schools have only 11 grades, and others have 13. Presently, Canada and the United States are very close trading partners. The natural resources of Canada are richly abundant, with large amounts of fertile farm land, mineral resources among the largest in the world, abundant fish and fur-bearing animals, and forests that make Canada the world's largest provider of paper. Geographically, Canada is divided into 7 major land regions, and it is surrounded by a number of islands around the 3 sides of its coast. The climate is cool to extremely cold for most of the year.

Causation. Students who have limited travel experience and are more removed geographically from Canada will have less knowledge of it and will have seen and felt less of its influence in their personal lives.

Implications. Canada and the United States are culturally quite similar and have traditionally been very friendly countries. Students need to explore why and how countries can coexist in close proximity and in harmony to understand why this sometimes does not happen with other countries.

CORRECTION Modify strategies for topical and learning needs.

1. *Neighborliness.* (Strand 3, *Skill:* Group Interaction)

    Discuss the concept of neighborliness. On the chalkboard, make 2 columns. In the first, list all the ways neighbors at home and in the classroom help students. In the second column, list all the ways neighboring countries help the United States.

2. *Canadian Money.* (Strand 2, *Skill:* Interpreting Information)

    Bring in some Canadian money and show the similarities and differences, discuss the values, and the costs of consumer goods in Canada compared to in the United States. VARIATION: Locate a Canadian newspaper from a major city and compare the costs of items from the ads. NOTE: Lack of difference in prices may reflect the value of the U.S. dollar.

3. *Two Governments.* (Strand 2, *Skill:* Analyzing Information)

    Make line drawings (structured overviews) of the U.S. governmental system and the Canadian system. Compare and display in the room.

4. *Canadian Country.* (Strand 1, *Skill:* Maps)

    Give students an outline map of Canada and ask them to locate the capital city and color in the primary land regions.

5. *Province Personalities.* (Strand 2, *Skill:* Summarizing Information)

    Assign groups of students a Canadian province to research and prepare a summary for oral presentation to the class. Members of the group should be assigned different parts to discuss and should be encouraged to make and use visual aids to summarize their main points.

6. *Canadian Consultant.* (Strand 1, *Skill:* Community Resources)

    Ask someone who has traveled in Canada to share his or her pictures and experiences with the class.

7. *Monarchy Members.* (Strand 2, *Skill:* Interpreting Information)

    Have students draw a family tree of the ruling monarchy of Canada. Display pictures of the family in the room and discuss its position in relation to Canadian politics, law, and government. Discuss how life would be as a prince or princess of a country.

8. *Olympic Fun.* (Strand 2, *Skill:* Summarizing Information)

    Canada has been a host of the Winter Olympics. Draw the flags of countries participating in the Olympics and label each with the name of the country. Make a list of the sporting events that occur in the Winter Olympics and discuss why Canada is a logical place to host them. Describe how competitions such as the Olympics bring people together.

9. *Canadian Conflict.* (Strand 2, *Skill:* Analyzing Information)

    Canada and the United States have had disagreements about air pollution problems from various industrial efforts. Research these problems and ask students to consider what will happen if we don't stop pollution. Ask students to have a mock United Nations meeting to solve the problems between our 2 countries.

50. OUR NEIGHBOR: MEXICO

DETECTION Students may have difficulty mastering key concepts if they:

- Have not traveled outside the United States
- Do not know where Mexico is located
- Cannot describe anything about Mexico
- Do not know why it is important to have strong allies
- Cannot describe any cultural features of Mexico

Description. Mexico borders the United States to the south, separated from our country largely by the Rio Grande River. Mexico City is the capital of Mexico, and is not only the largest city in that country but also the largest city in the Western hemisphere. Several hundred years ago, Indians built large cities and developed sophisticated cultures. The Aztecs were the last of the Indians to rule. They were conquered by Spanish invaders in 1521 and were a Spanish colony for the next 300 years. The Mexicans overthrew the Spanish in 1821 and established a democratic republican government, consisting of 31 states and 1 federal district. The head of state is the president, elected for one 6-year term. Mexico also has a congress, consisting of a Senate and a Chamber of Deputies, and a Supreme Court. There is no vice president. Mexico also has a federal constitution, which is comparatively much stronger than that of the United States. The official language of the country is Spanish and the majority of the citizens are Roman Catholic. Every city, town, and village has a market where people bring a variety of goods to sell and trade and bargaining is a highly practiced skill. Education begins in kindergarten and continues in elementary school for 6 years. Relatively few students go to college, but those who do attend high schools for 5 years before entering college for 3–7 more years of study. Corn is Mexico's most important food, with the best known product being the tortilla, a flat, round, corn meal, pancake-type food. Other important products include coffee, cotton, oranges, and sugar cane. Mexico is also rich in minerals and is one of the world's largest producers of silver. Geographically, Mexico has 6 main land regions, which differ greatly in altitude, climate, and plant and animal life. The terrain in these areas varies from desert to jungle and from flat to mountainous, including several active volcanoes. Many U.S. citizens have immigrated from Mexico.

Causation. Limited travel experiences and opportunities to meet people from other countries usually determines the knowledge base that young students have of other cultures.

Implications. Mexico is an ally of the United States and a key part of the Western hemisphere's defense and strength. Economically, the 2 countries are interdependent; culturally they are very different. Students need to learn that culturally different people can peacefully coexist and appreciate each other's differences.

CORRECTION Modify strategies for topical and learning needs.

1. *Spanish Language.* (Strand 1, *Skill:* Vocabulary)

     Many of the words we use in English are Spanish terms borrowed from the Mexicans. Make a bulletin board of Spanish words that we use in English. Examples: *patio, rodeo, canyon, corral, desperado, lasso.*

2. *Fiesta Time.* (Strand 3, *Skill:* Group Interaction)

     Divide the class into groups and plan a Mexican fiesta. One group should be responsible for food, another music, another games and entertainment. Make the fiesta as authentic as possible.

3. *Going to Market.* (Strand 3, *Skill:* Social Skills)

     Create a Mexican market by having students bring in things to buy, sell, and trade with each other. Demonstrate how bargaining can occur and encourage students to try out the system.

4. *Dress-Up.* (Strand 2, *Skill:* Summarizing Information)

     Ask students to wear any clothing or jewelry they may have that has Mexican influence. Discuss the characteristics that distinguish traditional Mexican dress from our own.

5. *Mexican Consultant.* (Strand 1, *Skill:* Community Resources)

     Ask someone who has lived or traveled in Mexico to share his or her pictures and experiences with the class.

6. *Sports Analysis.* (Strand 2, *Skill:* Analyzing Information)

     Mexico has several sports that are not played very often in the United States. Research these sports and discuss their rules and why they are popular among the people. Examples: Jai alai, bullfighting, soccer.

7. *Pesos and Pennies.* (Strand 2, *Skill:* Interpreting Information)

     Bring in some Mexican money and discuss the economic exchange rate from pesos to dollars. Explain why values fluctuate periodically.

8. *Indian Traditions.* (Strand 2, *Skill:* Synthesizing Information)

     Research some of the Aztec Indian traditions and show pictures of the pyramids built to worship the sun and moon. Have students build a replica of the pyramid to the sun located outside of Mexico City at Teotihuácan.

9. *Coat of Arms.* (Strand 2, *Skill:* Synthesizing Information)

     Compare and discuss the eagle symbol used on the Mexican coat of arms with that on the U.S. seal. Ask students to design or select a symbol and use it on a coat of arms for their classroom/school/town.

10. *Mexico Map.* (Strand 1, *Skill:* Maps)

     Give students an outline map of Mexico and ask them to locate the capital city, the 6 main land regions, active volcanoes, ancient ruins, and other significant features.

11. *Constitution Comparison.* (Strand 2, *Skill:* Analyzing Information)

     Obtain copies of the constitutions of the U.S. and Mexico (translated). Compare them and list the features that are alike and those that make them different. VARIATION: Ask students to make charts of the two governments and compare them.

51. THE SOVIET UNION

DETECTION Students may have difficulty mastering key concepts if they:

* Do not know that the U.S.S.R. and the United States are the 2 most powerful countries in the world today
* Have deep and irrational prejudices against the U.S.S.R.
* Cannot describe life, history, or the culture of Soviet citizens
* Do not know how the U.S.S.R. has contributed to world affairs, art, science, and social thought
* Do not have a sense of belonging to a world community

Description. Recent history and events have placed the United States and Soviet Union in world leadership positions in economic, political, and military affairs. Such eminence places a tremendous burden of responsibility upon these countries to establish a firm basis for harmonious cooperation. Because the U.S.S.R. is a powerful leader, it is appropriate to study the country, its history, language, and culture in order to develop greater understanding. The language, Russian, is an appropriate topic of study to break down barriers. Russian names can be anglicized and political, economic and legal practices can be explained in terminology more familiar to students. Geographic factors played a large part in Soviet history and in the development of agriculture, population growth, and industrialization. These factors influence and determine the way Soviets live, work, and spend their leisure time. The complex relationships between the United States and U.S.S.R. can be explained and efforts for building a cooperative, supportive coexistence described so that students can participate in these efforts as responsible citizens.

Causation. Ideological conflicts and lack of knowledge of the Soviet Union and its people have contributed to strong prejudices against it. Because of its great power, the U.S.S.R. is perceived as a threat to U.S. status in the world, which contributes to unrest and leads to suspicions and distrust about the Soviets. Often students have perceived these feelings from their families and reflect them in their own attitudes.

Implications. Young students will soon be leading the world and participating in making decisions that need to reflect a concern for world problems. Knowledge must replace hope that these decisions are well-founded and not based on fear and a limited world view. Including this kind of learning in the curriculum will help contribute to the creation of a peaceful world community.

CORRECTION Modify strategies for topical and learning needs.

1. *Break the Language Barrier.* (Strand 1, *Skill:* Vocabulary)

   Many Russian names can be anglicized: *Ivan* as *John, Andrei* as *Andrew,* and *Pavel* as *Paul.* Ask students to find other examples. Label things in the room with Russian vocabulary and learn some words of greeting. Listen to short recordings of Russian speakers.

2. *Dress-Up.* (Strand 2, *Skill:* Comprehension)

   Dress up in authentic Russian clothing or bring dolls to class in authentic costumes. Discuss Russian dress in terms of the climate, environment, and tradition. Supply pictures of modern Soviets and compare their dress to ours.

3. *Pen Pals.* (Strand 2, *Skill:* Personal Skills)

   Exchange letters with Soviet students or classes. Send pictures and describe school life. Vary the form of communication by sending audio- or videotapes.

4. *Story Festival.* (Strand 1, *Skill:* Comprehension)

   Plan a story day and read children Russian stories and other materials about the Soviet Union. Ask someone who has visited in the Soviet Union to show his or her pictures and tell about the trip.

5. *Typical Kid's Day.* (Strand 2, *Skill:* Analyzing Information)

   Ask someone who is familiar with life in the U.S.S.R. to compare a typical day for a Soviet student to that of a U.S. student. Discussion should include differences in how we live, customs, education, religion, and attitudes.

6. *Stereotype Demolition.* (Strand 2, *Skill:* Analyzing Information)

   Students have accumulated many stereotypical ideas about the Soviets. Ask them to call out their first impressions when the Soviet Union is mentioned and write them on the chalkboard. Discuss each one and determine the extent of the bias. Research aspects of some of the ideas to determine how accurate they are. Ask students to trace where and how they developed these ideas. VARIATION: Ask students to develop lists of questions they would like to ask about Soviets and their way of life.

7. *Food for Thought.* (Strand 3, *Skill:* Social Participation)

   Ask someone with knowledge about typical food in the U.S.S.R. and its preparation to speak to the class. Prepare some of the food and eat it in class. Discuss the tastes and why and how this food is important to the Soviet people.

8. *The Soviet Union in the News.* (Strand 1, *Skill:* Comprehension)

   Collect newspaper and magazine articles for a period of time about the U.S.S.R. Share these orally in class and post them on the bulletin board each day. At the end of a week, summarize the news and discuss the relationship that exists between the U.S. and the U.S.S.R. presently.

9. *Soviet Sports.* (Strand 1, *Skill:* Analyzing Information)

   Research what sports are popular in the Soviet Union and prepare a bulletin board with information about outstanding Soviet athletes.

52. JAPAN

DETECTION Students may have difficulty mastering key concepts if they:

- Have had limited experiences with other cultures
- Have not traveled beyond local areas
- Do not have a sense of the capacity for relationships to change over time
- Do not realize that cooperation and mutual benefit is possible even among previous enemies

Description. One of the best examples of how the world has grown smaller and brought people and cultures closer together is the present-day relationship between the United States and Japan. Today Japan is the third-largest investor in the United States, providing workers in this country with millions of jobs and stimulating the U.S. economy to high levels. Less than 50 years earlier, Japan and the United States were enemies in World War II. The Japanese attacked U.S. military bases at Pearl Harbor and a devastating war followed, resulting in the U.S. dropping 2 atomic bombs on the Japanese cities of Hiroshima and Nagasaki and near total destruction of the islands. After the Japanese surrender, the U.S. occupied Japan and reorganized its government, making it a constitutional monarchy. Although there is still an emperor of the country, he has no political power. Japan has 4 main islands and several smaller ones. It is located in the Pacific Ocean off the east coast of Asia. Mountains cover most of the islands and only a small area is available for people to live on and farm. Japan also has limited natural resources, making it necessary to import or trade for what is needed to sustain its population. The people of Japan have been its most valuable resource, using their skills to develop one of the most highly industrialized nations in the world. Recently, Japan has begun to establish factories all across the U.S. and mesh its economic future with that of the United States.

Causation. Many students may recognize and acknowledge the quality of such Japanese products as cars and televisions, radios, and other electronic products. They may have limited history knowledge to understand the significance of these products in our world today. If students have not had an opportunity to work with and talk to Japanese people, they will not understand or appreciate their culture.

Implications. More and more future jobs and services are Japanese related. Students must learn to understand the differences in the cultures and to appreciate that there are different ways of accomplishing tasks. It is through this kind of cooperation that students will learn to recognize the mutual relationship between human beings in satisfying each other's needs.

CORRECTION Modify strategies for topical and learning needs.

1. *Geography Scoop.* (Strand 1, *Skill:* Map and Globe Reading)

    Locate Japan and its present territory on the globe and a world map. Reproduce a map that will allow students to locate all the territory Japan occupied prior to World War II. After the treaty that ended the war, the Japanese territory was reorganized under Allied leadership. Ask students to research what occurred after World War II and what the present status of the territory is.

2. *Treaty Time.* (Strand 2, *Skill:* Synthesizing Information)

    Discuss the concept of a treaty as a contract to settle disputes. Research the provisions made in the treaty signed by Japan and the other 48 nations in San Francisco in 1951. Ask students to roleplay a common parent/child conflict or view a movie scene (*West Side Story* or other similar conflict) and write a treaty to solve the problems.

3. *Radio Round-Up.* (Strand 2, *Skill:* Evaluating Information)

    Ask students to bring from home any products they might have that are made in Japan or by Japanese companies in the United States. Discuss business practices of the Japanese, how they are different from those in the U.S., and why Japanese products are perceived to be of high quality.

4. *Exercise the Japanese Way.* (Strand 3, *Skill:* Personal Skills)

    It is customary in many of the Japanese-owned businesses in the United States for workers to begin each day with some form of exercise. Explain this custom to the class and begin each class session with some form of brief exercise. After some time practicing this custom, ask students to evaluate its advantages and disadvantages and tell why they think it is important or not.

5. *Karate Capers.* (Strand 3, *Skill:* Personal Skills)

    The word *karate* means "empty hand" in Japanese. Ask someone who is skilled in the sport to discuss and demonstrate various moves and the philosophy of the sport for the class.

6. *Business Impact.* (Strand 1, *Skill:* Analyzing Information)

    Ask students to mark the locations of several well-known Japanese businesses and industries in the United States. Discuss why the businesses have located in particular places. Ask a knowledgeable businessperson to visit the class and discuss some of the most important business philosophies of the Japanese and how they differ from the American point of view.

7. *History Outline.* (Strand 1, *Skill:* Arranging Information)

    Make an outline of all the major events of World War II involving Japan. Beside each event, make a note of its present status.

8. *People at War.* (Strand 1, *Skill:* Community Resources)

    If possible, locate someone who has firsthand knowledge of the camps Japanese citizens were placed in during the war. Simulate this situation by rounding up all the class members who have brown eyes and putting them in a separate place for awhile. Debrief the situation with discussion about how they felt about this experience.

53. THE ENVIRONMENT

DETECTION Students may have difficulty mastering key concepts if they:

- Do not know how the environment influences their lives
- Are not aware of how their behaviors can influence the quality of the environment
- Do not understand the interrelationships that cause environmental problems
- Do not recognize various forms of environmental pollution

Description. The environment comprises everything in the surroundings and conditions that influence living and nonliving things. Such factors as temperature, climate, food supply, soil and water conditions, and even the other people who live around us affect and determine the total environment. Ecology is the study of the quality and interaction of relationships among factors that influence the environment. One of the most serious problems facing the world today is pollution of the environment. Reducing pollution is a complicated process because much of what causes the most serious problems is also beneficial to people. Automobiles, factories, and solid wastes add tons of pollutants to the environment each day—all byproducts of increased technology that has greatly improved our way of life. Since the 1960s, people have become more concerned about the environment and have made important advances in protecting it. The Environmental Protection Agency (EPA) is an independent agency of the United States government responsible for protecting the environment from pollution. It establishes standards and conducts research on the effects of pollution. Other industrial countries have also taken action against pollution and some international controls have been developed. Individuals can help with the problems of pollution by recycling waste products and being willing to undergo some inconvenience and some changes in ways of life.

Causation. Education about the interrelationships in the environment and how individuals can contribute to solving some of the problems has been lacking. Thus, students do not recognize how they contribute to the problems or know what specific things they might do to help alleviate them.

Implications. Pollution of the environment is a serious and even life-threatening concern. Without awareness and information, students will not know what they can do as individuals to help solve these problems.

CORRECTION Modify strategies for topical and learning needs.

1. *Garbage Day.* (Strand 2, *Skill:* Analyzing Information)

     Ask students to bring their family's garbage from 1 day to school in a plastic bag. (Send a note home to parents explaining this project and asking them to supervise the collection of content.) Collect the garbage in an area outside the school or classroom where it can be opened and analyzed. Ask students to work in small groups and open the bags (not their own) and examine the waste products. Have them list the contents, categorize them according to recyclable or not, and deveop some conclusions that can be substantiated by the data.

2. *Visit the Dump.* (Strand 2, *Skill:* Summarizing Information)

     Take a fieldtrip to the local solid waste disposal area. Ask students to record their observations, trace or hypothesize the routes of the materials they see, and discuss their observations in class.

3. *Invent a Way.* (Strand 2, *Skill:* Synthesizing Information)

     Have students choose a particular pollution problem and design an invention for solving it and benefiting the environment. Have them draw or write about their inventions and share them orally with the class.

4. *Recycle Round-Up.* (Strand 3, *Skill:* Political Participation)

     Ask the class to organize and conduct a recycling project in their community. They should determine ways to advertise it and enlist the help of others. At the end of the project, evaluate the process and summarize the results and the advantages and disadvantages of the project.

5. *Private EPA.* (Strand 3, *Skill:* Political Participation)

     Ask students to form a schoolwide Environmental Protection Agency. Students would bring before the class all the problems they see in their local environment. The class can decide which of the problems they could solve and which they should report to the principal or the local community leaders for action.

6. *Wildlife Report.* (Strand 2, *Skill:* Interpreting Information)

     Ask students to investigate the consequences of various forms of pollution on wildlife. Examples of oil spills, large forests dying from air pollution, and contaminated waterways should be discussed in general prior to their research.

7. *Noise Pollution.* (Strand 2, *Skill:* Interpreting Information)

     Take a walk around the local area and note all the examples of noise pollution that are heard. List these on the chalkboard and have students determine the effects of this pollution and classify according to these categories: acceptable, annoying, possibly damaging to hearing.

8. *Write It Down.* (Strand 3, *Skill:* Political Participation)

     Have students debate the laws prohibiting smoking in public places and compose a letter to their state representative (or local mayor) regarding their position on the issue.

54. POPULATION GROWTH

DETECTION Students may have difficulty mastering key concepts if they:

- Have difficulty explaining the concept of population
- Cannot identify heavily populated countries in the world
- Have not studied population problems in other cultures
- Cannot recognize relationships between health and population growth

Description. During the early part of the twenty-first century, the world's population may reach 8 billion if trends continue and a major disaster does not occur. The rate of growth has been increasing and the total population has been growing larger. A birthrate of 40 persons per 1,000 population per year combined with a deathrate of 15 will produce an annual increase of 2%. Advocates of zero population growth cannot reach their goals unless the birthrate equals the deathrate. Ironically, the greatest population increases are in countries that are not highly industrialized and cannot provide adequate food and health care to take care of the expanding number of people. Other countries that are more developed have birth control and family-planning programs stabilizing population growth. People are living longer with improved diets and better medical care throughout the world. In the United States, the number of people over 40 will soon be greater than the number under 40. People are living in urban environments that have higher population densities as compared to rural living. Countries such as Japan have a high density of population as compared to that of the United States. India and China have more people than other countries in the world. Population problems will continue to increase until programs are implemented to raise the standard of living of undereducated people.

Causation. Special-needs students have difficulty understanding issues related to population growth due to the large number of concepts and lack of contact with the problems. A few may have experiences in large families and living in highly populated urban areas. These experiences are only minor illustrations of population problems that are more pronounced in other more distant countries.

Implications. The abstractness of population concepts must be transformed to more concrete learning to develop meaningful involvement. The severe problems in other cultures become a world problem that must be solved for future generations to maintain a high quality of life. Students must understand that only a certain amount of food and health care is available to all cultures and only when economic factors are also favorable.

CORRECTION Modify strategies for topical and learning needs.

1. *Population Growth.* (Strand 3, *Skill:* Social Participation)

    The world's population will double in the next 50 years. Explain to students that the space in the classroom represents the world. Move students to various parts of the room to take up the space. Invite another teacher's class into the room and make the comparison that adding this class represents doubling the world population. Discuss with students the consequences of having twice as many students in the classroom (world).

2. *Feast and Famine.* (Strand 3, *Skill:* Social Participation)

    Explain to students that many people in Africa and India do not have adequate food supplies. Around lunchtime, take the students to the lunchroom to watch others eat and not eat themselves. Discuss with students how they felt watching others eat.

3. *Food Shortage.* (Strand 3, *Skill:* Social Participation)

    Food and health care cost money and are thus not available in many countries. Distribute tokens at random (2 blue to one student and 1 red to the next student), representing money (assign value) to exchange for food and health care. About half the class will have enough (2 blue tokens) to purchase a cookie and a bandage while the other students become frustrated with not having the necessary tokens to make the same purchase. Discuss with students their feelings about this activity.

4. *Lifeboat.* (Strand 3, *Skill:* Group Interaction)

    Explain to students that the world is like a giant life raft with room for a certain number of people. Give students occupations, such as lawyer, doctor, scientist, construction worker, farmer, teacher, banker, and student. Use a large string to draw a life raft that has limited food and water supplies. Suggest that 2 people must be sent off on a smaller raft due to shortage of supplies. They must decide as a group who is to be sent off and explain why.

5. *Family Tree.* (Strand 3, *Skill:* Social Participation)

    Illustrate the effects of population growth by using the students to represent 2 families, the Smiths and the Joneses. The Smith family has 2 children per generation and the Jones family has 1 child per generation. Ask students to play the roles of the families in front of the class to illustrate these patterns of population growth. For instance, the Smith family has 2 children and their children will have 2 children. The Jones family has 1 child and this child will have 1 child. Students will see how quickly the families grow and the effect this has on population growth.

6. *Population Maps.* (Strand 2, *Skill:* Synthesizing Information)

    Have students select a specific country and illustrate its population on a map using dots to represent millions of people. Place the maps on the wall and give students a summary sheet. From the displayed maps, ask students to rank the countries from largest to smallest population.

55. COMMUNICATION

DETECTION Students may have difficulty mastering key concepts if they:

- Have difficulty understanding how communication impacts a global environment
- Cannot identify communication technologies
- Cannot explain importance of communication among countries
- Have not experienced the use of modern communication technologies

Description. Communication technologies have increased the amount and quality of information shared by countries. The world communication system has improved to the extent that people of different countries can now speak instantly with each other through a sophisticated satellite system. Communication used to take weeks to send messages across oceans and overland. Even packages and goods are delivered overnight with more efficiency with airplanes and automation. Television has had the greatest impact through the power of using visual messages for communicating ideas. Some cultures attempt to control access to information through strong governmental controls. In the United States, Great Britain, and other nations in Western Europe, the government has minimum control over the types of information that are exchanged in an open society. It is becoming increasingly more difficult to limit access to information due to the availability of newer, more efficient technology. For example, laser beams (controlled light waves) can pass information on thin fibers more efficiently than other technologies. Advanced technologies in computers have not only increased access to information but also have made us more able to store and retrieve information with increased speed and in smaller units. As countries continue to share information through various technologies, more cooperation and understanding should evolve in solving global problems. Space exploration will produce communication systems that will continue to advance to meet the challenges of an information hungry world.

Causation. Many students are users of many communication systems but are unaware of their complex technologies due to the transparent nature of these mediums. Students certainly lack a frame of reference for understanding the speed of communication as compared to historical, mechanical methods. Satellites are not easily visible nor is it easily understood how messages are sent and received this way.

Implications. Communication will continue to advance at a rate that will create new challenges for future generations. Students need to understand how to use communication systems in an information culture, especially since many students will spend their future worklife using these mediums.

CORRECTION Modify strategies for topical and learning needs.

1. *Communication Timeline.* (Strand 1, *Skill:* Arranging Information)
   Place the following words on the chalkboard: *laser beams, computers, telephone, telegraph, television,* and *smoke signals.* Discuss these modes of communication with students by giving examples of each. Ask students to mark use of each of the modes of communcation on a timeline.

2. *Communication Modes.* (Strand 2, *Skill:* Classifying Information)
   Challenge students to draw pictures of various modes of communication and place them on a bulletin board. Divide students into 3–4 groups and give each group 1 turn a day.

3. *Superpowers.* (Strand 3, *Skill:* Decision Making)
   Explain that the superpower countries, such as the United States and Soviet Union, are linked with communication systems. Discuss with students the importance of this communication, especially in a world of atomic warfare. Ask students to roleplay a conversation between 2 countries to set up procedures in case of a nuclear accident.

4. *Future Messages.* (Strand 2, *Skill;* Synthesizing Information)
   Advances in technologies will continue to improve the ways people communicate. Ask students to discuss the possibility of each person having a telephone small enough to wear like a watch. How would this change things?

5. *Censorship.* (Strand 2, *Skill;* Decision Making)
   Explain to students that some countries censor information. Take a newspaper article and darken certain sentences so that it is obvious that information is being hidden. Discuss with students the reasons why countries would not want everybody to have equal access to all information.

6. *Languages.* (Strand 3, *Skill:* Group Interaction)
   People speak over 3,000 different languages in the world, which makes it difficult to communicate with each other. Give students ideas to communicate to the group without speaking. Students may draw or act out these ideas. Discuss with students the possible ways that people developed language.

7. *Communication Development.* (Strand 1, *Skill:* Reference)
   Ask students to select a country in Africa or South America and compare their communciation systems with those of the United States. Students can share their information through a listing of various countries' communication modes.

8. *King of the World.* (Strand 3, *Skill:* Group Interaction)
   Pose the following challenge to the class: If you were king or queen of the world, how would you improve communication?

56. TRANSPORTATION

DETECTION Students may have difficulty mastering key concepts if they:

- Are not aware of the many new advances in transportation
- Have had limited travel experiences
- Are not interested in traveling
- Do not understand how transportation impacts the world's interdependence

Description. Modern transportation has made the world grow smaller. It is now possible to travel across oceans in a matter of a few hours—trips that once took weeks and even months to make only a short time ago. Airplanes, trucks and automobiles, rail systems, and waterway travel are the primary transportation systems today. The future will bring new forms of these systems and perhaps even completely different modes. Trains are presently being built that ride over a cushion of air and are pulled along by magnets at speeds of more than 250 miles an hour. Automobiles will possibly become more like robots, following electric or magnetic tracks that have sensors that keep them from crashing into one another. Air transportation between distant points is becoming faster and more efficient, and space travel is already taking place much more frequently and for new purposes. Boats that hover over the water rather than travel directly upon it are used more extensively to increase comfort and speed of travel. All the improvements that are foreseeable will make it possible for people to move and work more efficiently, increasing their production and bringing their products and service to more areas that need them. International agreements will need to be made and observed so that people can travel freely and safely and environments can be protected. Communication will also change as people will interact more with other cultures as they travel for pleasure and business.

Causation. The importance of transportation can best be demonstrated by real experiences. If these are lacking, students will need vicarious experiences through videos or fieldtrips to comprehend the need for efficient and safe transportation and participate in solving problems related to it. Often students are not interested because they do not see the relevance to their lives. Experiences related to their real-life problems must come first before they will appreciate the scope and develop a more world-view perspective.

Implications. Changes in transportation are quickly affecting the whole world. Each change ultimately causes another and students must be prepared to accept and adjust to these changes if they are to participate in the benefits that the changes bring. Travel is becoming safer and more time efficient, bringing the world closer together. Students will need to develop understandings, attitudes, and skills requisite for intelligent citizenship in a widening world community.

CORRECTION Modify strategies for topical and learning needs.

1. *Transportation Modes.* (Strand 2, *Skill:* Classifying Information)

     Provide a timeline ranging from the past to present and future. Challenge students to name and categorize various forms of transportation in historical order.

2. *Autorama.* (Strand 2, *Skill:* Decision Making)

     People in the United States are very dependent upon the automobile. What would happen in the United States if we no longer had automobiles? How would this change the way we live and do things? What advantages and disadvantages do other less developed cultures have without the automobile?

3. *World Shopping.* (Strand 1, *Skill:* Arranging Information)

     How does transportation bring different cultures together? Ask students to look at the labels on their clothes and determine the countries in which they were made. What other things are exchanged with other cultures? Students could collect pictures to illustrate this exchange. Finally, students could plan a world shopping tour and determine the appropriate mode of transportation.

4. *Gumball Express.* (Strand 2, *Skill:* Decision Making)

     Divide the students into 3 groups and give each group the following problem: They must ship 10 tons of bubble gum from their city to a city 1,000 miles away (teacher chooses a real city). They must use water transportation but can also use truck or rail systems to get the gum to and from the water. Provide maps and discuss each group's decision, advantages and disadvantages.

5. *Smaller World.* (Strand 2, *Skill:* Decision Making)

     Airplanes and rockets are going faster and faster, thus seemingly making the world smaller. Ask students to discuss how the speed of transportation seems to make the world smaller.

6. *Future Trans.* (Strand 2, *Skill:* Synthesizing Information)

     After collecting pictures of futuristic transportation, develop a class project to design a space station and the mode of transportation to go back and forth from it to earth.

7. *Future Car.* (Strand 2, *Skill:* Synthesizing Information)

     Explain to students that parking is becoming a major problem for the future car and new futuristic designs of cars (or mass transportation systems) will be required to address this problem. Provide each student with an opportunity to design a future car (or system) and explain the design. Also, ask students to determine the parking arrangements. Extend the activity by having students design supersafe cars.

8. *Pack a Bag.* (Strand 2, *Skill:* Analyzing Information)

     Explain to students that they will be going to another culture in Africa. They can fill a large trunk with things to take with them. Challenge students to take things that would be scarce in the new culture. They should read about this culture before making decisions. Give students an opportunity to explain what they would take.

57. CONFLICT (WAR AND PEACE)

DETECTION Students may have difficulty mastering key concepts if they:

- Are unable to reach compromise and settle differences with their peers
- Do not recognize the importance of establishing harmony within oneself as well as with others
- Do not recognize the importance of domestic tranquility
- Do not realize that values often conflict and that there are ways to settle differences and maintain peace and harmony

Description. From the beginning of time, people have fought against one another. Conflicts between people can vary from simple disagreements to declared war. As the world has become smaller, opportunities for disagreement have become more prevalent and the consequences have become more dangerous. At the end of World War II, the atomic bomb promised a future war, a nuclear war, in which we had the power to destroy the entire planet and poison the environment for thousands of years. Causes for wars have included desire for more land to live on, religion, more wealth and resources, increased power, and fear of being taken over. In order to restore peace, often a neutral party must negotiate between opposing forces to work out differences and write peace treaties that will satisfy all parties and promote general welfare. The responsibility of avoiding war and establishing and maintaining peace belongs to every individual at all levels of human interaction.

Causation. Students who have not had the freedom to work out their differences and make their own decisions may lack the attitudes and competencies for doing so. The issues for decision making must be within the maturity and experiential level for students to learn these skills. Students also may not have had opportunities for discussion and internalization of values that promote peaceful harmony.

Implications. The world community has a commitment to the principles expressed in the United Nations Universal Declaration of Human Rights: "All human beings are born free and equal. They are born with reason and conscience. They should act toward one another in a spirit of brotherhood." Unless people can learn to solve problems rationally, build consensus, and make compromises that promote the good of all people, hope for the future is dim. With the development and practice of those skills that resolve conflict, students will gain more social satisfaction, build positive attitudes, and have a stronger sense of control over their lives. They will become aware of value conflicts and realize that there are different sets of criteria and several points of view for evaluating alternatives.

CORRECTION Modify strategies for topical and learning needs.

1. *Write It Down.* (Strand 2, *Skill:* Decision Making)
    Choose a timely, debatable issue with which the class has some familiarity or propose a moral dilemma based on the experience level of the class. Provide the class with a values analysis chart to complete during and after discussion of the major concerns. First make a list of all the alternatives that are possible in this situation. For each alternative, think of the possible consequences. Examine each consequence from the desirability factors: moral, legal, aesthetic, ecological, economic, health, and safety. Then rank each alternative and form a consensus decision.

2. *Rank It.* (Strand 3, *Skill:* Personal Skills)
    Read the following question (or similar) to the class and write the choices on the board for the students to rank. Call on several students to give their rankings (allow students to pass) and after several responses, follow with a class discussion. Question: Which of the following issues would you give the lowest priority today? Choices: space race, world hunger, defense, ecology.

3. *Values Grid.* (Strand 3, *Skill:* Analyzing Information)
    Make a grid with 3 columns labeled Issue, Key Words, and Questions. In the third column (Questions), divide the space into 7 small spaces numbered from 1–7. Name 7 general world issues that students will have some knowledge of (for older students, hostage negotiation, sale of arms to foreign countries, apartheid, etc.). Beside each issue, students should write their initial thoughts in a few key words and then respond to the following questions by checking the box if positive and leaving it blank otherwise. Questions: Are you proud of your position? Have you publicly affirmed your position? Have you chosen this positon from alternatives? Have you chosen your position after thoughtful consideration of the pros and cons? Have you chosen your position freely? Have you acted on or done anything about your beliefs? Have you acted with repetition, pattern, or consistency on this issue? Divide the class into small groups and discuss their responses.

4. *Which Was Worse?* (Strand 2, *Skill:* Evaluating Information)
    Make a list of the major wars in history on the chalkboard. Ask students to choose 4 of these and read about them. After reading about each war, ask students to rank them according to which was the worst in terms of factors other than number of casualties. Students should report their decisions and tell why they ranked each as they did.

5. *Soldier's Diary.* (Strand 2, *Skill:* Synthesizing Information)
    Many personal insights about war can be gained from soldiers' letters written while they were at war. Ask students to select a particular war and battle situation and communicate information about the situation through a letter. They should also attempt to communicate the personal thoughts and feelings they predict a soldier might have.

58. THE UNITED NATIONS

DETECTION Students may have difficulty mastering key concepts if they:

- Do not understand the function of the United Nations as a peace-keeping force
- Have not learned respect for authority and those institutions that administer it
- Do not see the value in cooperation to attain goals
- Do not understand the need for collective and cooperative values setting

Description. "Let Us Beat Swords into Plowshares" is the motto of the United Nations and expresses its goal of world peace and human dignity. The UN is an organization of 145 nations that work together to find the causes of war and to eliminate them. The UN charter also defines several other major purposes: to aid nations in being just in their actions toward each other, to help countries cooperate in solving their problems, and to be an agency through which the goals can be attained. The UN is divided into 6 major divisions; the General Assembly is the 1 major organ in which all member nations are represented. Each nation has only 1 vote in the General Assembly and it takes a simple majority vote to decide most questions. The Security Council is another of the major divisions of the UN and its primary responsibility is keeping world peace. Disputes among countries are investigated and peaceful solutions are offered to the opposing sides. If settlement is not reached, the UN may ask other nations to stop trading with the countries, cut off communications, end contacts with the governments, or even send military forces to settle the dispute. The UN also works to make the world a better and safer place in which to live. Some of its activities have included providing various types of aid for countries and different groups of people, improving human rights, finding peaceful uses of nuclear energy, and working to improve pollution control. One UN agency, UNICEF, exists primarily to give children in the world food, clothing, and medicine.

Causation. Students who have not experienced the power of group efforts and cooperation in solving problems may not understand the significance of the UN. The rights and privileges of belonging to the UN also carry responsibilities to maintain world peace and to carry out the duties assigned by the charter. Students who have not been expected to maintain responsibilities in exchange for privileges are not likely to see the relevance of the UN for accomplishing peace.

Implications. The principles upon which the UN is founded are basic to maintaining peace among all individuals and groups of people. Working to help humankind also helps individuals increase their own sense of self-worth and human dignity.

CORRECTION   Modify strategies for topical and learning needs.

1. *Model UN.* (Strand 3, *Skill:* Political Participation)
   Assign each student a country to research and identify its major problems. Ask students to prepare a request for aid for its problems, stating reasons why the UN should support it. Present the requests to the whole class and make a decision by voting.
2. *Newspaper Events.* (Strand 1, *Skill:* Comprehension)
   Ask students to collect newspaper articles for a period of time about assigned countries and prepare a bulletin board (or folder) of all current articles that mention their country. Have students summarize the major events of their country in an oral presentation.
3. *Flags of the UN.* (Strand 2, *Skill:* Synthesizing Information)
   Make an authentic flag for each member country of the UN and display them in the classroom.
4. *Decision Time.* (Strand 3, *Skill:* Group Interaction)
   Have 2 students represent countries who are fighting over boundaries and/or resources. Have each present its case to the class, with allies who support each side. Ask the class to recommend several solutions for settling the dispute. Vote on the best solution.
5. *Language Barrier.* (Strand 1, *Skill:* Finding Information)
   Have students find out how UN members overcome the language problems in speaking and presenting their cases. What are the official UN languages and how are they heard by the members?
6. *Children of the World.* (Strand 3, *Skill:* Group Interaction)
   Organize the class for Trick-or-Treating for UNICEF at Halloween or create a fund-raising project to buy some UNICEF greeting cards.
7. *Good Deeds.* (Strand 2, *Skill:* Summarizing Information)
   Have students research some of the accomplishments of the UN, prepare a notebook summary of 3 of these accomplishments, and present 1 orally to the class.
8. *Veto Power.* (Strand 1, *Skill:* Finding Information)
   Ask students to research the veto rights of UN member countries and how this affects the decisions that are made.
9. *UN Problems.* (Strand 1, *Skill:* Finding Information)
   The UN has had difficulty in maintaining its role and functions. Ask students to find out what some of its problems have been, how the organization is supported, and how it carries out its responsibilities.
10. *Special Agencies.* (Strand 1, *Skill:* Study Skills)
    There are many specialized agencies within the UN and most are identified with abbreviations. Assign the following to students to identify and tell what each specialized agency does: FAO, IMCO, ICAO, IDA, IFC, ILO, IMF, ITU, UNESCO, UPU, WORLD BANK, WHO, WIPO, WMO, and UNICEF.

59. LEADERSHIP

DETECTION Students may have difficulty mastering key concepts if they:

- Have not had opportunities to be leaders
- Have difficulty understanding the purpose of leaders
- Cannot identify leaders of a few countries
- Cannot explain the differences between leaders and followers
- Cannot explain how leaders lose their power

Description. Leaders of countries have various titles, such as president, prime minister, premier, king, queen, and so on. Positions of leadership are obtained through election, revolution, religion, knowledge, and bloodlines. Leaders are identified in religion, academics, science, and many other fields. The styles of leadership can be viewed as democratic or autocratic. The democratic style is based on the fundamental idea that the followers have some say about electing or appointing their leaders. Democratic leaders obtain information from their followers before making decisions. An autocratic leader exerts power through the belief that the person at the top should make the decisions. Autocratic leaders can become dictators and exert great pressure to follow by using fear tactics. Countries have been successful with many diverse styles and combinations of autocratic and democratic practices. Most leaders have a council or advisory group to help make the many complex social, economic, and political decisions. Throughout history, leaders have exerted their power by trying to control other countries through economic or political pressures. Many wars have been fought to obtain greater dominance in the global community. Now it's possible that a full-scale war could actually destroy the earth and all its people due to the devastating effects of nuclear weapons. Due to improved transportation and economic systems, leaders have to maintain cooperative attitudes to participate in the world economy as well as to try to solve mutual problems.

Causation. Students form perceptions of leaders through their experiences with family, school, and world events. Due to the nature of media reporting, many views of political leadership are negative. Also, views of leaders in other countries are filtered through the culture that students live in. Students may have difficulty understanding various forms of leadership due to lack of concrete experiences.

Implications. Leadership is a very abstract term that is not easily explained but can be demonstrated to special students. The classroom is an excellent place for students to experience the tenets of democratic and autocratic leadership styles. As students compare and contrast various styles, the democratic style should be nurtured through students' participation in decision making. Students must be taught how to make decisions and to work with groups effectively.

CORRECTION Modify strategies for topical and learning needs.

1. *President's Cabinet.* (Strand 3, *Skill:* Group Interaction)

    Form groups of 3–4 students to represent the president's cabinet to advise on important issues. Select a current issue, such as hazardous waste or air pollution controls. The group must decide what action is necessary to resolve the situation. Ask the groups to report their actions.

2. *Great Leaders.* (Strand 2, *Skill:* Summarizing Information)

    Ask students to select a great leader in history to complete a leadership profile report. The leader may be from any number of fields: politics, religion, education, and so on. The profile should include the person's country, area of leadership, time period, accomplishments, and leadership characteristics. Students should share their findings with the class and display their profiles.

3. *Leader News.* (Strand 1, *Skill:* Arranging Information)

    Create a bulletin board for students to display newspaper or magazine articles and pictures about selected leaders from various fields. Categorize the leaders by their fields.

4. *Leadership Styles.* (Strand 2, *Skill:* Synthesizing Information)

    Explain that you are going to demonstrate the difference between autocratic and democratic leadership styles through roleplaying. Divide the class into 2 groups and give each student a styrofoam cup to decorate. Tell 1 group exactly how to decorate the cup with specific colors and diagrams, such as red circles and blue triangles. Explain to the other group that they can decide how to decorate their own cups. Discuss the differences in how each group's members felt about the activity.

5. *Leadership Slogans.* (Strand 2, *Skill:* Synthesizing Information)

    Challenge students to develop leadership slogans to reflect qualities of leadership. Slogans can emphasize decision-making ability, intelligence, skill, hard work, determination, and communication. For example, "One must risk in order to lead." Print the slogans with Print Shop or similar software on the computer or with colorful crayons. Give students the opportunity to explain their slogans.

6. *Leadership Music.* (Strand 2, *Skill:* Analyzing Information)

    Ask students to bring in songs that illustrate popular themes of leadership. Listen to the songs and have students explain how the lyrics reflect characteristics of leadership. Write these ideas on the chalkboard.

7. *Nobel Prize.* (Strand 2, *Skill:* Reference)

    The Nobel Prize is given for outstanding achievement in physics, chemistry, medicine, peace, literature, and economics. Ask students to find more information about 1 of the prize winners and report to the class, showing a picture illustrating the recipient's accomplishment.

REFLECTIONS

1. Students have difficulty understanding concepts about other countries due to the influence of the culture in which they live. Generate a list of concepts, such as religion, the arts, politics, and economics, as a strategy to help students compare and contrast their culture with other cultures.
2. Many adults and students are uncomfortable interacting with people from other cultures. Discuss with the class the reasons for this and possible ways of alleviating these feelings. Arrange to interact with people from other cultures to expand your point of view.
3. At the beginning of each chapter, observable behaviors are listed to help identify problems with understanding the concepts. Discuss the behaviors or other information necessary to make diagnostic recommendations for special students. Also, develop a series of interview questions to use as a diagnostic tool with a special learner.
4. Students are usually motivated if teachers demonstrate enthusiasm and interest in the subject they are teaching. Identify a country that you have visited or would like to visit and prepare a series of lessons. Pretend that you are going to take students on a tour, with the transportation and points of interests planned in detail.
5. Most systems have a curriculum guide specifying the social studies units for teaching about other cultures. Compare and contrast the information and ideas in this chapter with other curriculum guides. What ideas can you incorporate from this chapter to adapt the material to special students?
6. Special students can learn about other cultures through examining pictures in texts. Examine several textbook series and note the numbers and types of pictures used to display life in other cultures. Prepare a short lesson using a picture to teach a concept about another culture.
7. Religion provides the basis for many cultural beliefs and practices. Plan to attend a religious ceremony for a religion different from your own. Discuss this experience with other teachers as well as ideas for teaching about religions in other cultures.
8. Good teachers have a way of making social studies interesting through using various strategies. Arrange to observe two or three teachers who are teaching about other cultures. Make a list of effective strategies that you observe and could use.
9. Materials about other countries are readily available through the respective embassies. Send for this free material and determine its appropriateness for teaching special students. What adaptations are necessary to use the material with special learners?

10. A number of texts address the needs of special students. Compare and contrast information in these sources with the ideas in this section.

Herlihy, J. G., & Herlihy, M. T. (1980). *Mainstreaming in the social studies.* Washington, DC: National Council for the Social Studies.

Johnson, D. W., & Johnson, R. T. (1987). *Learning together and alone.* Englewood Cliffs, NJ: Prentice-Hall.

Maxim, G. W. (1987). *Social studies and the elementary school child.* Columbus, OH: Charles E. Merrill.

Mehlinger, H. D., & Tucker, J. L. (Eds.) (1979). *Teaching social studies in other nations.* Washington, DC: National Council for the Social Studies.

Michaelis, J. U. (1988). *Social studies for children.* Englewood Cliffs, NJ: Prentice-Hall.

Patton, W. E. (1980). *Improving the use of social studies textbooks.* Washington, DC: National Council for the Social Studies.

Polon, L. A., & Cantwell, A. (1983). The whole earth holiday book. Glenview, IL: Scott, Foresman.

Reardon, B. A. (Ed.). (1988). *Educating for global responsibility.* New York: Teachers College Press.

Remy, R. C., Nathan, J. A., Becker, J. M., & Torney, J. V. (1975). *International learning and international education in a global age.* Washington, DC: National Council for the Social Studies.

Smith, J. A. (1967). *Creative teaching of the social studies in the elementary school.* Boston: Allyn and Bacon.

Tiedt, P. L., & Tiedt, I. M. (1986). *Multicultural teaching: A handbook of activities, information, and resources.* Boston: Allyn and Bacon.

Winston, B. J. (1984). *Map and globe skills: K–8 teaching guide.* Macomb, IL: National Council for Geographic Education.

Index

ABOUT THE AUTHORS

LANA J. SMITH, Professor of Education in the Department of Curriculum and Instruction at Memphis State University, holds a Ph.D. from Southern Illinois University in Carbondale. In addition to the undergraduate and graduate courses she teaches in content subjects, diagnosis and correction of reading needs, language arts, and microcomputers, her experiences have included teaching English at the middle school and high school levels. Co-author of a content reading inventory, Dr. Smith has also published several articles in social studies, science, reading, and language arts, as well as presented numerous papers on reading and comprehension in the content areas, language arts, and computer instruction at state and national conferences. She has served as an editorial consultant and reviewer to several major publishing companies.

DENNIE L. SMITH has two decades of experience as an educator, consultant, and author. He holds an Ed.D. from Auburn University and is presently Professor of Education in the Department of Curriculum and Instruction at Memphis State University. Courses he teaches at the graduate and under-graduate levels include methods of social studies instruction, instructional strategies, and curriculum design and technology. Dr. Smith has served as president of the state council of The National Council for Social Studies and, at the national level, chair of the research committee. In addition, he has been a consultant for colleges, school districts, and businesses throughout the United States, and has published a social studies textbook and numer-ous articles in professional journals.

READER'S REACTIONS TO
SOCIAL STUDIES: DETECTING AND CORRECTING SPECIAL NEEDS

Name: _____   Position: _____

Address: _____   _____

_____   Date: _____

1. How have you used this book?

   ___College Text   ___Inservice Training   ___Teaching Resource

   Describe:_____

2. For which purpose(s) do you recommend its use?

3. What do you view as the major strengths of the book?

4. What are its major weaknesses?

5. How could the book be improved?

6. What additional topics should be included in this book?

7. In addition to the topics currently included in the *Detecting and Correcting* series—basic mathematics, classroom behavior, instructional management, language arts, reading, science and health, social studies, and speech and language—what other topics would you recommend?

8. Would you like to receive:

   _____a reply to your comments?

   _____additional information about this series?

Additional Comments:

THANK YOU FOR SHARING YOUR SPECIAL NEEDS AND PROFESSIONAL CONCERNS
Please send to: Joyce S. Choate, *Detecting and Correcting Series*
c/o Allyn and Bacon, 160 Gould Street, Needham Heights, Massachusetts 02194-2310